THE BONDS OF KINSHIP IN DAHOMEY

THE BONDS OF KINSHIP IN DAHOMEY

Portraits of West African
Girlhood, 1720–1940

JESSICA CATHERINE REUTHER

INDIANA UNIVERSITY PRESS

This book is a publication of

Indiana University Press
Office of Scholarly Publishing
Herman B Wells Library 350
1320 East 10th Street
Bloomington, Indiana 47405 USA

iupress.org

© 2025 by Jessica Catherine Reuther

All rights reserved
No part of this book may be reproduced or utilized in any form or by any means, electronic or mechanical, including photocopying and recording, or by any information storage and retrieval system, without permission in writing from the publisher.

First Printing 2024

Cataloging information is available from the Library of Congress.

ISBN 978-0-253-07142-2 (hardback)
ISBN 978-0-253-07143-9 (paperback)
ISBN 978-0-253-07144-6 (web PDF)

To Matthew,
whose love for our son Marius has shown me how parenthood
can be a choice and kinship supersedes biology

To "Maman" Melissa and Marius,
who accompanied me every step of the way

CONTENTS

Acknowledgments ix

Introduction: Portrait of a Girl and a Fabric Seller   3

1. The Value of Girls to the Royal Household of Dahomey, 1720s–1870s   23

2. Dashing and Entrusting Girls: The Atlanticization of Child Transfers during the Reigns of Kings Gezo and Glèlè, 1818–1889   47

3. Agbessipé and Her Mother: Female Wealth, Girl Pawns, and Enslaved Labor in Ouidah during the Era of "Legitimate" Trade, 1840s–1880s   65

4. A Runaway Girl amid the Turmoil of Conquest: Household Economies and Colonial Transformations in the Kingdoms of Hogbonou and Dahomey, 1880s–1890s   87

5. Entrusted or Enslaved?: Colonial Legal Debates about Girls' Statuses, 1900s–1930s   103

6. "Why Did You Not Cry Out . . .?": Sexual Assaults of Entrusted Girls in Colonial Dahomey, 1917–1941   125

7. The Télé Affair (1936–1938): Anxieties about Transformations in Girlhood in Colonial Abomey   141

   Conclusion: Obscured Histories of Girlhood   159

Glossary of Foreign Terms   167
Notes   171
Bibliography   231
Index   257

ACKNOWLEDGMENTS

I have accrued many intellectual and personal debts over the course of completing this book project. I am grateful to all the Beninese women, men, and children who showed me alternative perspectives on motherhood—in particular, the market women who called out to me and said, "Give me your son and I will give you one of mine." The exchanges that followed these informal encounters transformed my perspectives on entrusted children. These women sincerely wanted to invest in my child and have me invest in theirs. This was not a means to conceal trafficking; their motivations were in the best interest of their children. I only understood this many months into my research.

While in Benin, Euloge Akodjetin proved essential to the success of my research and became a dear friend. This research would not have been possible without his assistance. He started out as my Fon tutor and then became a mentor whenever I was in Benin. I thank Lucie Viakinnou-Brinson of Kennesaw State University for facilitating this connection. Euloge shared invaluable cultural insights into Beninese society and Dahomean history. He always frankly corrected any assumptions or conclusions that he believed were misguided. Euloge willingly made introductions on my behalf, introducing me to Felix Iroko, a historian at the Université d'Abomey-Calavi, and Romauld Michozzounou, the minister of education, both of whom shared their expertise in Dahomean history with me. Euloge also guided me through the day-to-day challenges of living and working in Cotonou.

I also wish to extend my sincere gratitude to Edna Bay and Doug Falen for sharing their expertise on Abomey. This proved invaluable while I conducted oral interviews there. I am indebted to Gracia Navé, my research assistant in Abomey, for her careful translation and patient explanations of cultural norms.

My favorite part of research has been the chance encounters with colleagues who become friends in the course of research in foreign archives. My research benefited from repeated overlaps in archival research with Lorelle Semley who tirelessly discussed the minutiae of Dahomean history with me. Her guidance and friendship have been invaluable. I also had the good fortune of developing friendships with Janet Horne, Sue Peabody, and Lisa Lindsay in far-flung archives. I hope they all realize how greatly they have contributed to my scholarship. They each encouraged me from the earliest days of research to my final ones.

Numerous archivists and librarians have assisted me over the years, many of whom I undoubtedly will unintentionally overlook here. I am grateful to the hardworking staff at the Archives Nationales du Bénin, the Archives du Sénégal, the Archives nationales d'outre-mer, and the Schomburg Center for Research in Black Culture. I want to thank Alphonsine Agwegwe, Blandine Behanzin, and Sonia Mahame from the Archives Nationales du Bénin, who welcomed and assisted me on a daily basis while I was working there. I wish to express my appreciation for the advice I received from Mamadou Ndiaye at the Archives du Sénégal.

This project started over a decade ago as a PhD dissertation at Emory University. Consequently, my committee members, Kristin Mann, Clifton Crais, and Pamela Scully shaped its initial form. Kristin has challenged me at every turn and guided me professionally even beyond the PhD. I could not have asked for a more dedicated adviser, mentor, and friend. I drafted the chapters on the colonial era as a graduate student at Emory. Kristin, Clifton, and Pamela left their marks on chapters 5 through 7. Their careful reading and guidance have enhanced all aspects of my scholarship. These chapters also benefited from the feedback of others in the African Studies community at Emory, including Susan Gagliardi and Jill Rosenthal. Though not an Africanist, Rebekah Ramsay also generously gave me feedback on drafts of the dissertation. My fondest memories of graduate school all involve Rebekah and her unflagging optimism.

The amazing institutional support from the Emory University Department of History in the form of the Joseph J. Mathews Prize for International Research made much of the research in Benin, Senegal, and France possible.

The Mathews Prize, along with Professional Development Research Support Funds from Laney Graduate School at Emory University, funded multiple research trips to Benin in 2012 and 2013–2014 as well as to Senegal, Switzerland, and France in 2013–2014.

At Ball State University, my colleagues Jennifer DeSilva and Abel Alves encouraged me to expand the project temporally to include a longer trajectory. This truly transformed the dissertation into a book. Jennifer's and Abel's support for the relevance of Africanist scholarship to the global early modern inspired me to tackle a few hundred more years! The ASPiRE Start-Up Grant Award from Ball State and research funds provided by the Department of History facilitated further research in Benin, France, and the United States in 2018 and 2019.

The early chapters of the book would not be what they are without the careful reading and critical feedback provided by Trina Hogg and Larissa Kopytoff. The three of us formed a virtual writing group that workshopped these chapters. Both Trina and Larissa made chapters 1 through 4 immeasurably better. I share any accolades for the prose of these chapters with them, though all mistakes are my own. The final version of chapter 3 was shaped by conversations with Erdmute Alber and other presenters at the Merian Institute for Advanced Studies in Africa (MIASA). The invitation to attend a MIASA conference at the University of Ghana came as I was making revisions. The entire manuscript benefited from conversations with other experts on gender in West Africa during this May 2023 conference, including Cati Coe, Jacqueline Bethel-Mogoue, Gretchen Bauer, and Marius Kothor. Other chapters benefited from presentations at numerous conferences over the years. There are just too many to mention here, but several commentators provided poignant insights. These individuals include Sara Berry, Kelly Duke-Bryant, Ruth Ginio, and Charlotte Walker-Said.

Last but not least, I want to acknowledge the support from my family. Matthew Wilson has borne the brunt of my frustrations as I transformed this from dissertation to book. He held my hand and encouraged me when I thought all hope was lost. "Maman" Melissa Vance made the dissertation research possible by accompanying me on my predissertation research and bringing Marius home from Benin. Melissa embraced my passion as her own. The unwavering support from Melissa and her husband, Greg Ziegenfuss, breathed life into this project and literally nourished me when I did not see a path forward. All of the quality childcare provided by Melissa Vance and Greg Ziegenfuss, Karen Milton, Megan and Randy Schumacher, Leo and Bre Reuther, and Mary Jo Anderson gave me the time to research and write significant portions of this book. I will never be able to repay them for their generosity. For many years, Norma Reuther, my grandmother, provided a home base for Marius and me to return and recharge. She taught me so much about mothering. She along with my parents Leo and Cathy Ziegenfuss Reuther shaped this through my memories of them. May my work be a tribute to them all.

This book began with the birth of my first son, who was born just three weeks before I commenced my PhD. I sent off the revised manuscript just weeks after the birth of my second son. These life events appropriately bookended this project. My experiences with motherhood gave me greater empathy for the biological parents and social mothers I encountered in the archives. Parenting is hard at all times and in all places. Parents struggle to do what is best for their children despite any personal sacrifices they may have to make.

THE BONDS OF KINSHIP IN DAHOMEY

"Une Marchande de Tissus" from Alexandre d'Albéca, *La France au Dahomey* (1895).

Introduction

Portrait of a Girl and a Fabric Seller

In the image titled "A Fabric Seller" or "A Female Merchant in Cotonou," a West African girl of about twelve to fourteen approaches a market woman who is reclining on her left hip with her legs tucked beneath her.[1] The girl is wrapped from bosom to knees in an unembellished *pagne*, a swath of cloth about eight feet long and four feet wide. The woman displays her meticulously folded and arranged wares, which are placed behind her left shoulder. These goods signal her profession, which one version of the title confirms—she is a fabric seller.

Alexandre d'Albéca, the image-maker, chose to portray this girl and woman in situ while they engaged in everyday activities rather than posing them in a staged scene. The printed lithograph of this image is a reproduction of d'Albéca's original photograph. While it is unclear to what extent d'Albéca intervened in framing the image, he was apparently trying to capture a candid reality as neither woman nor girl is looking directly at the camera. The woman and girl remained undisturbed by the camera's presence. The girl was focused on the woman, and the woman was looking at something to her left beyond the camera's range. The camera, like the French colonial administrator operating it, remained seemingly unobtrusive and only a minor intrusion on the lives of the woman and girl. Colonial photographers like d'Albéca, who aspired to be early ethnographers, often transformed African individuals into a representative "type" for their European audiences.[2] The woman becomes the embodiment of the "type" of African market woman, or *marchande*, a term that is part of all published versions of the title. Other than serving as an illustration for European audiences, what does the appearance of this anonymous girl and woman among the records tell us about them and their lived experiences? How can the history of Dahomey be told from their perspectives?

The Bonds of Kinship in Dahomey privileges the experiences, perspectives, and whenever possible voices of Dahomean girls, such as the one pictured. While girls are the central subject, the women who acted as guardians, mistresses, teachers, disciplinarians, and caretakers shaped girls' everyday realities, and they therefore make up a crucial component of this history as well. This book contrasts the forms of dependency that bonded girls to the households in which they lived and worked in Dahomey. Bondage—the state of being bound by or subjected to an external power or control—structured girls' lived experiences. *The Bonds of Kinship in Dahomey* explores the dual meanings of bonds as something that united individuals through common interests or goals and something that legally or physically constrained a person to a certain circumstance or status, such as enslavement. Individuals could be bound to households by coercive violence, legal agreement, emotional connections, personal circumstances, or a combination of all or any of these. By focusing on bonds, this book emphasizes that, regardless of dependent status in a household, girls sought to combat isolation, find support, create kinship, and facilitate belonging by whatever means necessary among their coresidents. It investigates the complex social norms of girlhood that distinguished one type of dependent status from another in the precolonial and colonial eras of Dahomey.[3]

In particular, this book focuses on girl transfers, a constellation of practices whereby girls were relocated from their birth home to unrelated households for an extended period or even permanently.[4] In these new homes, girls developed social kinship relationships, performed labor for the benefit of the household, and underwent socialization into adult womanhood. This book argues that, despite fundamental differences in each relationship, it is important to examine the range of the subservient statuses of these girls—enslaved, collected, dashed, entrusted, pawned, runaway, or borrowed, among others—to understand Dahomean girlhood on its own terms. Rather than analyzing a particular model of colonial or "modern" girlhood in West Africa, it examines girlhood as a Dahomean cultural construct that was dynamically restructured by the kingdom's and subsequent colony's involvement in international, transnational, regional, and local phenomena. It takes a *longue durée* approach to understanding the concept of girlhood as a historical, complex, social institution that was an essential part of all females' lives, one that both shaped and was shaped by African societies in response to external pressures and internal transformations.[5]

While the Kingdom of Dahomey shared its name with the French colony, the single name does not refer to the same geographic units. The territorial boundaries of the Kingdom of Dahomey and the subsequent colony of Dahomey were not coterminous. The borders of the late nineteenth- and twentieth-century colony vastly exceeded those of the kingdom. The Kingdom of Dahomey grew from a small, inland entity to a regional power that defeated surrounding rivals starting in the 1720s with the Kingdoms of Allada and Hueda (Ouidah). The colony of Dahomey combined the previously autonomous Kingdoms of Hula (Grand-Popo), Hogbonou (Porto-Novo), and Ketou as well as the Mahi confederation and Bariba city-states with the newly conquered Kingdom of Dahomey. This book focuses on the kingdom and its neighbors, which between 1894 and 1960 formed the colony of Dahomey; in particular, the precolonial Kingdom of Hogbonou featured prominently in this history along with Yorùbáland more broadly. This area is what is today the southern portion of the Republic of Benin in West Africa. *The Bonds of Kinship in Dahomey* provides new insights into the big themes of Dahomean history: the expansion of the Kingdom of Dahomey, the abolition of the transatlantic slave trade, the transition to "legitimate" trade, African households and colonization, the Great Depression in Africa, and the patriarchal bargain of colonialism.[6] The book reexamines how the major regional and global developments of the early eighteenth through mid-twentieth centuries affected girl transfers in Dahomey.

According to oral tradition, the girl in the image had likely been transferred to the fabric seller years earlier. In the late nineteenth century, Dahomean society recognized a variety of forms of dependent relationships among girls and women in households, such as mistress–enslaved girl, runaway girl–adoptive patroness, pawned girl–adult female in a credit-giving household, or entrusted girl–social mother. The first two relationships of dependence are widely understood, but the second two have more geographically specific definitions. In West Africa, credit could be secured using a human pawn, a person held as collateral for a loan while it was being repaid. The pawn resided in and labored for the household of the person giving the loan to a family member of the pawn. The pawnship arrangement differed from indenture because, first, the pawn's labor did not pay off the loan and, second, the debt was not, in general, the pawn's own since male elders often pawned girls and young women from their households. These pawned girls' labor was then supervised by a woman within the household who gave the loan to the pawn's family.[7] Pawning overlapped with entrusting in that both were forms of institutionalized girl transfer that were temporary in nature. Entrusting is a type of child fosterage whereby social mothers act as guardians for foster girls. Historically, Dahomean parents commonly entrusted their female children to social mothers to rear, nurture, educate, and discipline for many years, typically from the ages of seven to fourteen or so, though this varied widely.[8] The entrustment of girls to social mothers created relationships of indebtedness, which entailed reciprocal obligations over a protracted period. Each of these examples of servile relationships had distinct socially acknowledged and legally defined rights and obligations for both parties involved.[9] The details provided in the image do not give any clues as to the girl's position in the fabric seller's household.

The image of the fabric seller and the girl from the late 1880s to early 1890s represents a pivotal moment in the history of Dahomean girlhood; however, it does not signify the beginning of the evolution of girlhood norms that this book traces. Rather, *The Bonds of Kinship in Dahomey* starts in the 1720s with the expansion of the Kingdom of Dahomey southward from the Abomey plateau and ends in the 1940s when the era of so-called high colonialism came to a close. These three centuries encompassed the height of the transatlantic slave trade, its protracted abolition, the "legitimate" export trade in agricultural products, the expansion of intra-African slave trading and the associated internal regional diasporas, and the imposition of formal colonialism. Each of these transformations resulted in successive political economies that impacted West African societies.[10] Pressures from across the Atlantic world fundamentally changed the institutions of girl dependence and patterns of girl transfer in Dahomey.

The Bonds of Kinship in Dahomey asserts that in Dahomey, between the eighteenth and twentieth centuries, there were many distinct institutionalized forms of girl transfer. These varied forms defined girls' bondage in novel ways to meet the needs of specific adult constituencies ranging from the monarchy to market women. These adults collected, enslaved, dashed, entrusted, pawned, and borrowed girls as part of their strategies to successfully navigate the transformations upending the Atlantic world. Dahomeans responded creatively and innovatively to these economic and political changes. Despite these shifts, Dahomean adults continually relied on the unpaid labor of girls, legitimated through a variety of dependent, bonded statuses, to perform crucial tasks that ensured the household's day-to-day functioning and economic productivity. By examining both the spectrum of girl dependence and its evolution, it becomes clear that from the eighteenth to twentieth centuries, Dahomean girls' bonded labor proved essential to the economic, social, and political success of individuals, households, and institutions such as the monarchy.

Defining Girlhood in Dahomey

How did Dahomeans define girlhood? What made girls distinguishable from adult women, boys, men, or toddlers? What defining characteristics of Dahomean girlhood remained consistent, and which evolved? From the eighteenth to twentieth centuries, Dahomeans broadly defined girlhood as the period from when female children reached the age of awareness until they achieved full womanhood. In precolonial and colonial Dahomey, this roughly correlated with the ages of seven to fourteen. Dahomeans, however, defined this life stage based on the development of physical and social maturity rather than a numeric age.[11] At around the age of seven, girlhood began as a gendered life stage distinct from a younger, nongendered childhood. Before this life stage, young boys and girls played together indiscriminately under the watch of women in household compounds. At the age of awareness, gendered identities began to develop as boys were socialized with men and girls with women.[12]

Dahomean society deemed girls who had reached the age of awareness to be ready to take on greater labor responsibilities appropriate to their physical strength.[13] The age of awareness meant that they could be trusted to complete tasks with minimal supervision, navigate the streets independently, and handle small amounts of money. Girls' work typically included domestic chores such as sweeping courtyards, laundering clothes, cooking meals, fetching water and firewood, processing farm produce, creating handicrafts, selling goods in streets and marketplaces, caring for younger children, running errands, working in the fields and gardens, and much more, as household needs dictated. Younger girls of seven or eight could find and carry lightweight firewood and sell small items such as soap, oranges, or snack foods prepared by older girls or women. These items neither spoiled easily nor required that young sellers wield machetes to market them, unlike other produce such as pineapples, sugarcane, or coconuts. The goods sold by these young girls were of little monetary worth, so if they lost some items or a customer cheated them, they learned a lesson, but the financial loss was relatively minimal. Every day, girls displayed their social maturity through the tasks they performed and their associated responsibilities, such as fiscal matters or supervision of younger workers. As these girls gained experience, they could be given more physically demanding jobs and the greater responsibility of selling higher-value items that might require more price negotiation or attention. The performance of labor was a crucial and defining characteristic of each stage of girlhood. Labor roles within the household and marketplace functioned as one indicator of social age. For Dahomeans, female maturation was not simply a biological fact or a chronological age; it also functioned as a status that girls must earn through taking on additional responsibilities in the households, marketplaces, and streets where they worked.[14]

Awareness also marked the beginning of a life stage when Dahomeans considered harsher discipline to be important to girls' development. Upon reaching the age of awareness, Dahomeans believed that too much tenderness, affection, or indulgence would "spoil" young girls and render them incapable of enduring life's hardships in adulthood.[15] A biological mother's natural affection and supposed indulgent impulse toward her offspring justified the transfer of daughters to social mothers at the age of awareness.

Since at least the eighteenth century, one of the prevailing norms that defined girlhood in the Bight of Benin—the region of the West African littoral from the Volta River in the west to the Niger River in the east—was the shared belief that only during the earliest years of childhood did physiology dictate which women could fulfill motherhood roles.[16] After these initial years of life, biological limitations to motherhood no longer applied. Dahomeans, as well as other West African groups, believed that parental roles could be—and should be—divided among and delegated to nonbiological guardians. Throughout West Africa, biological parents shared and assigned parental roles among adults in multiple households operating on the assumption that it was hubris to believe that two individuals alone or one household possessed all the resources and skills to successfully form children into adults.[17] West African girls benefited directly and indirectly from their transfer into other households. The direct benefits included: building extended networks of close relationships they could rely on in times of hardship, acquiring skills or knowledge that her biological parents did not possess, and being disciplined with appropriate harshness so that they would adhere to societal expectations.[18] The voluntary transfer of girls created new relationships that transcended biology.[19] Most Dahomean girls spent much of their youth in a household through some form of transfer. The type of transfer depended on the girl, her natal family, and when the transfer took place. In contrast to voluntary transfers, forced transfers in the form of enslaved girls were not beneficial to girls or their natal families. Enslavement differed from other forms of girl transfer in that it involved violent capture, alienated the girl from her biological family, and did not have any safeguards to protect the girl from exploitation, violence, and sexual abuse.

All girls experienced some degree of labor exploitation as bonded dependents; many also suffered sexual assault and abuse as part of their girlhood. Historically whether or not Dahomean society condemned these acts of abuse as rape, assault, or illicit behavior depended on the girl's status and the relationship of the perpetrator to the girl. Dahomeans recognized the period from birth to ten years old as an age of innocence, during which one had no knowledge of sexuality or sex.[20] This ideal of associating girlhood with asexuality, however, did not match the reality. During the Atlantic Era from the sixteenth to nineteenth centuries, control of a girl's sexuality and reproductive abilities was another distinguishing feature that differentiated slavery from other forms of dependence.[21] An enslaved girl's mistress or master controlled her sexuality, which was put to both personal and economic use by their mistresses and masters; whereas a girl's guardian retained his claim to her sexuality when he transferred her as a pawn or entrusted girl to another household. The act of transferring did not grant any control over the girl's sexuality. During the colonial era, Dahomean girls engaged in the commonplace activities of street hawking or running errands were at a high risk for sexual assault. Many girls did not enjoy protection from sexual exploitation during their girlhoods.

Girlhood progressed into womanhood when females reached sexual maturity, married a spouse, bore children, established themselves as independent trader, and took on greater managerial responsibility in their marital household or even formed their own female-headed household. Girls gained social maturity and consequently female adulthood gradually through these experiences.[22] Alongside these physical developments and status markers, girls' labor and domestic responsibilities also evolved to reflect their maturation. These female life events normally occurred when a woman reached her mid to late teens and continued into her twenties. Dahomeans rarely relied on age alone as the defining characteristic of girlhood; more commonly, a group of factors indicated social age markers.[23] Maturation was an individual process, so some of the "girls" discussed in this book may have passed the chronological age of fourteen but were not yet recognized as adult women by their society. In Dahomey, this general definition of girlhood as a developmental stage lasting from the age of awareness until womanhood remained consistent over the centuries. This stable, normative base, however, encompassed a sociohistorical construct that evolved within a constant state of flux due to the larger political, economic, and social transformations of the eighteenth through twentieth centuries.[24] During this period, Dahomean households built their wealth on the unpaid labor of both free and captive girls. Girlhood in Dahomey diverged into two paths depending on whether the girl was born in Dahomey or if she was a foreign captive brought to the kingdom. The lives of both Dahomean and foreign-born girls who had reached the age of awareness were shaped by the institutions of dependence that dictated the terms by which they were incorporated into Dahomean households.

Bondage, Kinship, and Girlhood: Institutions of Household Dependence

In recent years, the history of African girlhood has developed around materially wealthy and theoretically sophisticated case studies focused on colonial girlhood during the twentieth century in former British colonies. These works provide important insight into how colonialism attempted to "modernize" girlhood, with an emphasis on the imperial efforts to "save" girls from customary practices that Europeans and some groups of Africans considered harmful, such as clitoridectomy, debt bondage, street hawking, early marriage, and child prostitution.[25] Through these works, we learn more about what Maria Lugones has termed "the colonial/modern gender system" and African attempts to engage with that system rather than about indigenous girlhood norms.[26] They also reveal more about adult agendas to transform girlhood than they do about girls' lived experiences.

While the scholarship on colonial girlhood has enriched the latter chapters of this book, the two distinct but overlapping fields of scholarship on the anthropology of child fostering and the history of women's and children's enslavement in Africa have provided an overarching theoretical framework and informed the analysis of the entire temporal period under consideration here. The various forms of academic study of child fostering in West Africa have a decades-long history in both Anglophone and Francophone scholarship. From the late 1970s into the 1990s, Mona Étienne, Esther Goody, Caroline Bledsoe, and Suzanne Lallemand published foundational ethnographic scholarship on child fostering in Côte-d'Ivoire, Liberia, Ghana, and Togo, respectively.[27] Goody and Lallemand applied the theoretical approaches of descent and alliance theory, respectively, to the subject of child fostering. In her book *Parenthood and Social Reproduction*, Goody argues that the various component roles that make up parenthood can be divided and allocated among parental figures. She proposes seeing parenthood as concerned with fulfilling certain tasks, many of which need not be completed by a single set of biological parents.[28] Lallemand argues in *La circulation des enfants* that the circulation of children among households was structurally similar to and interconnected with marriage. She argues that the British functionalist explanations of child circulation that reduce it to its socioeconomic dimensions are unsatisfactory. Alliance theorists, such as Lallemand, conceptualized marriage and child fostering as opportunistic forms of alliance building among strangers or nonrelatives.[29]

The Bonds of Kinship in Dahomey draws on both Goody and Lallemand and their respective paradigms in a hybrid approach that builds on the "new kinship studies" model. Erdmute Alber and other new kinship scholars have appropriately criticized both the descent and alliance models developed by Goody and Lallemand for ignoring the everyday reality of lived parenthood in order to sketch out the idealized norms of fosterage. Both Goody and Lallemand fail to consider the conflicting interests and motives of biological parents, foster parents, and foster children as they existed in specific times and places.[30] In addition to exposing the vast possibilities of the practice of fostering, new kinship studies provide a fresh set of terms for what anthropologists have previously referred to as "fictive" or "constructed" kinship. New kinship studies prompted scholars of kinship to abandon the foundational assumptions that biology and consanguinity determined kinship and to reorient kinship around experiential dimensions that have creative and dynamic potentialities. Kinship can therefore be based on sentiment, substance, and nurturance, and it can transcend contradictions between "real" and "fictive" or "biological" and "social" or "natural" and "constructed." New kinship scholars claim that kinship is better understood as the ongoing process of developing relationships and a sense of belonging.[31] The girls featured in *The Bonds of Kinship in Dahomey* all built kinship around experiential dimensions.

Through focusing on kinship as process, new kinship studies challenge the perspective that kinship and enslavement are fundamentally opposite concepts.[32] This view of kinship as process recognizes the resourcefulness of enslaved individuals and better represents the fluidity of kinship structures in "open" slave societies.[33] Dahomey was an open slave society, which meant that enslaved people and their children were gradually incorporated into a clientship or kinship arrangement within their mistress's or master's household. Over time, this integration obscured the previous enslaved status of a person. Social mobility for enslaved persons and their descendants was encouraged in certain situations.[34] Africans in these societies saw the incorporation of most outsiders as a way to expand their retinue of dependents and retainers.[35] This does not mean that the institution of enslavement in Dahomey or any open slave society was in any way harmless, especially during the initial years. Enslaved individuals did, however, create meaningful and enduring connections in their new life situations that evolved into kinship.[36] It was especially important for child slaves to create stable relationships with the adults who became their kin, protectors, and mentors. Bonds of enslavement and kinship were closely connected in open slave societies like Dahomey.[37] Kinspeople were simply persons who acknowledged a connection among themselves that was recognized by their society and whose lives were interwoven for a meaningful period.[38] The process of household formation in Dahomey produced kinship in ways that superseded biological ties.[39]

The degree to which scholars of child fostering and enslavement considered the intersection of gender and age has varied in the existing literature. All experiences of child dependence and bondage were heavily influenced by the gendered divisions in both labor and socialization into adulthood. Furthermore, in addition to the gender-specific labor they performed, girls had a distinct and unique value that boys did not—the possibility of being a permanent part of the household by marrying a male household member. This opportunity divided girls' loyalties from birth because they were socialized to serve a lineage other than their biological one[40] while also leaving them vulnerable to sexual exploitation and impregnation. Much of the important research on domestic slavery has transformed our understanding of the social relationships and ideology of servility by incorporating gender into its analysis. However, this same research has left largely unexamined the significance of age as a factor in captivity, servile relationships, and the ideology that justified servility.[41]

Portraits: New Approaches to Telling the History of African Girlhood

The major methodological challenge to writing a history of girlhood concentrated on the views and experiences of girls in Dahomey is that the archives of the precolonial kingdom and subsequent colony lack any sources written by these individuals themselves. How can historians navigate around the elite Dahomean men whose views influenced the European-authored archive from the seventeenth century to the twentieth century to gain a deeper understanding of girls' and women's perspectives? *The Bonds of Kinship in Dahomey* asks: How can historians bring the experiences of girls and women to the forefront? How do historians deconstruct the many layers of male mediation—both African and European—to prioritize girls' and women's points of view to discover what was important to them?

The Bonds of Kinship in Dahomey recenters the history of Dahomey around girls and girlhood through using images as mediums to refract written and oral sources. In physics, refraction refers to a transformation in form of a medium after it has passed through an interface that changes its direction. The refractive process bends sound or light to change its path. This book uses images, such as "A Fabric Seller" featured at the beginning of this chapter and on the book's cover, as an interface through which to refract sources to change the direction and foci of the historic narrative. This process results in a series of narrative portraits that are likenesses of individual West African girls who lived in the Kingdom or, later, the colony of Dahomey.

As Beninese historian Luc Garcia has observed, the European men who visited the Bight of Benin region during the Atlantic Era as well as the colonial administrators and ethnographers who traveled to the colony of Dahomey produced an "excess of riches" of source material. Since the early eighteenth century, the Kingdom of Dahomey was a "globally facing society" embedded in transnational trading networks that extended in multiple directions across the Atlantic and Indian Oceans, the West African region, and the Sahara Desert.[42] The sustained trade relationship that developed among Atlantic slave traders and the Kingdom of Dahomey produced a rich archive of written sources. These written sources changed in fundamental ways with the imposition of French colonial rule in 1894 and its subsequent shift from conquest to an institutionalized system of governance. Over three centuries, these records documented a male, Eurocentric narrative that, at best, marginalized girls and, at worst, ignored them completely.[43] While the records from the eighteenth through twentieth centuries are diverse and span the Atlantic and colonial eras, they share the commonality that European men produced almost all of them. These men gathered their information while they lived in or visited the area. They traveled to the Kingdom of Dahomey for various reasons including trade, diplomacy, religious missions, and, in the twentieth century, colonization.

This abundance paradoxically masked its shortcomings in its bounty.[44] These men produced a wealth of material about Dahomey, focusing on the political history of the region, the king and his palaces, commercial exchanges, and exotic rituals. This bounty of documentation created blind spots on certain subjects, such as girlhood, because European men had limitations on their interactions with African girls and it was beyond the scope of their primary interests. Histories of girlhood are among these obscured subjects within Western sources, which often reveal more about adult men's perceptions of girls than how these girls experienced girlhood as a life stage.[45] These white men's observations, experiences, prejudices, and discussions with elite West African men shaped their views on Dahomean girls and women. European men and their mostly male Dahomean interlocutors had a significant influence over the narrative preserved and reproduced in the archives.[46] And although some European men formed close and enduring relationships with Dahomean women, neither they nor their Dahomean counterparts had firsthand experiences of girlhood. Despite the extraordinary richness of the records of the precolonial Kingdom of Dahomey, the history of its girls and their experiences are largely neglected. Where does one start to deconstruct the European, masculine gaze and narrative authority over the history of African girlhood?

The first step is to analyze the medium before it is bent through knowing the sources, their biases, their agendas, and the historiography. This was done in the previous section. Then the second step is to find an interface and start there; in this case, the interface is the image. While d'Albéca controlled the framing and the timing of the image capture, the two females pictured created the substantive elements of the visual composition. With d'Albéca, the fabric seller and the girl coproduced a multiauthored visual artifact.[47] The image is a cross-cultural creation incorporating elements that exceeded the intentions of the European colonists in Africa.[48] D'Albéca's desire to document life in Africa, rather than staging the image, allowed for the subjects to nonverbally express themselves. The fabric seller and girl chose their clothes and accessories as well as the positioning of their bodies. D'Albéca did not orchestrate these aspects of the image. The image documents how, in their everyday lives, the fabric seller and girl expressed themselves through sartorial language. In the late nineteenth century, inhabitants of the Bight of Benin relied on visual status markers, such as cloth, to differentiate themselves from the recent large influxes of enslaved persons and other bonded dependents. Both women and men placed great emphasis on cloth's power to communicate their social positions.[49] In the image, the fabric seller and the girl express their statuses through their clothing, accessories, and hairstyles.[50] The fabric seller adorns her body with either two pagnes layered on top of each other or loose, light trousers under a pagne.[51] Even in a grayscale image, the fabric seller's over-pagne almost gleams in the sunlight, which emphasizes its pristine condition. The market woman's conspicuously higher-quality pagne with ornate bands of thin horizontal lines makes the girl's clothing look inferior, almost dull, with no decorative pattern. Their attire differentiates them as individuals and within a larger society.[52] The fabric seller visually conveys her elevated social position through her choice of garments and accessories. Similarly, the girl's simpler clothing establishes her subservient status. The attire of the fabric seller and girl tell a story of their own that sheds light on their lived experiences and social standing. In focusing on their choices, rather than d'Albéca's, their contributions to authorship in producing this image become clear.

Beyond their clothing, their hairstyles offer clues to their daily routines and statuses. The fabric seller further demonstrates her high standing with an elaborate, coiffed hairstyle. The sculpting of her tresses into a cone-like shape serves the twofold purpose of pleasing the eye and communicating her elevated standing within her household hierarchy that exempted her from carrying loads balanced atop her head. In contrast, the younger girl wears a simple band of cloth that conceals her presumably nonstyled hair. This headgear also served a practical purpose: the girl could coil it into a disc to protect her hair and cushion the goods that she carried on her head. It would facilitate her day-to-day activities of carrying atop her head pots of water from a river to her home or of hawking goods in the streets and markets, two onerous tasks that took up significant amounts of girls' time each day.[53] Without such cushioning, the friction from the baskets, trays, and pots that she balanced for extended periods each day could rub a bald spot on the crown of her head, an uncomfortable disfigurement.[54] This brief analysis supports the assertion that images, especially those that portray an everyday moment, have the "capacity to go beyond what is obvious in the visible itself and open up something far less evident."[55] The social connotations attached to these visual details reveal two things: first, how individuals conveyed their status to everyone they met and, second, the complexities of how female hierarchies operated within households.

The preceding analysis sketches out the ways in which images can bend the narrative and focus it on girls and their lived experiences. The next step is asking questions that the image cannot answer. The image raises at least one important question that it does not address: What was the relationship between the girl and the woman? The analysis of the image only narrows down the possibilities. The girl's position between the woman's home in the background and her market stall on the roadside implies that she has access to the home and that the two might live there together. The clear inequality in social positions suggests that the relationship between the two is not familial, such as biological mother-daughter, sisters, or even cowives since family members would likely display their statuses in similar ways. More plausibly, the two females were bound together by some form of servile household relationship.

Each chapter begins with an image, typically a photograph, but the initial chapters include engraved lithographs. Beginning a chapter with an image serves several purposes. First, it allows readers to directly and immediately engage with relevant primary source material. Second, it embraces the flexibility of the photographic medium to generate a platform for exploring new analytical spaces.[56] The interpretation of visual cues in photographs can vary among historians because visual perception is both culturally formed and historically informed.[57] The unstable nature of this visual genre generates questions and empathy, both of which assist in reorienting the narrative around girls. Third, taken together with textual and oral evidence, visual sources produce a collection of fragmentary data that both fills in some gaps and reveals other omissions.[58] By creating a dialogue among these separate but sometimes overlapping gaps, one can uncover a wealth of thought-provoking histories of girlhood in Dahomey.[59]

Often these images are of anonymous girls. The opening passage of each chapter connects the image to a named individual girl whose story written sources have in part preserved. The biographies featured are based on "partial, fleeting, or disjointed" narratives contained in the archives.[60] The established conventions of the genre of biography as a cradle-to-grave comprehensive life story is impossible for most Dahomean girls.[61] Instead, this book alternates between two approaches selected to enhance the richness of the data in the archives instead of focusing on the limitations of the source material. Chapters 2, 5, and 6 take a collective biography approach that acknowledges the unique individuals who make up a particular group. In these chapters, short-prose biographical accounts of Dahomean girls with some sort of characteristic or experience in common drive the narrative. Chapters 3 and 4 rely on prosopographically inspired methods to analyze the limited primary source information in ways that improve on the existing evidence.[62] Chapter 7, which is neither a collective biography nor a prosopography, presents a biography of Télé Acapovi, the most well-documented girl in the Beninese archives.

Collective biographies and prosopographies are conceptual approaches to life stories that overlap methodologically and analytically—so much so that some scholars use the two terms interchangeably. Both collective biography and prosopography seek to understand the common background characteristics of a specific group of historical actors. Prosopography, however, is the study of shared biographical details of individuals taken in aggregate, whereas collective biography is a profile of a particular group or a collection of individual biographies. Prosopography is an alternative approach to life histories or individual biographies. It is specifically designed for situations where there is insufficient primary source evidence to write an individual life history or a collective biography. *The Bonds of Kinship in Dahomey* relies on what might be called a prosopographically inspired approach because, unlike traditional prosopography, the data on female householders and their dependents in nineteenth-century Ouidah or girl runaways from conquest-era Dahomey to French colonial Porto-Novo cannot meet any specific numerical requirements, which is a key feature of prosopographies of the elite.[63] Once the important characteristics of lived experiences that justify aggregating the data sample were identified, data-based inferences recenter the chapter narrative around a single individual's life portrait.

Chapter Overview

Chapter 1 functions in part as a prologue in that it lays out the ideological foundations and pragmatic reasons for girl transfers from the point of view of the Dahomean monarchy. Subsequent chapters focus on individuals and take biographical approaches to center each chapter around the life of a girl or a small group of them. Chapter 1 explores the many ways the Dahomean royal household built a political economy around its ability to capture and collect girls by various means. It shows how the palace used specific forms of girl transfers to emphasize its exceptionality and project its power. The monarch also participated in widespread practices of child circulation, such as entrustment, to serve as an exemplar for popular ideals. Chapter 1 describes how, from the eighteenth century onward, royal policy required that guardianship of children of both genders be separate from their biological parenthood. Families willingly and unwillingly gave their daughters to the palace as part of the population's obligation to the king. Girl captives recently seized in conquered territories or areas targeted for annual raids added to this number from within the kingdom. The girls sent to the palaces of the Dahomean king fulfilled a variety of economic, military, ritual, and domestic roles.

Chapters 2 and 3 temporally overlap, and both cover the nineteenth century. Chapter 2 argues that during the nineteenth century, Dahomean monarchs Gezo and Glèlè, who reigned from 1818 to 1858 and 1858 to 1889, respectively, continued to play a crucial role in dictating the patterns of forced and coerced child transfers. As international abolitionist rhetoric influenced Atlantic politics, the Dahomean royal household and its interpreters as well as European visitors developed a new Atlantic vocabulary that distinguished a rich repertoire of norms about child transfer. Chapter 3 moves away from the royal palaces of Dahomey to the kingdom's commercial center of Ouidah. The chapter focuses on the lives of Agbessipé and her enslaved Yorùbán mother. Agbessipé rose to become one of the wealthiest female entrepreneurs in Ouidah during her lifetime. Crucial to Agbessipé's commercial empire were both pawned and enslaved girls. As the history of this remarkable woman shows, girls' servitude and bondage to women was not a consequence of these women's attempts to gain economic independence; rather, it was a prerequisite for it.

Chapters 1 through 3 examine the value of girls to the precolonial political economy, and chapters 4 through 7 shift the focus to the sociocultural history of girls' labor in the colonial era. The scope of these latter four chapters extends beyond the historic Kingdom of Dahomey to include the surrounding kingdoms, city-states, and confederations that were part of the colony of Dahomey. Chapter 4 looks at how girls coped with the changes of the late nineteenth century, a time of economic volatility and political upheaval ushered in by the conquest era. Through the life story of Aholoupé, this chapter examines how girls were not just helpless victims of slave trafficking; they also took advantage of the chaotic time to renegotiate their dependence, transform their status, and change their identity.

Chapters 5 and 6 examine how the colonial economy continued to rely on the precolonial practice of entrusted girls. Chapter 5 analyzes how the meaning of human trafficking of girls has changed over time, revealing how, by the 1930s, colonial officials were questioning whether entrustment was enslavement. Dahomean women, however, effectively defended the practice of entrusting girls in colonial tribunals. They based their arguments on claims about the precolonial custom of entrusting girls to social mothers and their understanding of the established colonial definition of the crime of *traite*, or human trafficking. Chapter 6 further explores the caregiving roles of social mothers toward entrusted girls who were experiencing the aftereffects of rape. Despite growing hostility in tribunals and low rates of conviction for rape after the 1931 judicial reorganization, social mothers continued to demand justice from colonial tribunals, and girls persisted in sharing their experiences of sexual assault in these legal forums. Women acting as the girls' guardians showed their concern for their wards by consistently supporting their claims of sexual assault.

Chapter 7 examines an extraordinary potential threat to girls—human sacrifice. In April 1936, Télé Acapovi, a thirteen-year-old girl, disappeared in Abomey, Dahomey. The documentation of Télé's young life is exceptional. Colonial administrators attempted their own version of prosopography as the investigation into Télé's disappearance remained open and unsolved for years. Colonial administrators drew their own conclusions about the actions and experiences of girls like Télé and defined what "type" of girl she was based on their views of the attributes they considered most fundamental to her identity. Rumors circulated that Chief Justin Aho, a district chief and member of the royal family of Abomey, had performed a sacrifice of the girl. The investigation into Télé's disappearance uncovered concerns about the changing norms regarding girl transfers in the context of colonial society. West African families struggling with the global Great Depression of the 1930s often transferred their daughters to unfamiliar households with whom there was no established relationship of trust. This arrangement became known as "borrowing." Chapter 7 discusses the fears and concerns surrounding the abuse and possible sacrifice of Télé.

"The King of Dahomy's Levée" by Francis Chesham from *The History of Dahomey* by Archibald Dalzel © British Library/AKG Images, Ltd.

1

The Value of Girls to the Royal Household of Dahomey, 1720s–1870s

In a 1726 letter to King George I of England, King Agaja of Dahomey observed, "But we think it very strange, that your God's Laws and Customs, confine so great a King to one Wife." He later explains why this appeared peculiar to him: "As we esteem our selves, and are looked upon [b]y all neighbouring Nations to be greater or richer, the more *Women* we have."[1] In "The King of Dahomy's [sic] Levée," an eighteenth-century Dahomean king— either Agaja, who reigned from c. 1708 to 1740, or Tegbesu, who ruled from 1740 to 1774—ostentatiously displayed his wealth through surrounding himself with his *ahosi* or wives.[2] In this fanciful 1793 image inspired by Archibald Dalzel's text *The History of Dahomey*, the engraver Francis Chesham featured the monarch as the central figure; however, the strikingly beautiful ahosi are the most eye-catching element in the scene. While Chesham never set foot in West Africa, Dalzel was an expert on the region. He spent extended periods over thirty years living in West Africa, and from 1767 to 1770, he served as director of the English-controlled William's Fort at Ouidah in the Kingdom of Dahomey.[3] Chesham's image combines Dalzel's firsthand experiences in the court of Tegbesu with slave trader and sea captain William Snelgrave's description of the court of King Agaja in 1727. Dalzel had incorporated extant passages from Snelgrave in his account, inextricably linking the two eighteenth-century sources. The image transforms Agaja's statement into a visual representation of what scholars have designated as the wealth in people paradigm, whereby in many African societies wealth was embodied in the accrual of interpersonal dependents of all kinds including wives, children, clients, pawns, and slaves.⁴ As the details of the image suggest, this wealth was not simply about quantity of dependents.⁵

The text of the letter and the composition of the engraving emphasize the value of adult women to the king. Chesham faithfully produced a rendering of an eighteenth-century diplomatic audience with the king of Dahomey, who was overshadowed by his entourage of ahosi. Dalzel described the women of the royal court:⁶

> All the women were finely dressed from the middle downwards; the upper part of the body of either sex, remaining, in this country, generally uncovered: their arms were adorned with many large manellos, or bracelets of gold, of great value; and round their necks, and in their hair, were abundance of beads, of divers colours ... which are in as great esteem with the negroes, as diamonds among the Europeans. ... The neck, arms, and ancles [sic] are adorned with beads and cowries; and rings of silver, or baser metal, encircle the fingers. The ears are pierced so as to admit the little finger, and a coral bead of that size stuck into each⁷

Chesham portrayed the wives in proximity to the king as beautiful women draped in sumptuous cloth and adorned with necklaces and headdresses decorated with beads, jewels, and cowrie shells as well as armbands and bracelets made of precious metals. These women literally adorned themselves with currency. During the early modern era, Europeans purchased human captives with the *manellos* (metal bracelets) and cowrie shells. Chesham embellished the wives' hairstyles and transformed their attire into Greco-Roman-inspired togas rather than a pagne wrapped around their bosoms, the more common attire of West African women. While the women's hairstyles and adornments may not have been entirely authentic, many of the details came directly from Dalzel's text.

This visual representation emphasizes the ahosi's beauty, but as the image shows, their importance to the king went beyond superficial aesthetics. These women contributed their talents and labor to the successful domestic, political, and economic functioning of their marital households. Both Chesham's image and Dalzel's text confirm that these wives performed practical roles during diplomatic exchanges between eighteenth-century Dahomean kings and European officials. Ahosi facilitated and enforced royal protocol. For example, no visitor approached "nearer than twenty feet to the King's chair. If they wished to speak to him, they first kissed the ground; then whispered their pleasure into the ear of an old woman, who communicated it to the King, and brought his answer."[8] Kings inherited their predecessors' ahosi, who had entered the palace as girls or young women and remained there until their death. This "old woman" that Dalzel observed had been part of Agaja's court and continued to serve Tegbesu as a trusted member of his inner circle. Palace protocol prohibited visitors from speaking directly to the monarch. Elder female ahosi mediated access to the king.[9] In the image, the wife shown at the king's left shoulder holding a fan near her face likely served this function. Chesham, though, does not make her appear older than the other ahosi pictured. The other ahosi fulfilled other roles, such as the wife who knelt in front of the king with a golden spittoon for him to expel tobacco waste.[10] Another two stood behind him with fans to cool him. Other roles were less visually evident: some wives functioned as official record-keepers or living archives, painstakingly committing to their memories an accurate transcript of all that transpired for the king's subsequent reference. In a society that prized oral communication, these women fulfilled vital roles, preserving official ledgers, documenting negotiations, and serving in integral bureaucratic capacities. These women's direct access to the ruler reflected their place at the apex of palace hierarchy and their powerful positions in the governance structure.[11]

The Kingdom of Dahomey has an exceptionally rich and well-documented history of elite royal women.[12] However, these privileged ahosi, such as the dozen or so who surround the king in Chesham's image, represented the minority of the thousands of women and girls who resided in the palace. Ahosi literally translates from Fon, the official, indigenous language of the Kingdom of Dahomey, to English as wives of the king; however, the English term *wife* is not truly synonymous with this capacious category that refers to any subordinate dependent of the king female or male who was not born into the royal family. Estimates vary, but in 1724, at least two thousand ahosi were part of the royal household of Dahomey. In the 1726 letter to King George I of England, Agaja bragged that he had seven thousand wives distributed among seven palaces. He further specified that this figure did not include household slaves.[13] Since wives could be of captive origin, how Agaja distinguished household slaves from wives in the palace is unclear. While Agaja's figure seems unlikely so early in the rise and expansion of Dahomey, even the more modest two thousand number represented an enlargement of regional royal palace norms in the Bight of Benin.[14] For example, the kings of Allada and Hueda, two kingdoms to the south of Dahomey, which were conquered by their expanding northern neighbor in 1724 and 1727 respectively, had hundreds of wives compared with Agaja's thousands.[15] Dahomey's higher numbers reflected the wealth that accompanied the kingdom's position as one of the leading slave traders, which allowed the monarchy to amass and support a large household.

The Dahomean royal household was almost exclusively female; the only biologically male individuals who lived there were the king; perhaps a few very young princes; and, through the eighteenth century, a small number of eunuchs.[16] The palaces were veritable small towns of women and girls since, as Agaja claimed to British trader Bulfinch Lambe, "no Man sleeps within the Walls of any of the [seven royal palaces] after Sunset, but my self [the king]."[17] Most of these thousands of women would not have been among the elite entourage regularly interacting with the king or participating in statecraft. Chesham's image depicts a second distinct but less ostentatious group of ahosi in the background. On the right side of the image, wives of lower status bring in prepared food to serve to guests or perhaps to sell to onlookers at the public ceremony. The majority of ahosi in the palace fulfilled the more mundane and less glamorous roles of cooking vast quantities of food, laundering clothes, transporting water, counting cowries, staffing the royal workshops, or serving in the king's female army corps.

Often overlooked is how the king acquired these female dependents in such immense numbers. Scholars have investigated the functions performed by adult women in the political economy of the kingdom. Yet the roles these women fulfilled during their girlhood and adolescence in the palace are not as well understood.[18] Where did these women and girls come from? How did Agaja and his descendants obtain the thousands of women and girls needed to run his many households, staff the workshops that held royal monopolies on producing certain handicrafts, or fulfill the necessary quotas for the battalions of female soldiers? What labor contributions did girls make to the royal household, the Dahomean economy, the kingdom's military, and the political economy? This chapter examines the influx of female children to the palace and investigates the evolution of the roles girls played both politically and economically in Dahomey. In the process of expanding and centralizing their state, Dahomean kings built a political economy around existing regional norms that validated the transfer of children as essential to a proper upbringing. The palace as a gendered space placed a premium on the collection and capture of girls whose socioeconomic value increased as royal demands for them intensified.

This chapter sheds light on some of the various youthful fates of the thousands of collected and captured girls who lived the remainder of their lives within the palace confines. It relies primarily on written sources from 1669 to 1871. During this time, at least twenty European men visited the Kingdoms of Allada, Hueda, and Dahomey and wrote a collection of travelogues, letters, and journals about their visits. Most of them failed to mention, or did so only in passing, the royal collections of girls. Three notable exceptions were *Voyage to the Coast of Guinée* by Pierre LaBarthe published in 1803, *Memoirs of the Reign of Bossa Ahádee* by Robert Norris, and *Description de la nigritie* (Description of the Land of the Blacks) by Antoine Edme Pruneau de Pommegorge, both published in 1789. LaBarthe was chief of the Colonial Bureau dealing with Africa and the Orient from 1794 to 1808. His travelogue was based on his 1788 trip to West Africa. Norris was actively involved in the slave trade from the 1750s to the 1780s. During the time he lived in Dahomey, he learned to speak Fon.[19] Pommegorge resided in Dahomey for an unheard-of period, from 1748 to 1764, while working for France's Compagnie des Indes. He served three tours of duty at France's fort Saint Louis in Ouidah. Both Norris and Pommegorge commented extensively on the kingdom's collection of girls during Tegbesu's reign from 1740 to 1774. Both men's extended stays in the kingdom allowed them to witness the collection of children at least once.

In addition to these contemporary written sources, I have relied at pivotal points on the oral history of Tegbesu's reign recorded in the mid-twentieth century by Édouard Dunglas, a colonial functionary and politician who spent almost two decades stationed in Dahomey from 1934 until his death in 1952.[20] His informants came from two of the ten royal sublineages; specifically, those descended from Kings Glèlè and Béhanzin. As Edna Bay has rightly cautioned, oral histories of Dahomey reflected the perspective of the ruling class and were, therefore, inherently self-serving.[21] Dunglas's informants were not part of a lineage descended from Tegbesu; rather, they had personal incentives to discredit Tegbesu to bolster their ancestors' claims to legitimacy and their own claims to power. Dunglas recorded a history of Tegbesu's reign that, though unsubstantiated in the contemporary written record, revealed unexpected insights into the actions of an eccentric monarch. This recorded oral history has proved fruitful in exploring new paths of inquiry and different ways of understanding the existing data.²²

Ideals of Child Fostering along the Bight of Benin: Princely Life Histories in the Seventeenth and Early Eighteenth Centuries

Oral tradition insists and the fragmentary evidence from written precolonial sources suggests that parents chose to send their children to reside in other households because they recognized this experience as a valuable practice for socialization into adulthood. Unfortunately, during the seventeenth and early eighteenth century, very little is known about girls' lived experiences in the kingdoms of Hueda and Allada. The oral histories preserved rich details about the experiences of princes in these kingdoms. The life histories of royal princes proved that child circulation in West Africa was a more complex phenomenon than simply a matter of crisis fostering.²³ Royal families had both long- and short-term goals when they willingly transferred princes to residences and families outside the kings' palaces. In the seventeenth and eighteenth centuries, the biographies of young princes in the kingdoms of Allada and Hueda articulated the underlying ideals that justified the practice of sending children away from their birthplace and biological family. Though these ideals transcended gender and class boundaries, it is important to acknowledge that the transfers of princes out of the royal household for their formative years differed from the experiences of transferred girls in that upon reaching adulthood, the princes would return to their natal home, the royal palace, whereas transferred girls normally joined their marital home upon maturation rather than returning to their biological kin's household.

Allada and Hueda were two of the "little kingdoms" that populated the seventeenth-century Bight of Benin. These kingdoms were hardly more than city-states, encompassing only several dozen square miles each. The Kingdom of Allada was established around 1575, and by the early seventeenth century, it was the most powerful of the kingdoms of the region.²⁴ Allada's dominance was fragile and frequently contested by erstwhile allies such as Hueda and its powerful neighbors to the east, the Kingdom of Benin and the Oyo Empire. Hueda was established at approximately the same time as Allada, in the mid- to late sixteenth century.²⁵ The coastal Kingdom of Hueda bordered the Kingdom of Allada, and both participated in the Atlantic slave trade with competing ports at Ouidah in Hueda, and Offra—or, after 1692,

Jakin—in Allada.²⁶ The highly competitive and tense environment of the Bight of Benin necessitated diplomatic alliances among these kingdoms. The transferring of children created interlineal networks that further solidified these alliances. Fostering royal children was a politically meaningful process that created relationships of mutual obligation and, perhaps, even personal affection or respect.

Princes in the royal lineages of Allada and Hueda spent their childhoods in households and institutions away from the royal court.²⁷ Their life histories show that it was neither expected nor desirable that children would spend their entire youth in their natal homes. For example, King Tezifon, ruler of Allada in the 1660s, spent his youth on São Tomé, an island off the Atlantic Coast of West Africa in the Gulf of Guinea.²⁸ São Tomé was uninhabited until the Portuguese arrived there around 1470. In the late fifteenth century, São Tomé became one of Portugal's first settler colonies along the coast of Africa.²⁹ The length of Tezifon's stay and the exact dates of his residency are unknown, though he likely spent several years there.³⁰ While in São Tomé, Tezifon received a European-style education at the Catholic seminary on the island.³¹ He spent enough time at São Tomé to become conversant in Portuguese and was one of the Alladan elite who spoke the language flawlessly.³² As part of his education, he learned the tenets of Catholicism, though he declined baptism.³³ Tezifon accepted the religious education as part of the price of learning the Portuguese language. Throughout the early modern era, missionaries provided one of the few educational opportunities for Africans to formally learn European languages such as Portuguese, the lingua franca of the Euro-African coastal trade at the time. Being conversant in Portuguese was an important diplomatic and commercial skill for the elite of Allada.

Local West African traditions of child fostering effortlessly incorporated the São Tomé seminary into the existing system. Alladans recognized the linguistic and cultural skills Tezifon gained there as being valuable to their economy as it became integrated into Atlantic trade. African rulers strengthened their networks with Europeans by transferring children, such as young Tezifon, to European religious institutions, but they also relied on their children's circulation within indigenous networks to solidify local alliances. In the seventeenth and eighteenth centuries, Europeans entered into existing social systems as just one more participant in a network.³⁴ As the most powerful kingdom in the region during Tezifon's childhood, Allada sought to expand and integrate Europeans more fully into its system of alliances.

Due to the cultural connections and ethnic commonality between the kingdoms of Allada and Hueda, it is not surprising that princes in Hueda also spent their childhoods outside the palace. The political and social situation in the Kingdom of Hueda at this time, however, differed significantly from that in Allada. Child circulation of princes within Hueda helped to unite and stabilize the kingdom. This was particularly important after the death of King Agbangla in 1703. Over the next two and a half decades, succession crises plagued the kingdom, and no king was able to successfully consolidate power. At the turn of the eighteenth century, King Huffon spent his childhood with a foster family within the Kingdom of Hueda, as did his son. King Huffon was born around 1695, and in 1709, he ascended to the throne at the unusually young age of fourteen.[35] In the intervening years, a foster family raised the prince. The skills Huffon acquired from his experience differed radically from those of Tezifon. Huffon did not learn a European language or familiarize himself with Christianity; rather, he acquainted himself with the day-to-day lives of his future subjects. He guarded the pigs belonging to his foster father.[36] Throughout his childhood with a humble foster family, the heir to the throne was unaware of his royal status and destiny. The fostered prince gained firsthand experience in agriculture, the economic base of the kingdom.[37] This intimate knowledge of his subjects' daily lives most likely made him a more effective ruler than he might otherwise have been.

His experience proved so formative and politically important that Huffon had his heir fostered with a provincial family. The choice was not Huffon's alone, though. The elite of the kingdom helped the king choose which family would raise the young prince—in this case, a chiefly family in the frontier province of Zingué.[38] Huffon wanted to build closer ties with this province and integrate the chosen family into the kingdom. Kings sent children to these areas to solidify alliances and establish far-reaching, diverse networks. These personal relationships often proved to be important resources for princes into adulthood and assisted their successful accession to the throne.[39]

Princes in the kingdoms along the Bight of Benin spent their childhoods residing outside the palace.[40] As these examples prove, child fostering was not stigmatized as an indication of low socioeconomic status whereby only children from poorer backgrounds were transferred to wealthier households. The Alladan and Huedan princes' childhood experiences show that ideological justifications and practical motivations for child circulation already existed in the mid-seventeenth and early eighteenth centuries before the southward expansion of the Kingdom of Dahomey. These examples from Allada and Hueda show a fundamental willingness among peoples of the region to transfer their children to foster families and, in turn, accept transferred children. These royal childhood biographies are not representative of commoners' childhoods or child circulation in either kingdom. However, they do showcase the normative ideologies that were widely accepted by the general population. During childhood, princes circulated within social networks that commoners rarely accessed.

Girl Transfers into the Royal Palaces of Allada, Hueda, and Dahomey Compared

Kings along the Bight of Benin and their royal households participated in a political economy that included child transfers as a crucial part of both alliance building and wealth generation. As Agaja explained to King George in the Bight of Benin, there was a gendered element to royal households' accumulation of dependents. Transferred girls possessed a unique long-term value to their foster families. Girls could be permanently incorporated into these adoptive households through marriage rather than being returned to their natal family, as was the norm for boys. Royal palaces of the region preferred girls over boys because of their productive and reproductive abilities. Additionally, households socialized girls to belong to a lineage other than their natal one, which was not the case with boys.[41] While the ideals that justified the transfer of children were gender neutral, royal households enacted policies that placed a premium value on girls.

Royal households sought to accumulate a large number of female dependents as evidence of their far-reaching networks as well as an outward expression of their wealth and prestige. The demands of royal households for female children created an environment whereby ever larger numbers of girls migrated in a one-way, permanent transfer. The king of Hueda appropriated girls as one manifestation of his royal privilege that distinguished him from other elite men of the kingdom. Girls in the Kingdom of Hueda were vulnerable to the arbitrary and forced recruitment into the king's household. William Bosman, a merchant with the Dutch West India Company stationed in the Gold Coast, visited Hueda in the 1690s. He saw how the king gained his hundreds of wives, explaining: "For whenever they [three of the king's principal captains] see a beautiful Virgin, they immediately present her to the King, which none of his Subjects dare presume to refuse or contradict."[42] Bosman contended that Huedan girls did not consider being incorporated into the king's household a favorable distinction. According to Bosman, the king took the "honor to lye with her twice or thrice; after which she is obliged to pass the remainder of her Life like a nun."[43] Bosman, a Protestant, found such a fate revolting. Not all of the hundreds of girls absorbed into the palace serviced the sexual demands of the king, as Europeans such as Bosman salaciously suggested. In royal households with attached harems, girls played diverse and essential roles that did not always involve sex.[44] The women and girls ensured the functioning of the household, the execution of official ceremonies of state bureaucracy, and the success of the royal economic enterprises.

Since its founding in the early seventeenth century, the Kingdom of Dahomey participated in this regional system of royal households amassing large numbers of girls and women within its palaces.[45] Around 1625, King Ouegbedja formed the Kingdom of Dahomey in the inland plateau region of Abomey.[46] At this time, it was as small as its southern neighbors Allada and Hueda. The Kingdom of Allada's power began to decline during the mid-seventeenth century, and political turmoil engulfed Hueda at the turn of the century. From the 1700s to the 1720s, the monarchs' power in both Allada and Hueda diminished and proved more aspirational than effective.[47] Both kingdoms continued to prosper economically despite the weaknesses of their monarchs.[48] The political powerlessness of both kingdoms combined with their wealth derived from agriculture and the transatlantic slave trade made them attractive targets for an ambitious, expansionist rival—the Kingdom of Dahomey. In the eighteenth century, Dahomey grew quickly in size and military strength. The upstart Kingdom of Dahomey took advantage of the region's political turbulence, a by-product of the increased volume of slave trading spurred on by the Caribbean sugar revolution of the 1640s through 1680s.[49] In the early eighteenth century, the Kingdom of Dahomey transformed from an insignificant inland polity into a dominant regional power that through its militaristic zeal either conquered or terrorized its neighbors in the Bight of Benin. King Agaja expanded the Kingdom of Dahomey southward beyond the central plateau region to the Atlantic Coast. Agaja conquered the rival kingdoms of Allada in 1724 and Hueda in 1727. In just those few short years, Dahomey doubled in size and became a key player in the transatlantic slave trade.

The kingdoms of Allada, Hueda, and Dahomey all placed great diplomatic, social, and economic importance on girls' incorporation into their royal palaces. The Kingdom of Dahomey, however, expanded this system to an unprecedented scale. The kings of Allada and Hueda had hundreds of wives in their palaces, whereas the eighteenth-century kings of Dahomey had thousands. Immediately after conquering these two neighboring kingdoms, the king of Dahomey established his effective authority by demanding their recognition of his triumph over them.[50] According to Bulfinch Lambe, who had been held captive in King Agaja's court from 1724 to 1726, King Agaja explained that after he conquered Allada, he took the former king's wives and moved them to his own household. He did this because Dahomey and all of the neighboring kingdoms considered the number of royal wives to be indicative of his power and the wealth of his kingdom.[51] King Agaja and his successors were not satisfied with the former king's wives; they also demanded the surrendering of girls from both kingdoms as part of the subjugation process. During the eighteenth century, transfers of girls to the expanding Dahomean state regularly occurred as part of tribute payments from newly conquered territories.

The king demanded a large number of girls for both symbolic and pragmatic reasons. In addition to the social capital they conferred on the king, they also performed crucial economic roles that supported the monarchy's stability. West African households, including royal ones, were commercial units in which labor was divided by both gender and age. Girls performed a variety of economic functions that contributed to the financial viability of the royal household. These functions included working and weeding the king's fields and fetching water to irrigate them.[52] Women and girls also spent countless hours processing the agricultural harvests, working together to grind the staple grains of the regional diet: maize, millet, and sorghum.[53] Grinding harvested grains was just the first step in a longer process that could take many days to produce staple foods. The day-to-day sustenance of the thousands of residents in the palace required an untold number of girls to cook meals.[54] Beyond feeding the population of the royal palace, the girls also prepared "provisions for the King's ministers and principal men, who, although they live in their own houses with their families, yet are all furnished with food by the King, which is prepared in the palace." The male and female ministers' ranking as elite ahosi of the king entitled them to provisions from the lower-ranked "wives" of the king. Ministers were given such benefits to highlight their dependence on the king and his retinue of servants and slaves.[55]

In addition to the household duties necessary for day-to-day life, girls contributed to the proper functioning of the palace's rituals. Girls helped prepare the massive amounts of food required for the elaborate, months-long ritual events of Hwetanu, an annual celebration for the royal ancestors.[56] In the early eighteenth century, King Agaja introduced Hwetanu as an element of both ritual observance and political statecraft. Politically, Hwetanu reinforced Agaja's authority and legitimized his ascension to the throne.[57] Massive feasting was an integral part of these lengthy rites, which assembled Dahomean notables, ambassadors from across West Africa, and all Europeans living in the kingdom.[58] In addition to their sacred value, the Hwetanu rituals contributed to the kingdom's political stability, economic prosperity, judicial function, and military success. The importance of these annual ceremonies to Dahomean life cannot be overstated. Hwetanu expressed the totality of Dahomean civilization and was at the heart of the very foundations of the political institutions and social organization of the kingdom.[59] On a smaller scale, girls and women cooked provisions for any visiting diplomatic party. European traders relied on the meals the king's wives sent to them and their entourage. Older girls strong enough to carry large loads on their heads also assisted in the distribution of daily and occasional food deliveries. Several European observers went so far as to say that the king's wives were "principally" and "constantly" engaged in "carrying food in immense gourds or calabashes" or water in pots on their heads.[60] Girls assisted palace women in the preparation of food for sale, for the palace's consumption, for ritual festivals, and for visitors' sustenance while in the kingdom.

Many of the thousands of ahosi entered the palace as young girls whose labor allowed the state to carry out its duties. Girlhood in the Bight of Benin region changed in significant ways during the eighteenth century due to reconfigurations in the political economy of the expanding Kingdom of Dahomey. Dahomey built on existing traditions and innovated them as well. The royal palace did not create a brand-new practice but rather applied a different logic to a preexisting system.[61] The king of Dahomey strategically used girls to increase the palace's wealth, demonstrate his prestige, fulfill royal ritual responsibilities, and ensure the day-to-day functioning of the palace. The royal household served as a model proving that a household could thrive in its domestic and economic functions with a labor hierarchy that excluded men by dividing the labor among a hierarchy of girls and women.

"Children Belong to the State": An Emerging Ideology during the Reign of Tegbesu (1740–1774)

While the palace relied directly on girls' labor, it did not focus only on controlling the circulation of girls into the palace. The 1740s were a period of internal challenges for the Kingdom of Dahomey, and children were crucial to resolving many of the resulting predicaments. King Agaja died in 1740, and a bitter struggle for succession ensued among many of the surviving princes. Avissu, the youngest of the claimants, emerged victorious, taking Tegbesu as his reign name.[62] Throughout the first decade of his rule, Tegbesu struggled to consolidate his authority.[63] Upon assuming power, he had to overcome political divisions within Dahomey and a bankrupt treasury. Surmounting these obstacles called for drastic action.[64] Under his guidance and vision, the monarchy created new ideologies of power along with an increasingly centralized state.[65] Part of this strategy was to expand the palace's bureaucracy and opulence. Since the palaces were almost exclusively female spaces, this meant amassing more wives, more female guards, and more female slaves.[66] This led to an extraordinary demand for collected girls in Dahomey and for captive girls and women within the palace. Additionally, this policy of centralization aimed to regulate the circulation patterns and foster alliances among the ministers' sons. Dahomey recognized the power of children and their distribution as a type of currency that formed the foundation of kinship allegiance networks.[67] Controlling the transfers of children especially among the elite further strengthened Dahomey's authority over newly conquered areas and their existing structures of power.

Robert Norris, a British slave trader, described Dahomey during Tegbsu's reign as an autocratic and tyrannical state.[68] Norris was an exceptionally well-informed eighteenth-century European who spent eighteen years as a slave trader who frequently visited Dahomey and learned the Fon language.[69] Norris observed that during Tegbesu's reign, the Dahomean monarch's absolutism took new forms due to Dahomey's consolidation as a preeminent regional power. Dahomean kings claimed to "own" the heads of their subjects.[70] Norris stressed that the king's subjects were no better than slaves, inferring that exporting slaves from the region to the Americas improved the lives of West Africans.[71] An unexamined aspect of this patrimonial conception of royal authority was the claim the king as owner of these slave-subjects had over their offspring. Norris stated: "Children belong to the state, or rather are the property of the king."[72] He went on to explain: "The motive for this, is, that there may be no family connections or combinations; no associations that might be injurious to the king's unlimited power. Hence, each individual is detached, and unconnected; and having no relative for whom he is interested, is solicitous only for his own safety; which he consults, by the most abject submission, and obedience."[73] This comment aligns with Dahomey's worldview of a strong monarch owning all forms of wealth in the kingdom, including humans.[74] Was this mere rhetoric? How did Tegbesu enact such a policy?

In addition to being an extension of the absolutist monarchy, this new expression of an existing ideology might have had its roots in a more personal matter for Tegbesu. Some oral traditions assert that Tegbesu was impotent or nearly so.[75] If this was true, it certainly sheds light on possible motivations for some peculiar actions that transpired during his reign. Despite Tegbesu having thousands of wives, he had only three or four children.[76] Oral tradition also reveals that one of these potential heirs, Adjokpalo, was rumored to be the result of an affair between his wife and a lover and therefore not Tegbesu's biological offspring. Adjokpalo's mother was executed for her adulterous relationship, which seemed to prove that Adjokpalo was likely illegitimate.[77] It also cast doubt on the paternity of the remaining sons.

Tegbesu's alleged impotency also renders legible one of his more capricious acts. In 1754, when Tegbesu had finally conquered his rivals and quelled internal opposition, he faked his death. In Dahomean history, there was no precedent for such an action. Three years earlier, Tegbesu had explicitly expressed his desire for succession by naming his son Junipera as his *vidaho*, or heir apparent.[78] Tegbesu stayed out of the public eye for six months to see if anyone challenged Junipera's accession to the throne. He told French Resident Guestard that his ruse was designed to draw out any enemies who might take advantage of his death.[79] While this scenario is plausible, Tegbesu's actions make more sense if rumors had begun to circulate about his impotency. Adjokpalo's parentage and Tegbesu's alleged impotency cast doubt on the legitimacy of the three or four children he claimed as his progeny. He might have feared that his royal line would not continue after his death. Regardless of whether Junipera was his biological son, he wanted to know if the kingdom would accept his designated heir. After six months of this subterfuge, Tegbesu resurrected himself and took on official responsibilities once again. He felt that he had learned all that he could by this experiment.

Junipera's death in 1764 and rumors of Tegbesu's impotence prompted him to take radical action.[80] Norris describes how Tegbesu redefined parent-child relationship norms to minimize the importance of consanguinity: "Here, paternal affections, and filial love scarcely exist. Mothers, instead of cherishing, endeavor to suppress those attachments for their offspring which they know will be violated, as soon as their children are able to undergo the fatigue of being removed from them."[81] This attempt to discount maternal affection may reflect Dahomean women's attempts to adapt to the new reality of "children belonging to the state" in ever-greater numbers. Norris states: "Children are sent away from their parents at too young of an age to recollect them."[82] After 1764, the Dahomean monarchy began to collect Dahomean children, expanding the levée to include not only recently subjugated people but all families in the kingdom. During the eighteenth century, these collections were sporadic based on the whims of the palace.

Norris further elaborates on the reasons behind these separations of parents and children by stating that the government bureaucracy "distributed [children] in villages remote from the places of their nativity; where they remain subject to his [the king's] future appropriation of them, with but little chance of their being ever seen, or at least recognized by their parents afterwards."[83] Presumably, the king kept many girls in his eight palaces and distributed others to loyal subordinates throughout the country. It is less clear what happened to the collected boys. The only evidence of their fates comes from Snelgrave's account from eight decades earlier. When Dahomey conquered Hueda, Snelgrave observed an "abundance" of boys following the soldiers as they performed drills. His linguist explained that "the King allowed every common Soldier a Boy at the publick charge, in order to be trained up in Hardships from their youth."[84] This justification for privation and hardship as a necessary component of childhood corresponded with later rhetoric validating other institutionalized forms of child transfer.

A new ideology about parent-child relationship norms developed in Dahomey during Tegbesu's reign. Throughout the eighteenth century, the Kingdom of Dahomey began systematically collecting children from within the kingdom to meet the palace's labor needs and gain control over the interlineal connections among ministers created through child circulation. This may have reflected Tegbesu's desire to create different conceptions of parenthood due to his impotency. The new understanding of children belonging to the state relaxed as Tegbesu's successors produced heirs whose patrilineage went unquestioned.

Following Dahomey's expansion in the 1720s, the neighboring Oyo Empire contested Dahomey's consolidation of power over its conquests.[85] A 1730 treaty agreement between the two adversaries transformed Dahomey into a tributary state recognized and protected by Oyo.[86] From 1730 until the 1820s, the Kingdom of Dahomey demonstrated its deference by providing tribute to its political superiors.[87] Oyo demanded girls, among other forms of wealth, as an acknowledgment of Oyo's sovereignty over the Kingdom of Dahomey. Throughout its history, Dahomey received and provided girl captives as tribute. The tribute system was a crucial part of diplomacy between the competing kingdoms. The type and amounts of payments would vary based on the power and economic imbalances between the subordinate region and the dominant power. From 1781 onward, Oyo required more women and girls as part of the yearly recognition of its power.[88] Tegbesu's successors Kpengla (r. 1774–1789), Agonglo (r. 1789–1797), and Adandozan (r. 1797–1818) faced challenges asserting their legitimacy because of these ongoing demands and ruled from positions of precarity.[89] Further compounding these difficulties, Tegbesu's alleged lineage faced significant challenges due to the prevailing famine and economic depression in Dahomey at the end of the eighteenth century.[90] Adandozan in particular governed from an extremely weak position because, during his reign, both the French and British abandoned their slave-trading forts in Ouidah.[91] These events further solidified in oral tradition that Tegbesu's line had cursed the country with extraordinarily bad luck. In 1808, the dire straits of the Dahomean economy made it almost impossible for Adandozan to pay the requisite tribute to Oyo.[92]

European travelers to Dahomey confirmed that the monarchy after Tegbesu continued to sporadically collect Dahomean children. Pierre Labarthe, who visited in 1788, observed that the culture of the kingdom socialized Dahomean children to believe that the king had the right to "dispose of his person in any way he [the king] pleases."[93] Labarthe disagreed with Norris about whose children Tegbesu appropriated and redistributed. "All the boys and the girls born to the [king's] ministers were handed over to the hands of the king, who placed them at his convenience; he kept in his *seraglio* the girls, as many as for his pleasures as for service and to guard the palace."[94] While Tegbesu may have started this practice for personal reasons, subsequent kings found it advantageous to continue collecting female children.

While Tegbesu's official ideology pertained to all children, his successors showed a disproportionate preference for girls over boys. In the late eighteenth century, the monarchy reduced and eventually stopped its collection of boys. It is unclear whether this change originated from a widespread refusal to surrender sons or if the monarchy simply required fewer boys. The transfer of girls remained an important component of the political economy throughout the precolonial period. Dahomean families resented the increased burden of having to provide more daughters to the expanding palace. Pruneau de la Pommegorge observed the population's discontent with the growing demands of the state for their daughters.[95] What had once been an honor was now a burden because of the scale of the demands. Girls living along the Bight of Benin were increasingly vulnerable to being transferred to the Dahomean palace over the course of the eighteenth century.

Recruiting Young Agojie, Female Soldiers in Training

In the nineteenth century, Kings Gezo (r. 1818–1858) and Glèlè (r. 1858–1889) sought to collect Dahomean girls on an unprecedented scale. They employed some in domestic and economic tasks, but many more became *agojie*, or female military corps. The ranks of the agojie rapidly doubled from approximately 3,000 in 1793 to more than 6,000 in the 1840s.[96] Europeans who visited Dahomey at this time estimated that its army comprised 6,000–10,000 professional female soldiers.[97] These numbers, however, may not have reflected the youthful auxiliaries attached as trainees. The number of young female recruits drafted during this era increased due to concurrent disastrous defeats and epidemic diseases among the female soldiers. In 1847, smallpox ravaged Dahomey, causing significant loss of life among its population, including male and female troops.[98] In 1848–1849, the inhabitants of Abeokuta, a city in modern-day southwest of Nigeria, decimated a female regiment when they successfully repelled the agojie's attack on the city.[99] Gezo lost approximately 2,000 agojie in this assault, resulting in a loss of one-third of his ranks.[100] The considerable losses caused by disease and warfare required Gezo to establish a new system of collecting girls once every three years.[101] Throughout the eighteenth century and into the early nineteenth century, Gezo's predecessors Kings Tegbesu, Kpengla, Agonglo, and Adandozan managed to staff their households and recruit for the agojie through sporadic collections of girls that were not routinized. During the 1840s and 1860s, the king imposed heavy taxes on households by forcibly recruiting hundreds of girls during the triannual collections. In an effort to quell popular discontent with the increasingly frequent royal demands for daughters, Gezo elevated female soldiers from a subsidiary position to one of parity with the male troops.[102]

Most of the thousands of female troops came from within the kingdom. During a visit to the kingdom in 1851, Auguste Bouet observed, "Nearly all the Amazons are daughters of the chiefs [elite men]." Europeans commonly described the agojie as Amazons, the famed female warriors from the ancient Greek world. Bouet noted that Dahomean men gave up their daughters to Gezo when the girls were eight or nine years old.[103] This age might have been the norm, but there is evidence that the palace recruited younger girls as well, perhaps as young as six.[104] The young ages of those drafted ensured the agojie's absolute devotion to the king.[105] These girls saw themselves as "'the king's daughter[s],' under his protection," and they felt a certain filial loyalty to him.[106] New recruits explicitly articulated this dedication to the monarch in a pledge when they performed for him at the annual Hwetanu. "With bow in hand, these sweet children, directed by a little Amazon of ten-years-old at most, come for their turn to twist and turn at the feet of the king . . . they promise in the future to be faithful guards devoted to his person."[107] This indoctrination during their youth as well as their limited ability to form relationships outside the palace resulted in adult agojie being stalwart supporters of the king and fierce warriors for his causes.

Like his father, Glèlè faced similar catastrophic losses to his female military corps and struggled to replenish his forces. During the second year of his reign, an epidemic of smallpox swept through his kingdom, and just three years later in 1864, the annual campaign suffered further losses of its female corps.[108] Glèlè changed the collection of girls from a triannual event to an annual one.[109] While Gezo "kept the corps clear of the servile and the captive," Glèlè, his son and successor, could not adhere to this practice. Although native girls were preferred, during Glèlè's reign, a secondary stream of foreign-born girls supplemented Dahomean conscripts.[110] These young captive girls whose parents had been killed or sold as slaves were raised in the palace and later incorporated into the agojie.[111] After suffering devastating losses in rapid succession throughout the 1840s and 1860s, Glèlè could no longer maintain their ancestors' custom of using only girls born in Dahomey.

The youngest female draftees started their martial training as *gohento*, or archers.[112] In 1861, explorer Richard Francis Burton estimated that Glèlè had a newly chosen company of about two hundred girls.[113] Europeans saw the young gohento perform at royal celebrations and repeatedly praised their skills as archers and dancers. "Nothing is more gracious than the slow movements and rhythm of these pretty children guided by soft and monotone chanting."[114] For public performances, the girls dressed elegantly in blue tunics with embroidered white skullcaps that featured a blue caiman or agama lizard. On her left arm, each gohento wore an ivory bracelet over which she slid the arrow as she aimed her bow.[115] The king's gifts of these clothes and jewelry elevated the gohento over their female peers, who wore nothing on their upper bodies and never owned ivory jewelry.[116] The ivory bracelet was particularly remarkable because, in the 1860s, elephants in the region had become exceedingly rare to the point of facing extinction.[117] This distinctive adornment was visible evidence of the gohentos' exalted status.

The young recruits did not directly participate in warfare until they could handle a musket, usually by the time they were in their upper teens.[118] During the "war season" of January through March, girls accompanied adult agojie on campaign, serving as scouts and porters to assist the military in intelligence gathering and carrying supplies to the battlefront.[119] Throughout the year, apprentice agojie lived in the royal palace, trained alongside the adult women, and supported the palaces' daily operations as a household and economic unit. Even though Burton observed that "the Amazons are everything in this country," these girls and women did not lead idle lives in the months between war campaigns.[120] The king reserved agricultural work for slaves and exempted military recruits, as performing agricultural labor would have diminished their status among the population.[121] In addition, the corps would have had difficulty putting aside agricultural labor when they went to war or during the Hwetanu ceremonial cycle, in which the agojie and their apprentices participated.

When living at the palaces from April to December, these youthful recruits helped women fetch water.[122] Water was a precious commodity in the inland plateau surrounding the capital Abomey because it was scarce.[123] It was needed for personal consumption, cooking, handicraft production, and agriculture. The kings' wives and the agojie in training spent numerous hours of their days walking to the water source, filling a jar one calabash scoop at a time, and then carrying it back to the palace—a "long operation" that also involved filtering the swamp water that came from outside of Abomey.[124] English geologist J. A. Skertchly saw five members of the agojie who were not the "fighting Amazons, but camp followers" carrying water near Cana, the site of a royal palace.[125] These "camp followers" included female recruits who could not yet handle a musket. The apprentices residing at the Cana palace had to walk half a mile to the southeast for water.[126] When weighed down with a large jar of water on their return to the palace, carriers could only manage a pace of half a mile an hour.[127] Girls and women residing at the Abomey palace had to walk three to four miles each way; the return trip alone was six to eight backbreaking hours of balancing jars of water on their heads.

Girls produced a variety of handicrafts while living at the palace, working in artisanal workshops to create dyestuffs, pottery, and clay pipes, all of which were royal monopolies.[128] Agojie also made carved calabashes and serving utensils, which were not a royal monopoly.[129] Manufacture of all products stopped when the agojie were at war or performing at extended rituals. Agojie also did the appliqué work for some royal regalia including the king's iconic umbrella and the enormous So-sin pavilion.[130] The Hwetanu ceremonies rotated between two variants, the So-sin (horse tie) and the Attoh (platform), which took place in alternate years. The So-sin ceremony featured an elaborately decorated tented structure known as the elephant shed that was reserved exclusively for the king and his ahosi entourage.[131] In 1871, Skertchly observed agojie completing the appliqué work on the So-sin pavilion which was covered in a "blood-red, white, and black cotton cloth," with each colored stripe separated by a narrow strip of blue calico. On the white stripes, "three black elephants with green ears and yellow tusks, pointing downward! Were displayed; the animal being cut out of cloth and sewn on the white ground,— all the needlework of the Amazons."[132] There is evidence only of the agojie doing the appliqué work for the So-sin pavilion and the royal umbrellas; however, they were likely responsible for all of the appliqué work on their uniforms because this craft required a high level of skill.

During the nineteenth century, the female corps of soldiers suffered repeated and devastating losses, forcing the monarchs to increase the frequency of drafting new juvenile recruits from within the kingdom and—by Glèlè's reign—beyond to bolster the ranks. These losses were compounded by the steady decline of the region's population from 1700 to 1850 due to the Atlantic slave trade. This demographic situation increased the importance of the remaining girls and women as military troops and economically productive members of the royal household.[133] Agojie and their recruits performed seasonal labor. Some of their tasks were mundane, like carrying water, while others required skill and increased their prestige, such as creating pottery and performing appliqué work. The revenue-producing crafts and royal ceremonial items that the king assigned to the agojie and their apprentices could be completed on a seasonal basis and set aside while on military campaigns. The role of the female warrior in training involved more than simply learning the martial arts required to eventually participate in annual campaigns.

Conclusion

The life histories of Alladan and Huedan princes provide concrete examples of the fact that child transfer was not a phenomenon limited to girls in the period before subsequent Dahomean innovations. In the eighteenth century, Dahomean monarchs manipulated the existing ideology to justify the circulation of children to meet the palaces' labor and military needs as well as to centralize state power. The eighteenth- and nineteenth-century kings mapped a different logic onto preexisting norms of child fostering. The exact number of girls demanded by the palace depended on the strength and requirements of the respective monarchy at any given moment. After their successful conquests of the neighboring kingdoms of Allada and Hueda, Dahomean kings fundamentally changed patterns of girl transfers in the kingdom by increasing the demands for girls to an unprecedented scale. Tegbesu introduced new norms of relationships among parents, children, and the monarchy. During Tegbesu's reign from 1740 to 1774, the Dahomean state he personified laid claim to all children born in the kingdom. While Tegbesu's policy was that all "children belong to the state," his successors focused their efforts on demanding only girls to incorporate into the palace in a variety of roles. In the early eighteenth century, during a period of rapid growth, Dahomean kings collected both boys and girls. By the late eighteenth century, either King Kpengla (r. 1774–1789) or King Agonglo (1789–1797) stopped collecting male children and exclusively demanded female children for the palace's use. The palace absorbed thousands of young female dependents from its conquests and state-sponsored collections of native dependents.

Royal diplomacy and wealth depended on the state's ability to attract, collect, acquire, and capture large numbers of girls.

Women of the palace generated wealth through their economic endeavors. This revenue stream was particularly important because of the fluctuations in the slave trade. Part of the compositional logic of the enormous expansion of the palace was practical. Women in the palace wanted to increase their revenue streams to support the king as well as the women at the top echelons of the palace hierarchy. The shift to the feminization of child collection in the last decades of the eighteenth century coincided with the pinnacle of authority held by royal women in the kingdom.[134] Girls became a crucial resource to the royal household of Dahomey, and by the end of the eighteenth century, the palace demanded female children exclusively. If the goal had been simply to accrue a certain number of girls regardless of status, the palace could have easily retained the slaves it captured in raids and warfare. However, the palace sought a specific compositional logic that included girl transfer from within the kingdom as a sign of submission to the king. Enslaved captive girls could not fulfill all the roles within the complex household hierarchy, such as the agojie prior to the nineteenth century, though certain kings had to make exceptions to rules. These gendered changes to child transfers began within the Dahomean palace but soon had implications beyond the cloistered walls of the king's household. The royal palaces of Dahomey showed the larger Fon society that entire commercial enterprises could be staffed by girls and several experienced women supervising them. This became a model for other households to emulate in terms of labor recruitment.

The royal household was both exceptional and exemplary to the Dahomean elite and perhaps commoner households. These households emulated the royal one and its strategies for economic success on a smaller scale.[135] As the compounded effects of the transatlantic slave trade produced an increasingly feminine majority population in the kingdom, the royal household, though always incomparable in scale, created a household labor hierarchy that served as a model for large households in the kingdom. These households, like the royal one, functioned as corporate economic units, dealing with and adapting to the demographic reality of the era. Between 1700 and 1850, the region experienced a steep decline in its population; however, this was skewed in a gendered fashion.[136] Historian Patrick Manning estimates that the gender ratio might have been imbalanced, with two women for every man or perhaps closer to sixty-five men per one hundred women (approximately one man for every 1.5 women).[137] This shortage in men and their labor led to an increase in women's and girls' productive activities.

The transfer of girls remained important to the political economy of Kings Gezo (r. 1818–1858) and Glèlè (r. 1858–1889). A crucial component of the palace's nineteenth-century success was the strategic deployment of girls as objects of tribute, domestic laborers, market sellers, porters, water carriers, and apprentice warriors. The palace, however, did not simply accumulate dependents. It also judiciously transferred the girls—and boys—that it controlled. The next chapter examines these outward-bound transfers of children the palace bestowed on Europeans. These transfers brought about a new vocabulary surrounding child dependents. The Atlantic politics of abolition heavily influenced this terminology, with Dahomeans going to great lengths to distinguish certain forms of bondage from slavery. The palace experimented with and promulgated novel terms to differentiate the various dependent statuses of girls from enslavement.

"Sarah Forbes Bonnetta" by N. M. Hannare from *Dahomey and the Dahomans: Being the Journals of Two Missions of the King of Dahomey . . . in the Years 1849 and 1850* by Frederick Forbes, public domain.

2

Dashing and Entrusting Girls

The Atlanticization of Child Transfers during the Reigns of Kings Gezo and Glèlè, 1818–1889

On July 5, 1850, King Gezo "dashed" an eight-year-old girl to Captain Frederick Forbes, a British diplomat visiting the Kingdom of Dahomey. During the fifteenth through eighteenth centuries, the term *dash*, from the Portuguese *dação*, had developed a colloquial meaning in the Atlantic world. In this context, to dash meant to bestow a gift as an introductory or supplemental component to a later exchange.[1] Dashing objects had long facilitated Atlantic trade relationships. Since the time of Agaja (reign c. 1708–1740), Dahomean kings had given women and girls away as gifts, though Europeans did not record these acts as "dashed" until the mid-nineteenth century.[2] This linguistic convention marked an important shift in Atlantic relationships. Gezo (r. 1818–1858) and Glèlè (r. 1858–1889) demonstrated their status by awarding human captives as gifts to favored individuals. This exclusive royal prerogative visibly demonstrated the king's status and communicated to witnesses the unequal relationship between the king and the recipient. The king hoped these dashes would ensure the recipients' loyalty and service to the monarch.[3] Using the term *dash* to conceal the fact that the gift was of an enslaved human further Atlanticized the idea in the context of the abolitionist movement. Atlanticization was the process of sustained circum-Atlantic exchanges that resulted in the creation of an integrated zone spanning Atlantic West Africa, the Caribbean, the Eastern Seaboards of North and South America, and Western Europe where multicultural influence impacted cultural practices, social norms, linguistic conventions, political systems, and economic policies. This differed from Atlantic forms of creolization in that it was not a hybrid derivative. Atlanticization inspired innovation in Atlantic societies themselves that was not always a compilation of elements. In this instance, abolitionist discourse emanating from traders and politicians in Europe prompted the Dahomean king, or perhaps his translators, to craft terminology. This allowed British representatives to save face by using more palatable terminology to plausibly deny that the British emissary participated in human trafficking through the use of a euphemism.

The girl in question had been given the Yorùbán name of Àìná seven to eight days after her birth.[4] The name means "brought from heaven" and was bestowed on a girl based on the complicated circumstances of her delivery.[5] Àìná's difficult birth around 1843 foretold a harrowing childhood. In 1849, Dahomean troops attacked Okeadan, the village where she lived, captured her, enslaved her, and brought her to Abomey. She lived and worked in the royal palace for the next eighteen months or so before Forbes's visit. In the nineteenth century, Àìná was just one of the many girls and women "absorbed in the capacious maw of the various palaces" of Dahomey.[6] During this time, the royal court's demands for female laborers, warriors, and bureaucrats grew inordinately. As discussed in chapter 1, thousands of these women and girls were born in Dahomey, but an untold number, including Àìná, were captured from neighboring regions. Some were moved to Dahomean palaces for short periods before being redistributed to Europeans and Dahomeans favored by the king; others remained permanently within the palace walls.

Gezo had a practical reason for dashing a girl of this age to the visiting diplomat. Forbes explained that Gezo presented him with the girl so that he had someone to wash his clothes.[7] After all, Forbes, a foreign dignitary, was a bachelor traveling in the kingdom and, from Gezo's point of view, needed at least one juvenile female servant to perform domestic tasks. The labor system of Dahomey assigned roles to girls that were exclusive to them and crucial to the economic functioning of local and international trade. As historian Beverly Grier argues in gender-neutral terms, in precolonial, colonial, and postcolonial Africa, both male and female child laborers were sought as workers in their own right and not simply as supplemental to adult laborers. Adults perceived juvenile workers as uniquely valuable because of the relative ease with which children assimilated into the household either permanently or temporarilyThe compositional logic of nineteenth-century Dahomean households required at least one juvenile girl to complete certain tasks. Gezo could not imagine how European men could travel without one at their disposal.

In addition to the practical rationale for this "gift" of a girl, Gezo also wanted to create a bond between himself and Forbes, to establish a special relationship of trust, intimacy, and solidarity. Gezo anticipated that this association with Forbes might eventually benefit him in negotiations with the British government and its traders. Forbes's acceptance of the girl communicated to Gezo that Forbes agreed with this arrangement.[8] The irony of this episode was that Forbes had traveled to Dahomey in hopes of convincing the monarch to stop participating in the transatlantic slave trade. Notably, almost all of the male European visitors from the 1840s through the 1870s mentioned having children dashed to them after their meetings with Gezo or the son who succeeded him, Glèlè. While Forbes and other British representatives had their abolitionist agenda, Gezo had another. In 1797, France vacated its fort and ceased trading with Dahomey until the 1840s. Great Britain followed suit in 1812, staying away from the kingdom until 1837. Gezo sought to rebuild the broken connections between Dahomey and European powers by involving European visitors in two separate forms of child transfer: dashing and entrusting. Dashing was a gift that anticipated, though did not require or guarantee, that additional gifts or favors would be given to the king. In contrast, when the king entrusted a child from the royal household to a European visitor, he intended to build an enduring relationship between himself and the recipient or the cultural and commercial group that the recipient represented. The verb *entrust* means to assign the responsibility for doing something to someone else, or to put something or someone, in this case a child, into someone else's care or protection. It was explicitly understood that the child would be returned once a certain goal was achieved. The terms of entrusting required ongoing interactions between the parties involved.

Àìná became known in Great Britain by the Anglicized name Sarah Forbes Bonetta, an appellation Forbes bestowed on her. In Forbes's travelogue, a portrait of the dashed girl, seen at the chapter's opening, shows her in English-style clothing. She wears a long-sleeved, full-length plaid dress with some smocking around the waist and wrists. Under the dress is a white undergarment that goes up to her neck. She also wears stockings and European shoes. How strange it must have been for Àìná to wear such restrictive clothing after a childhood spent wearing only waist beads or a small cloth wrapped around her waist. What did she think of the shoes? Did she stumble? Was this an opportunity for self-reinvention that she welcomed? Or did she feel forced into attire not of her choosing? After living in Okeadan and Abomey, she might have only seen such clothing occasionally on foreigners. Upon reaching Ouidah with Forbes, European-style attire would have been more prevalent. Shoes, however, were still reserved for the monarch and foreign dignitaries, so wearing them may have been both physically and psychologically uncomfortable—or perhaps exciting. Did Àìná embrace her new identity as Sarah and adapt to English-style clothing as a way to move on and start over? Was this her way of seeking new forms of belonging within her new community? All of these questions haunt this image. Much more is known about Àìná's life in Great Britain and Sierra Leone, but details about her time in Dahomey as an enslaved girl remain obscure.

Àìná's young life was not exceptional for Yorùbá girls of the era. The Yorùbá lived in the region to the east of Dahomey. During the nineteenth century, Yorùbáland endured frequent slave raids that depleted its population. Àìná's fate and that of others like her was shaped by two interrelated events: the gradual abolition of the transatlantic slave trade from 1807 to 1863 and the forced migration of a large number of Yorùbá from the 1820s to 1870s.[9] During the first half of the nineteenth century, the international consensus on the transatlantic slave trade changed. Initially, a minority of Atlantic powers condemned the trade in human cargo. Eventually, however, all Europeans and Americans, some begrudgingly, agreed that the slave trade out of West Africa should end. This was a gradual process, and the trade continued into the 1860s.[10] In the first half of the nineteenth century, four hundred thousand enslaved Yorùbá embarked on the Middle Passage, and an untold number remained enslaved in West African kingdoms such as Dahomey.[11] During this era, Europeans did not condemn slavery itself within Africa. No European power proposed intervening in African slave systems.[12]

Àìná's early life illustrates how British abolition efforts had unintended consequences in West Africa. In Dahomey's case, these efforts prompted the retention of a large enslaved Yorùbá population within the kingdom. One of the ironies of the Atlanticization of West African economies in the nineteenth century was that freedom for Black children (and adults) in the Americas resulted in the widespread expansion of child slavery in Africa.[13] This chapter examines the impact of Atlantic abolition on Dahomean society before the eventual cessation of the trade in human cargo in 1863. In the wake of abolition, several new patterns of migration developed that affected

Dahomey.¹⁴ One diasporic community left a deep and lasting impact on Dahomean society—the Yorùbá. The massive influx of Yorùbá peoples was fundamentally different than the incorporation of other groups into Dahomean society.¹⁵ Although some of the Yorùbá migrants were traders who voluntarily relocated to pursue economic opportunities, the majority were enslaved persons. It is difficult to estimate how many Yorùbá individuals were part of this diaspora, but it is clear that the retention of such large numbers of enslaved persons from a single ethnic group altered the classifications of social hierarchy in Dahomey.¹⁶

During Gezo's reign from 1818 to 1858, new vocabularies emerged around child transfer and juvenile subservience. In the Atlantic world, West Africans' engagement with abolitionist ideas prompted them to develop terminologies in their intercultural exchanges that distinguished an array of arrangements of child transfer from child enslavement. Many of these child transfer practices likely predated Europeans' initial recordings of the distinct terms, but due to a lack of European visitors from around 1800 until the 1840s, historians have limited evidence of the transformations taking place in Dahomey during these decades.¹⁷ From the 1840s onward, two groups, British diplomats and Christian missionaries, produced the majority of documentation on the rapid transformations occurring in the kingdom. From the 1840s to the 1870s, British diplomatic emissaries recorded their experiences with the phenomenon of dashed girls. Christian missionaries from several European nations stationed at Ouidah in Dahomey and Porto-Novo in the neighboring Kingdom of Hogbonou, described having child novices entrusted and dashed to them. The historical record left out mentions of child entrustment taking place between Dahomean families.¹⁸ European outsiders to the kingdom did not record their observations about entrustment arrangements that they did not participate in because they were not privy to the terms of these intra-African arrangements.

This chapter traces the development of a shared transatlantic terminology regarding African child transfers. It shows how international pressures adapted child transfer practices to fit into local and European moralities in ways that Atlanticized them.¹⁹ Based on the collective biographies of Àìná and her contemporaries who remained in West Africa as either dashed or entrusted children, this chapter argues that during the mid-nineteenth century, the Dahomean monarchy was central in dictating the patterns of forced, coerced, and voluntary child transfers. The royal household in collaboration with its interpreters developed a newly recorded Atlantic vocabulary concerning child dependence. From at least the 1850s onward, Atlantic populations in Dahomey carefully distinguished among different forms of child subservience. In particular, the terms *dashed* and *entrusted child* became accepted categories in exchanges between Dahomeans and Europeans. *Dashed* was understood as a euphemism for *slavery*, whereas *entrusted* emerged in the written record as a practice distinct from enslavement. Alongside the development of this Atlanticized vocabulary concerning child transfers, local linguistic innovations occurrred in the Fon language regarding the social standing of Yorùbá agricultural laborers. The shift from exporting human captives to palm products changed Dahomean understandings of servile statuses and increased the distinct institutions that bonded individuals to households.

Transatlantic Abolition and the Forced Yorùbá Diaspora in the Kingdom of Dahomey, 1820s–1860s

Starting in the 1790s, the Oyo Empire's power began to decline, and the western areas of Yorùbáland became attractive targets for Dahomey's annual slave-raiding campaigns.[20] The stream of Yorùbá captives into the Atlantic trade and the Kingdom of Dahomey swelled when in 1823, Dahomey revolted against Oyo and liberated itself from paying tribute to its formerly powerful neighbor.[21] After Dahomey gradually conquered Mahi country in the 1820s and 1830s, the king's armies turned their full attention to Yorùbáland.[22] Dahomey preyed on these vulnerable areas, turning them into a storehouse for human captives who would be sold abroad and retained within the kingdom. Àìná's village of Okeadan was just one of many Yorùbá villages where Dahomean troops captured Yorùbá girls, boys, women, and men. Before the 1840s, most of these captives had been exported across the Atlantic. As the British Royal Navy's West Africa Squadron exerted ever-greater pressure on the kingdom to cease its exports of human cargo during the 1840s and 1850s, the demography of Dahomey evolved as larger numbers of Yorùbá became integrated into the Fon-dominated society.[23] During the nineteenth century, the enslaved population outnumbered the free one in Dahomey.[24] During the transition to "legitimate" trade, Forbes estimated that only 10 percent of the kingdom's population of two hundred thousand was "free."[25] Even if his estimates were inaccurate, his comments indicated that most people were enslaved or in some form of dependence that differed from Forbes's definition of freedom. This large number of recently enslaved people resulted in the formation of new social stratifications and had a significant impact on Fon society.

The sheer number of enslaved Yorùbá people and their unique skills had a considerable influence on Dahomean culture and society. In the eighteenth century, Yorùbá influences permeated Dahomean court life and laid the groundwork for easy acceptance of Yorùbá cultural norms among the larger society. The Dahomean elite had already adopted some elements of Yorùbá religion, governance principles, and prestige items, which conveyed status on the owner. Tegbesu spent his youth either as a captive or a foster child in the Oyo court. He selectively imported elements of Yorùbá royal protocols and religious practices.[26] Dahomean society and the monarchy valued Yorùbá expertise in religious divination, various skilled crafts, such as metal work and appliqué arts, and the cultivation of palm orchards. This last area of expertise proved essential to the nineteenth-century commercial revolution when the slave export economy shifted to palm products. The labor performed by enslaved Yorùbá children, women, and men transformed Dahomey's landscape by creating plantations of palm groves. In the mid-eighteenth century, Archibald Dalzel, director of the English Fort in Ouidah from 1767 to 1770, remarked that palm trees, though "prodigious," remained in a semiwild state that were not at that time grown on Dahomean plantations.[27] In the latter part of Gezo's reign and throughout Glèlè's reign, both kings established agricultural villages where they settled enslaved war captives to tend royal plantations and process palm oil.[28] For example, when Gezo conquered the Yorùbá village of Leflefun in 1843, he moved the young and healthy members of the population to a royal plantation in Dahomey to cultivate the king's palms.[29] This flood of Yorùbá laborers, who were already skilled in growing palm trees in their home villages, contributed to the flourishing of palm orchards and their growth in the Dahomean heartland. Frequent visitors to the kingdom were shocked by the speed at which the landscape had changed. In 1856–1858, palm plantations reached northward from the coast to Cana and, by 1863, from Cana all the way to Abomey.[30] In the 1850s and 1860s, the land that stretched from Cana to Abomey was "the garden of Dahomey" planted with a "succession of palm orchards and grain fields belonging to the King and his ministers."[31] All this produce would pass through Ouidah to be wholesaled in European, Brazilian, and indigenous factories.

The Yorùbá diaspora affected the demarcation of servile statuses and resulted in a proliferation of terms indicating specific forms of enslavement, descent from enslaved persons, and household dependence. All enslaved persons fell into the broad Fon category of *kannoumon*, or "people of the cord." This large group could be divided into smaller, more specialized groups based on occupation or the reason for their enslavement.[32] In the nineteenth century, some of these subcategories evolved. For example, the subdivision of enslaved persons known in Fon as *gbablito*, or puncheon rollers, was an occupation that arose with the new palm oil export industry. From the 1840s, European, Brazilian, and African wholesalers needed a large group of laborers to roll the wholesaled oil in barrels from their factories in Ouidah, Godomey, and Kotonou to the beaches where canoes awaited to cross the roadstead and then transfer the produce to ships bound for Europe.[33] Yorùbá slaves supported the emerging plantation economy in Dahomey by producing, processing, and transporting palm products.

Dahomean armies forcibly resettled most Yorùbá children, women, and men onto royal plantations to work for the king, his ministers, and other favored elites.[34] The enslaved people who performed agricultural labor on these plantations were known in Fon as *glési*, or "the wives of cultivated land." The first generation of glési also had the status of *kannoumon*. Over the nineteenth century, the category of glési comprised enslaved persons working in agriculture and their descendants, who remained a separate, oppressed, serf-like group in society.[35] The glési were descended from these enslaved persons whom the king ordered to remain tied to the land their enslaved ancestors had worked in perpetuity.[36] These subsequent generations of glési were distinguished from other slaves by their Dahomean birth. This afforded them a modicum of protection because they could not be legally resold outside of the kingdom. The term *glési* eventually became synonymous with *farm laborer* because, by the late nineteenth century, agricultural work in the kingdom was predominantly done by this special category of slave-descended serfs.[37]

Most of these individuals are unnamed in the historical records, and there is little evidence of the experiences of child glési on Dahomean plantations. Yet they are an important part of the history of captive Yorùbá girls and boys as well as their descendants. The fates of a handful of Yorùbá children living in Dahomey and attached to the palace were better documented. Like Àìná, these young individuals are mentioned briefly in travelogues and missionary accounts as dashed children, most often with their indigenous names lost to history and only their ethnic identities and latinized names preserved for posterity.

Dashed Children: The Fates of Captive Yorùbá and Mahi Children in Dahomey

Throughout West Africa, relationships were based on gift-giving. In Atlantic West Africa, dashes were essential to establishing the foundation for a relationship that would open the negotiation of a commercial exchange. In the seventeenth through nineteenth centuries, Europeans commonly dashed items to the Dahomean elite that included cloth, liquor, hats, chairs, flags, and umbrellas. High-ranking Dahomeans reciprocated with dashes of water, foodstuffs, cloth, liquor, and prestigious insignia such as *récades*, carved staffs used instead of calling cards. Dahomeans considered Europeans who participated in the political economy of dashes to be part of the indigenous hierarchy who submitted to the reigning king's supremacy and appealed to his beneficence as the sovereign.[38] By the nineteenth century, this long-established practice of dashing formed the basis of intercultural exchanges and relationship-building in the kingdom. In 1864, Richard Burton remarked, "The dash in these regions ... is omnipotent."[39] A gift, in theory, is the uncoerced bestowing of a commodity to another person; however, a gift's voluntary nature can be a social falsehood, as was the case with dashing.[40] Some mid-nineteenth-century European visitors tried unsuccessfully to oppose this centuries-old norm. Two years after Forbes's failed mission, Great Britain sent Vice-Consul Louis Fraser to Dahomey with the expressed purpose of convincing King Gezo to end the transatlantic slave trade. Fraser expressed his strong dislike for the dash system and tried to avoid participating in it. Fraser's Dahomean informants explained to him that he "*must* dash the King" in order to make Gezo his "friend."[41] Dahomeans anticipated a return on their investment in gifts, but the gift was ostensibly independent of the later exchange. It built goodwill and proved that the gift-giving party valued the friendship of a prospective business partner.

Dashed children were never "properly Dahomean," meaning they were not born in the kingdom.[42] According to Europeans' recorded ethnic information, all dashed children were taken from communities that had recently been attacked, such as Yorùbá or Mahi. By the nineteenth century, European visitors were familiar with the "country marks" used to distinguish one group from another.[43] West Africans displayed their ethnic identities through the practice of facial scarification.[44] Facial scarification was remarkably varied and easily identifiable. For example, the Fon people scarified their children with three short perpendicular cuts on the temples, whereas Mahis had a long single slit running from the hairline to the top of the nose. Yorùbá identities were more localized, with less uniformity in the scarification and a variety of patterns.[45] If Europeans did not recognize a particular mark, they could ask their interpreters about the origins of dashed children. Other visitors could identify their origins from the languages they spoke.[46]

In the nineteenth century, the meaning of the Atlantic loan word *dash* was changed to include gifts of enslaved persons. After Britain so publicly condemned the slave trade and championed abolition internationally, humans could no longer be gifted to Europeans as slaves.[47] This led Dahomean translators, and perhaps even the king himself, to apply the term *dash* to human captives gifted to European emissaries and the Dahomean elite. This etymological shift reflected Dahomean sensitivity to the changing political landscape.[48] In the 1850s, Dahomean interpreters began to actively conceal slavery from visiting Europeans. Fraser remarked that the term *slave* had never been used in his presence. He did, however, state that *Black* had become synonymous with slave status.[49] In this case, the term *Black* did not refer to physical appearance, as Dahomeans only categorized certain Africans as Black.

Translators also served as crosscultural brokers, and Madiki Lemon, Fraser's Dahomean interpreter, was undoubtedly aware of the politics surrounding the term *slave* in English.[50] Madiki could have "softened" this "hard" word by changing *slave child* to *dashed child*.[51] Madiki knew the established British abolitionist agenda. The men of the Lemon family had served as liaisons and translators to British traders and diplomats in Dahomey for generations. Madiki was appointed "Governor" of the English Fort by the king after Madiki's father, who previously held the position, passed away. Fraser's mission was the fourth in which Madiki had served as a guide, interpreter, and translator.[52] The previous British diplomats who had employed him had repeatedly tried to convince King Gezo to prohibit the transatlantic slave trade to no avail.[53] Madiki knew what British missions of the era thought of slavery and avoided using this terminology in his translations. The linguistic convention of "softening" words was not limited to Dahomean-British interactions, nor was it fleeting. French missionaries told Richard Burton over a decade later in 1861 that their Dahomean linguists always translated "master and slave" as "white and black."[54] European visitors collaborated with their African interpreters to create a transatlantic vocabulary that replaced *slave* with euphemisms such as *Black person* and *dashed child*.

The king dashed both boys and girls to British visitors, who had limited options of what to do with these captive human gifts upon their return to Great Britain. As Àìná's situation shows, a very small number of dashed children accompanied their new masters to Europe. Most, like Amelia and Emma, whom Glèlè dashed to Commodore Arthur Parry Eardley Wilmot in 1862 or 1863, remained in Dahomey. Wilmot left twelve-year-old Amelia and sixteen-year-old Emma with the wife of John Beecham, a missionary stationed in Ouidah.[55] Beecham could sympathize with the girls' situation. Beecham was captured by the Dahomean army when he was a child and was taken from his home in Mahi territory. Subsequently, Gezo dashed the boy to the visiting Wesleyan missionary, Thomas Freeman.[56] Freeman decided to bring the Mahi boy, whom he named John Beecham, back to the Cape Coast Castle in modern-day Ghana to be educated.[57] Fifteen to twenty years after he had been dashed to Freeman, Beecham became the guardian of the girls Glèlè dashed to Wilmot. Amelia and Emma joined Philip, Isaac Nahum, Laja (Elijah), Hoole, Sosu, and other "slave boys of English Town," all of whom had been dashed to the Reverend Bernasco, a predecessor of Beecham at the Wesleyan Mission in Ouidah.[58] Beecham's alternating between *dashed* and *enslaved* when referring to the children's status indicated that West Africans commonly merged these two categories and understood them as interchangeable. The Wesleyan mission in Ouidah relied on these dashed children as laborers, linguists, cultural interpreters, and pupils for their fledgling school.

The king dashed enslaved children to European visitors and Dahomean subjects with no expectation of the children being returned. He also did not articulate that dashed children's masters had any obligations to said children. King Glèlè made these norms explicit when, in 1871, he dashed four Mahi girls to J. A. Skertchly, an English zoologist and traveler who resided in the Kingdom of Dahomey for eight months as the unwilling "guest" or prisoner of the Dahomean monarch. Glèlè explained that he gave these girls to Skertchly so they would cook his food, wash his clothes, and wait on him. Glèlè justified dashing these girls in the same way that Gezo had before him. Bachelors, such as Skertchly and Forbes, needed young girls to perform certain domestic tasks. The king also clarified that Skertchly had permission to flog them for their misdeeds because "they were in my [Skertchly's] hand and I was their master."[59] The designation of Skertchly as their master confirmed the girls' enslaved status. As Glèlè's statement to Skertchly shows, these human gifts served their masters' every need and could be severely punished for their failure to do so. Glèlè gave these girls to Skertchly in perpetuity with no conditions to infringe on his use of them.

Both European men and Dahomean kings understood the status of dashed girls as domestic servants and enslaved individuals in all but name. This does not reflect a new practice but rather a new vocabulary Europeans and their African intermediaries used to talk about the gifting of captives. Dahomey, as an Atlantic kingdom, was tied into the discourses on abolition. Dahomeans innovated linguistically and created euphemisms to conceal forms of dependency deemed illicit in the Atlantic community. While the kingdom's political and commercial elite resisted the abolition of the transatlantic slave trade as an economic system, it internalized the cultural transformations occurring in debates around slavery and child transfers. Despite these accommodations to Atlantic politics, neither Europeans nor Dahomeans saw any reason to eradicate African child enslavement—it was simply an accepted part of the household operation.

Entrusted Dahomean Children: Defined Responsibilities and Limited Time Frames

Not all forms of child transfer were coerced, like royal collections, or forced, like dashing. West African societies valorized voluntary forms of child circulation that households willingly negotiated. To emphasize the intimacy involved in such exchanges, Dahomeans and other Africans used the idiom "entrusting" when referring to them.[60] Entrusting one's children to others created networks based on ongoing and long-standing relationships, though often unequal ones.[61] Precolonial Dahomeans defined *entrusting* as a limited-duration transfer of a dependent from one household to an unrelated individual for an expressed, valuable purpose, such as professional instruction, personal discipline, skill acquisition, medical treatment, or all of these. The social legitimacy of entrusting children rested on the benefits children purportedly gained from the arrangement. Youths profited throughout their lives from the professional skills they acquired in their foster homes. They also had lifelong access to additional nonfamilial financial and emotional support in times of need.

To be dashed and to be entrusted were distinct statuses for children in Dahomey. The difference in status was explained in Freeman's account of his final meeting with King Gezo on March 16, 1844. Just before leaving Abomey, the king "presented, for Her Majesty the Queen of England, two handsome cloths of native manufacture, and two little slave-girls."[62] In 1844, Freeman did not use the term *dashed* as his successors in the next decade would do so. This terminology was not yet agreed on and was still being discussed. Freeman and his companion were also "presented" with one slave girl each. The verb *presented* means "to bring, offer, or give, often in a formal or ceremonious way."[63] Such an action marked the human object as property or a commodity that Gezo gifted to the recipient in perpetuity. This exchange was theoretically completed at this point.

The king also "placed under" Freeman's "care two boys and two girls from his [Gezo's] household." Gezo instructed Freeman to "take them to Cape Coast, and give them an English education; and when they were prepared for it, to return them to him."[64] The verb *placed* means "to put in a suitable place for some purpose" or "to put into particular or proper hands."[65] The choice of *placed*, rather than *presented*, suggests that the king may have used the Fon term *vidomégòn*, which is translated into English as "placed child."[66] The king explicitly stated that this arrangement was temporary. He did not give a time frame, but he expected the four children to remain with Freeman until they received an English style education, after which they would be returned. In 1844, Freeman did not use the terms *dashed* or *entrusted*. However, in the decade that followed, the language used to describe this status became standardized. European visitors consistently used the term *entrusted* to describe Dahomean children whom the king expected to return to the kingdom after a specific purpose was achieved. At this time, the statuses of dashed and entrusted children had not yet been agreed on in a transatlantic context. Freeman could not do what he wished with these children. Gezo made clear, and Freeman understood, that these children were not his property to be used or disposed of as he pleased. Freeman stated: "This was to me an extraordinary mark of confidence on the part of the King, and proves at once that he really wishes to cultivate a good understanding with England."[67] Gezo obviously cared about the fate of these children and felt responsible for them. Years after the children's entrustment, he asked Freeman's British compatriot John Beecroft about them before permitting Beecroft to leave Abomey. He reprimanded Freeman in absentia for not keeping his word and returning the children. Gezo reminded Beecroft that the children had been at Cape Coast for five years at that point—although it had actually been seven years, according to the Gregorian calendar. He also had apparently inquired about the children through other channels because he knew one had died while at Cape Coast.[68]

Despite Gezo's frustration with Freeman's failure to comply with the terms of entrustment, Gezo tried again in 1856 to entrust children of his household with European emissaries for educational purposes. Gezo sent for French naval officers A. Vallon and Pierre-Clément Repin, who were then in Ouidah. These men traveled to Abomey at the king's request to pick up two boys to take to France for education.[69] Gezo literally placed the hands of the two children Housson and Dossou in Vallon's hands. Gezo asked Vallon to be "their father until they arrived in France." Vallon, like Freeman, agreed with enthusiasm.[70] Vallon discovered that "the two children entrusted to him" were not the sons of Gezo or Bahadou, the princely heir to the throne; rather, they belonged to a family toward whom Gezo had a great deal of affection.[71] Vallon seemed bothered by the fact that the boys entrusted to him were not princes. There was no reason to send members of the royal family to learn European languages and other skills acquired through an English education, such as writing or bookkeeping. Dahomean kings did not need to be fluent in European languages because they never spoke directly to European diplomats. The king employed servile dependents as cultural intermediaries and linguistic translators with European emissaries, not royals.

The opportunity to gain an education was one of the primary justifications for entrusting children of the royal household to Europeans, as it had been for Alladans two centuries earlier. In the mid-nineteenth century, Europeans established missionary schools in Dahomey where a select few Dahomean children could learn basic literacy and some tenets of the Christian faith. The king had long entrusted children in his care to indigenous *vodun* religious institutions and subsequently treated Christian establishments in a similar fashion.[72] Nineteenth-century kings patronized and supported Christian religious institutions within the framework of established norms. Both entrusted and dashed boys formed the backbone of the Christian community in Ouidah. These young captive and free boys along with several dashed girls, such as Amelia and Emma, were crucial to the success of European missionary endeavors in Dahomey.[73] The Catholic mission did not always treat these two groups differently. Father Francesco Borghero, the first European Catholic missionary in Dahomey, recorded in his diary the distinction between captives "given" to the mission and free persons "entrusted" to the mission for either education or medical care. Notably, many former captives rose to positions of responsibility within the mission's hierarchy. Joao Pinheiro Taparica, a wealthy slave trader in Ouidah, gave the Catholic mission his youngest slave Roberto to act as a servant to the missionaries. Roberto's linguistic talents made him an invaluable translator for these early missionaries. This enslaved boy spoke all the "normal languages of Dahomey including Portuguese, Fon, and Yorùbá." Borghero had such trust in Roberto and other boys that he asked them to check the accuracy of the official translations during his meetings with the king.[74]

Entrusting children of the royal household, like dashing captive children, fit into a larger system of royal patronage. These limited examples of Dahomean children entrusted to Europeans confirm that entrustment was a status distinct from that of an enslaved person dashed as a gift. The entrustment arrangement had a limited duration that was determined by the expressed, specific purpose legitimating the transfer, and the entrustment of a child created a kinship relationship. Guardians of entrusted children understood that they were responsible for giving their wards a practical education and properly socializing them into adulthood.

Conclusion

With the return of European traders, diplomats, and missionaries to Dahomey in the late 1830s and early 1840s, King Gezo sought ways to solidify alliances with the English and French.[75] Despite the changing attitudes of the nineteenth century, girls remained at the heart of the Dahomean political economy. Kings Gezo and Glèlè expressed their power and authority through their strategic gifting of dashed girls and placing of entrusted children, while also demanding the Dahomean elites' daughters for their personal households in ever-greater numbers. Nineteenth-century Dahomean kings dashed captives and entrusted royal children to a variety of constituencies to build relationships. These kings were not simply giving away boys and girls. Gezo and Glèlè strategically reallocated precious commodities in these child transfers.[76]

The period of the 1840s–1870s proved crucial in the development of a crosscultural, shared Atlantic vocabulary of West African juvenile dependence. As the slave trade declined, West Africans, Europeans, and Brazilians collaborated on and adapted the colloquial meaning of *to dash* to include human gifts. These human gifts most often took the form of young captive girls from the Yorùbá and Mahi regions bordering Dahomey to the east and north, respectively. During this time, Europeans became more sensitive to the gradations of child dependence and recorded a greater variety of child transfer arrangements. Identifiable and consistent terminology distinguished *dashed* from *entrusted* children. In the nineteenth century, West African girls and their divergent experiences of transfer begin to show up in the records. These experiences included dashed children, such as Àìná, Emma, Amelia, and John Beecham, given as human presents to the Dahomean elites and European visitors, as well as entrusted children, such as Housson and Dossou, temporarily fostered with the expressed purpose of being assisted in some way over a set duration. The Atlantic language surrounding the variations of child transfer emerged in the context of a rapidly changing Dahomean society transformed by the waning and eventual end of the transatlantic slave trade.

This chapter opened with the story of Àìná, the Yorùbá girl who became known in the Atlantic world as Sarah Forbes Bonetta, the Black goddaughter of Queen Victoria of Great Britain. Àìná's life story shows how the Atlantic world functioned as "an integrated zone" of exchange, meaning, and debate within which Africans actively "appropriated, revised, and indeed transformed" Enlightenment ideals.[77] The Kingdom of Dahomey did not simply or passively accept European ideas. During the nineteenth century, Dahomeans engaged in debates and established rhetorical conventions around abolition, freedom, and enslavement. During the transitional decades of the early nineteenth century, the abolitionist impulse affected transatlantic cultures' discourses surrounding slave labor, forced migration, and household dependence even before the trade ceased. From at least the 1850s, both West Africans and Europeans understood the entrusting of children to be distinct from enslaving children. This distinction would go unquestioned for the next eighty or so years.

Àìná was one individual in a large-scale forced Yorùbá diaspora to Dahomey. Her Yorùbá compatriots who remained enslaved in Dahomey faced a much different fate from hers. Chapter 3 focuses on one such enslaved

Yorùbá woman's life and that of her daughter Agbessipé. It examines the wider impact that this Yorùbá diaspora had on the kingdom and its practices of girl transfer. In addition to pressures created by Europeans' policies regarding abolition, the widespread Yorùbá diaspora in Dahomey introduced new norms of girl circulation that overlapped with the accepted practice of entrusting. The nineteenth-century Dahomean economy benefited from the forced labor of Yorùbá girls, women, boys, and men who were the workforce behind the export-based economy in agricultural products. Beyond innovations occurring at the level of palace interaction with elite European and Dahomean communities, changes in girl transfer norms also took place at the popular level among these newly incorporated Yorùbá. Yorùbá women manipulated existing arrangements of girl transfer to meet their labor needs. They also used a compositional logic similar to that of the royal household by making both free and captive Dahomean girls essential elements in their household hierarchies.

"Porteuse d'amandes" from *Trois mois en captivité au Dahomey* by E. Chaudoin, public domain.

3

Agbessipé and Her Mother

*Female Wealth, Girl Pawns, and Enslaved Labor in
Ouidah during the Era of "Legitimate" Trade, 1840s–1880s*

In the late 1820s or early 1830s, a Yorùbá woman gained the title "Agbessipé's mother" when she gave birth to a daughter whom she named Agbessipé.[1] The Yorùbá ethnic group practiced teknonymy whereby they renamed parents after their children, hence this name represented an honor that had cultural significance. Agbessipé's mother was among the Yorùbá captives taken from Yorùbáland during the late eighteenth or early nineteenth century, the decades of cataclysmic decline and the eventual implosion of the Oyo Empire.[2] For the first several years of Agbessipé's life, her mother, like any other in Dahomey, would have secured the young girl to her back by wrapping two pagnes around her. The image "Carrier of Palm Kernels" shows a nineteenth-century woman of the region carrying her child in this manner. Mothers, including enslaved women, ensured that their babies thrived in their early years by keeping them close to them until the child was around two or three years old. Agbessipé's mother dedicated herself and her resources to keeping Agbessipé healthy and happy.[3]

The woman carrying the palm kernels smiles, seemingly happy, as she wears her baby on her back and balances a large basket atop her head. Her lack of accessories or hairstyling indicate that the woman occupied a dependent status at the lower levels of the social hierarchy. Openly engaging in head porterage of goods where a European can capture her image further supports that the woman, like Agbessipé's mother, was enslaved in the Kingdom of Dahomey. During the nineteenth century, most of the population of the kingdom was both female and enslaved. Europeans estimated that perhaps as much as 90 percent of Ouidah's population was enslaved.⁴ How these foreign observers arrived at these statistics is questionable since Dahomey was an "open" slave society that sought to gradually incorporate outsiders, including slaves, into the dominant group instead of keeping them enslaved for generations.⁵ Agbessipé's mother and the woman in the image would have begun striving for their social ascent from the early days of their enslavement, if not for their immediate benefit, then for the benefit of their children. Because Agbessipé was born in the Kingdom of Dahomey, she was free, a status that protected her from being sold into the Atlantic slave trade or becoming a glési, an oppressed stratum of society of slave descent forced into serf-like agricultural labor. The stigma attached to slave descent, however, was not easily overlooked.⁶ Agbessipé was subject to a coercive relationship of patronage with her mother's master. Her ongoing dependence on this patron-client relationship was difficult to escape despite her "free" status.⁷

In the early years of her daughter's life, Agbessipé's mother, like all enslaved persons, conveyed her culture and history to her offspring.⁸ Enslaved persons never forgot their ancestral cultures, and their status did not diminish their connections to the customs and traditions of their homeland.⁹ The large Yorùbá population in Dahomey made it easier to maintain and pass on these traditions. Over the previous century, the Fon-dominated society had internalized many aspects of Yorùbá culture and religion that would have been familiar to Agbessipé's mother.¹⁰

Tender moments between mother and daughter in the child's early girlhood would likely have been replaced by a more detached relationship once Agbessipé approached the age of awareness at approximately seven years old. Her mother would have readied her for their separation and disciplined her in ways that would prepare her for future hardships. She also would have thought carefully about to whom to entrust her daughter. How did mother and daughter adjust to the transition from being within reaching distance during toddlerhood to living separately just a few years later? Did Agbessipé remain in Ouidah during her girlhood? Was she able to see her mother frequently? How did Agbessipé's mother choose a foster home and social mother for her daughter? Did she select a Yorùbá woman to keep her daughter connected to her maternal natal culture? Was Agbessipé's entrustment a positive experience that helped her and her mother form a network of social kinship in Dahomey?

There is no record that Agbessipé's mother did entrust her daughter, but tradition supports the fact that she did so for several years. Mothers commonly entrusted their daughters to social mothers from the age of seven until marriage at around fourteen or fifteen. Her mother must have made strategic decisions that gave Agbessipé a solid foundation to build on in adulthood. Incredibly, despite her humble origins, Agbessipé became one of the most independently wealthy female entrepreneurs in Ouidah during her lifetime.

There are few recorded details about Agbessipé's early life and her mother's entire life. The 1917 census of Ouidah is the only source that mentions Agbessipé by name. The governor-general of French West Africa tasked Reynier, district administrator of Ouidah, with researching the organization of the indigenous leadership in the city. Reynier interpreted these instructions to mean recording the family histories of notable households in each of Ouidah's neighborhoods. He justified this approach based on his belief that there existed "a very old social organization established on venerable traditions."[11] Reynier recognized and included several women in these "venerable traditions" of leadership.[12] He described the families he selected as politically influential and historically interesting. Reynier's brief entry on the history of Agbessipé's house consisted of a three-paragraph summary of her life after she had risen to the pinnacle of Ouidah's merchant community.

Because of the limited data available, this chapter adopts a prosopographically inspired approach to reconstruct the history of Agbessipé's household.[13] After collecting and analyzing information about women with similar backgrounds to Agbessipé or her mother, much of the chapter relies on inferences about female householders' life experiences in Atlantic West Africa to add significance to the basic details of Agbessipé's life and that of her mother. This approach veers into informed speculation as a theoretical method.[14] In particular, the history pieced together posits that the unnamed *femme du pays*, or "country wife," in Frederick Forbes's travel account *Dahomey and the Dahomans* was in fact Agbessipé. After carefully examining all of the female-headed lineages listed as existing in Ouidah in 1917 by Reynier, all data points to Agbessipé as the most likely candidate for the unnamed femme du pays of an Englishman discussed in Forbes's account. The available data makes this inference plausible and probable, though not definitive.[15] This chapter builds a chronology of Agbessipé's life based on the assertion that she is the femme du pays. This means that she would have been in her late teens or twenties in 1849–50 when Forbes visited, and she was born in the 1820s or early 1830s.

This data-based inference that Agbessipé and the unnamed country wife are the same person is neither arbitrary nor fictional. It aligns with the available information from historical records while also acknowledging the inherent limitations of the primary source material in order to empathetically consider the lived experiences of Yorùbá women in nineteenth-century Dahomey, individuals who left few written records and remain marginal in oral historical data.[16] This speculative work yields productive results as it enables a female-centered perspective of the history of Ouidah's transition to "legitimate" trade, an otherwise elusive point of view.[17]

This chapter examines the exceptional life, economic success, and political downfall of Agbessipé, a wealthy female householder who acquired almost five hundred dependents. While her life was extraordinary, she also represented the larger population of Ouidah at the time—overwhelmingly female with exogenous ancestry and only a generation removed from enslavement. During the mid- to late nineteenth century, Yorùbá women living in Ouidah prospered as independent entrepreneurs in the palm oil trade.[18] The nineteenth-century political economy of Dahomey evolved with the cataclysmic economic shift from an Atlantic-oriented export-based economy concentrated on the slave trade to one centered around palm oil. Initially, this presented women with opportunities because palm oil processing was traditionally a female enterprise. Agbessipé, attained unparalleled wealth as a plantation owner and large-scale palm oil and kernel producer, as well as from other endeavors such as market trading and brothel keeping.

Through Agbessipé's life history, this chapter explores the importance of the Yorùbá diaspora in Dahomey to the process of Atlanticization. While scholars have long acknowledged that much of the religious innovation in the Kingdom of Dahomey resulted from the incorporation of voluntary and forced migrants and their beliefs, less attention has been paid to the other areas of innovation, including credit-giving systems.[19] This chapter argues that Yorùbá women and their daughters, such as Agbessipé, reintroduced forms of credit-giving known in Yorùbá as *iwofa*, and more commonly across West Africa as pawning, to the Kingdom of Dahomey. Pawning occurred when a male with authority over a dependent, typically the patrilineage head or father, transferred that person, often a female child, to another household to obtain a loan. The pawnship contract stipulated that the person pawned was to remain in the credit-giving household until the sum was repaid. The creditor's household benefited from the pawn's labor for the duration of her stay.[20] The period of a debt's repayment depended on the loan amount and the prevailing economic conditions. A few days or several years could elapse, or a debtor could indefinitely default.[21]

West Africans pawned humans in the seventeenth through early twentieth centuries across much of Atlantic Africa, though the practice was not universal. While traditions of fostering and entrusting existed throughout the Kingdom of Dahomey's history, monarchs prohibited commercial pawning in Ouidah from shortly after the eighteenth-century Dahomean conquest until the mid-nineteenth century.[22] Pawning reappeared as a credit arrangement with the expansion of legitimate trade in palm products. Yorùbá women needed to create their own forms of credit because they were marginalized within the established systems dictated by the monarchy.

Agbessipé's commercial empire depended on both pawned and enslaved girls. Like the royal household, elite households such as Agbessipé's relied on a compositional logic that required various types of dependents to function at their most profitable. Agbessipé employed pawned and enslaved girls in ways that benefited her enterprises. In nineteenth-century West Africa, the enslavement of women was foundational to male ascendancy.[23] Women, however, built their economic power on the pawning and enslavement of girls.

Enslaved Women in the "White Man's Town"

Ouidah established itself as a culturally and racially mixed community and was part of a cosmopolitan trading network along the West African littoral that attracted a variety of foreign communities, all of which created a heterogeneous, multiethnic society.[24] Europeans built trading forts, sometimes called castles or factories, in Ouidah starting with the French in 1671, followed by the English a decade later in 1681, and the Portuguese in 1721.[25] The three forts were close to one another and near the lagoons, which ran parallel to the Atlantic Ocean.[26] European traders and the immigrant Africans they employed lived there for limited periods.

After the Dahomean conquest of the Kingdom of Hueda in 1727, this port city along the coastal lagoon developed as a uniquely administered region within the kingdom. While Abomey was the political and ritual center of the kingdom, Ouidah was its commercial capital. Its economy revolved around all aspects of export trade, from amassing large numbers of slaves in the barracoons to growing provisions in the vicinity of the city to feed the enslaved captives and fort personnel while they remained on the coast. Historians conservatively estimate that "well over one million" slaves passed through these forts and embarked on slave ships anchored off the shores of Ouidah. This number made Ouidah second only to the port of Luanda in terms of the volume of human cargo traveling across the Atlantic.[27]

Agbessipé's mother was not a palace slave, like Àiná, nor was she a glési, like the majority of enslaved Yorùbá in Dahomey. Agbessipé's mother was a "fort slave" in one of the European-established slave forts in Ouidah. Fort slaves, also known as castle slaves, performed a range of services that facilitated the functioning of the transatlantic slave trade and provided domestic services to the visiting Europeans in residence.[28] Female fort slaves also attended to the day-to-day needs of fort residents by preparing food, shopping and negotiating for groceries and other locally produced goods, laundering clothes, carrying water, translating cultural and linguistic exchanges, and, depending on their age, fulfilling the sexual desires of their employers.

Around the turn of the nineteenth century, Agbessipé's mother arrived in Ouidah as it was undergoing profound changes. Political upheaval in metropolitan France and its Caribbean colonies prompted France to abandon its fort there in 1797. Britain's activism in abolishing the transatlantic slave trade resulted in the withdrawal of British officials and traders from William's Fort in 1812.[29] Abolition of the transatlantic slave trade and its enforcement proved to be a complex and protracted process in the Bight of Benin.[30] The Portuguese fort São João Baptista remained a thriving center of the trade in human cargo between Ouidah and both Brazil and Cuba. Due to its prosperous commerce in human cargo, the city had long attracted a variety of *yovos*, a Fon term for foreigner or outsider. This diverse yovo community of Europeans, multiracial Africans, and Africans from Sierra Leone and the Gold Coast (modern-day Southern Ghana) contributed to the cosmopolitan environment of this Atlantic trading center. The term *yovo* developed a racial connotation and was often used to refer to the identity of whiteness. However, yovos were not exclusively phenotypically white. A large proportion of the city's residents were African foreigners who had been awarded certain "white" privileges at the king's indulgence. Some of these concessions included wearing shoes, traveling in a hammock, sitting in a chair, religious freedom, access to missionary education, and bowing at the waist rather than placing one's face in the dirt when meeting with the king. "White" privileges were conspicuously enacted and displayed by individuals in Ouidah to indicate their status. By the nineteenth century, Ouidah had developed the reputation of "a white man's town."[31] This designation referred to the fact that the three European-controlled forts and their appended neighborhoods formed a core semiautonomous component of the city.

Among these "white" residents was Adjanmiaglo, Agbessipé's father. He was a visiting Gold Coast canoe man employed by the fort that had enslaved Agbessipé's mother. Europeans employed itinerant, West African canoe men to help them cross the rough coastal waters of the Bight of Benin in order to land their goods ashore or transport human cargo and goods to their ships. For centuries, the shoreline from the Volta River in the west to the Niger River in the east had the reputation of being "the most difficult [shore] to land" because European ships could not get closer than "within two hundred yards" of the coast. Vessels had to anchor in the roadstead, transfer all goods and people to indigenous-built flat-bottomed canoes and rely on Gold Coast canoe men's expertise navigating the coastal waters to carry passengers and cargo ashore.[32] Despite these men's skills, many boats still capsized. Like fort slaves, Europeans could not have engaged in the transatlantic slave trade without the crucial support that these migrant laborers provided them. Some canoe men visited the same port for several seasons; others stayed for longer periods, engaging in various trading enterprises before returning home. How long Adjanmiaglo remained in Ouidah or if he returned on a seasonal basis is unclear.

While European traders and foreign-born free Africans entered and left the forts on a regular basis, fort slaves lived there permanently as support personnel. The employment of fort slaves enabled the export trade—first in slaves and then in agricultural products—to flourish through their support of the European trade community.[33] Throughout Atlantic Africa, fort slaves occupied a distinct and paradoxical position in coastal societies. The social and commercial importance of the slaves belied their relatively small numbers.[34] Each fort in Ouidah had a diverse community of several hundred to approximately one thousand African fort slaves (or individuals descended from them) attached to it. The surrounding residential neighborhoods where enslaved persons and free-born fort dependents lived formed communities based on their or their ancestors' connections to the European fort.[35] The permanence of fort slaves' residency gave them a certain degree of power because the success of European trade in Africa relied on this community to facilitate communication through their translation services as well as navigating cultural practices on both sides of the exchange. Even more fundamentally, African fort personnel supported Europeans in their very survival along the coast, nursing them through illness and preparing meals to sustain them.[36]

Adjanmiaglo stayed long enough to marry a Yorùbá slave who bore him a daughter named Agbessipé.[37] As both were foreign born, it is unclear which marital rites they adhered to, if any at all, or if they more casually established a household and lived there as husband and wife. The couple had a daughter in the late 1820s or early 1830s.[38] As the slave trade ebbed and relocated to less infamous ports of the slave trade in Agoué, Porto-Novo, and Lagos, Ouidah's population declined in the early 1840s to approximately ten thousand, half of its 1803 number of twenty thousand.[39] These must have been financially challenging and economically lean years for those who remained. Fortunately, a new opportunity arose in the global marketplace: palm oil export. During Agbessipé's childhood, she witnessed the transitioning of the European forts from slave barracoons to abandoned relics of a bygone era and, finally, during her young adulthood, to wholesale factories for the gathering and transshipment of palm produce.

Agbessipé's diasporic ancestry and her connections to both exogenous European and African communities exemplified the distinct history of Ouidah in the nineteenth century. Agbessipé's birth in the Kingdom of Dahomey granted her the status of being free. However, familial attachments to forts and the communities that developed around these centers of trade endured across generations in evolving relationships of dependency. Agbessipé used this association with both European and African diasporic communities to her advantage.

Agbessipé: A Country Wife in Nineteenth-Century Ouidah

Agbessipé's mother built on both her and her husband's connections to the European communities in Ouidah in ways that shaped her daughter's life. As the family history of the Lemons showed in chapter 2, African residents such as Madiki Lemon remained attached to these communities despite the decades-long absence of European personnel. During Agbessipé's youth, the slave trade waned, and the Europeans all but abandoned their forts. Her mother may have gained nominal freedom at this time, but her servile status and relationship with the indigenous fort personnel endured. The 1840s brought new opportunities in "legitimate" trade to Ouidah and the Kingdom of Dahomey. Legitimate trade referred to the export of agricultural products as opposed to the illicit—from the European point of view—trade in enslaved humans. For this region of West Africa, the legitimate trade in palm products developed as the dominant export.

Agbessipé was able to benefit from her parents' connection with the "white" community when the palm oil export business brought European traders back to their derelict national forts. Thomas Hutton, a British merchant, reoccupied William's Fort in 1838, and the Regis trading firm of Marseille resettled the French fort Saint Louis in 1842.[40] In the mid to late 1840s, Agbessipé reached her teen years and became the femme du pays of her father's European employer.[41] Throughout their history of trading in West Africa, Europeans had taken African women as country wives to help them with trading and other responsibilities.[42] Europeans considered their conjugal relationships with country wives to end when they left the coast of West Africa, and they did not grant their partners the same status as that of a spouse in a Christian marriage. In other parts of Atlantic Africa, *signare* (West African women married to European merchants or soldiers stationed in the Senegambia region) or *cassare* (interracial unions between West African women and Danish men in the Gold Coast region) lineages developed whereby female-headed households encouraged their mixed-race daughters to marry visiting European traders and soldiers, oftentimes in serial succession upon the permanent departure of one husband for Europe. There is no documentation to support the existence of cassare or signare lineages in Atlantic Ouidah as there was along the Gold Coast or on Gorée Island.[43] Both these locales developed beyond the orbit of a powerful West African central state, whereas Ouidah was tightly controlled and monitored by the Dahomean monarchy, which prevented the establishment of such lineages. For example, Sophia Olivier (d'Oliviera), a woman of mixed African and European ancestry, was married to Joseph Olivier, commandant of the French fort during Tégbesu's reign (1740–1774). She was not allowed to independently negotiate a series of marriages with Europeans as signare and cassare did. Upon Olivier's return to France, Sophia entered King Kpengla's harem and became one of his wives. Upon Kpengla's death in 1789, she was inherited by his successors, Agonglo (r. 1789–1797) and Adandozan (r. 1797–1818).[44] As a result, European men in Ouidah began seeking relationships with African women instead of developing a preference for multiracial women.

Agbessipé's husband was likely among the earliest European traders returning to Dahomey in the late 1830s or early 1840s when there was a surge in the legitimate trade in palm products. There are no direct records that describe the nature of Agbessipé's relationship with her husband, but, like elsewhere in West Africa, European traders in the early to mid-nineteenth century formed relationships with African women for various reasons. Some of these European men developed a sincere affection for the African women who acted as their business associates, domestic companions, and sexual partners.[45] By the time Frederick Forbes visited in 1849–1850, Agbessipé and her husband had established a prosperous household. Their relationship seems to have been one of mutual and genuine fondness. Six decades later, oral tradition described the generosity of Agbessipé's husband, stating that he "showered her with gifts" throughout their relationship.[46] The infusion of her husband's capital enabled Agbessipé to expand her business dealings. With the rise in the demand for palm oil for export in the 1840s, Agbessipé embarked on a new business venture. Coastal women outside of the Abomey plateau region entered the palm products trade as artisanal producers of palm oil. Women in and around Ouidah did not face the same barriers—scarce water, difficult transportation, and direct palace authority on a day-to-day basis—that Abomeyan women did. This represented a substantial new economic opportunity for them.[47]

Initially, the burgeoning palm oil trade offered unprecedented commercial opportunities for women, the group who had historically controlled palm oil. For centuries, women had processed palm oil in small artisanal batches for household consumption and regional trade. The palm export trade began with these same women selling relatively modest amounts that they made in excess of these demands. To expand their production, they needed to attract workers. Creating credit systems was key to securing this labor and financing the expansion of their commercial endeavors. Women, especially nonroyal women, were largely kept out of the existing credit systems in the kingdom.

Yorùbá Influences on Female Credit-Giving in Dahomey

Agbessipé needed more workers to help process the palm oil. Throughout Ouidah's history, free labor had always been scarce and difficult to procure. A woman with two migrant parents, one of whom was enslaved, would have been marginalized from child entrustment networks. She may have had capital, but she did not have social status. She relied on a system to recruit dependent workers familiar to both her Yorùbá mother and her Gold Coast father, namely, pawning. Diasporic Atlantic Africans continuously reinvented themselves to build on familiar concepts from their natal cultures.[48] Agbessipé's acceptance and deployment of the institution of pawning would not have been unusual due to her lineage. Both her parents came from societies that widely accepted pawning as a means to secure labor or credit.[49] Agbessipé's mother, as well as Yorùbá men and women living in Ouidah, would have readily accepted child pawning or iwofa as a legitimate form of child circulation that was common among their forebearers in Yorùbáland.[50] Iwofa overlapped with other Fon norms of child circulation; notably, entrusting. Both iwofa and entrusting valorized the training, discipline, and socialization that foster parents provided to children in their care. The primary difference between entrusting and iwofa was that the latter attached an explicit monetary transaction with the transfer of the child.

In most of Atlantic Africa, the institution of pawnship laid the foundation of the trade relationship between European slave dealers and their African trading partners. The pawn process ensured that once the African trader went inland to purchase slaves, he would return and pay the debt, thereby redeeming their kin.[51] Human pawning as a credit system was fundamental to the slave trade in West and West Central Africa. It was taking place in the Kingdoms of Hueda and Allada before the expansion of the inland Kingdom of Dahomey.[52] In addition to suspending pawning, Agaja banned the related practice of *panyarring*, which involved a creditor seizing a debtor's family member and holding them hostage until the debt was repaid.[53] The Dahomean monarch forbade the selling of a family member as a slave or pawn.[54] This prohibition aligned with the king's larger objective to assert centralized control over both interlineal connections and credit-giving institutions. Dahomean monarchs throughout the eighteenth century and into the nineteenth century prohibited pawning because it circumvented the king, the ultimate owner of all things, persons, and land within the kingdom.

This ban was easier to enforce when a small group of elites controlled the slave trade than when more egalitarian principles allowed women to enter the palm oil trade as small-scale producers. During the period from King Agaja's conquests in the 1720s until the 1840s, Ouidah was an exception in Atlantic Africa. Despite the Kingdom of Dahomey's high-volume participation in the transatlantic slave trade, commercial pawning did not play a role in facilitating the commerce in enslaved humans.[55]

Favorable circumstances for male and female independent traders in Ouidah prevailed during the reign of Gezo (r. 1818–1858). This was due in part to the group of Ouidan merchants led by Francisco Félix de Souza who had supported Gezo in his usurpation of the throne from his brother, King Adandozan.[56] During the early decades of Gezo's reign, the commercial community in Ouidah, including male and female traders of modest means, achieved greater autonomy.[57] The development of the palm oil export industry required the extension of credit to persons who were not already a part of the palace's credit systems. Gezo's decision not to enforce the current ban on pawning allowed the ever-increasing Yorùbá population to use culturally accepted forms of credit-giving. Dahomean society easily incorporated the Yorùbá iwofa (in Fon, *gbanú*) because of how closely the ideals of the practice resembled child entrustment. Presumably, the connections between families that were strengthened by entrusted children could have also been a source of financial support to both parties. With the iwofa arrangement, this monetary backing coincided with the girl's transfer rather than taking place at a different point in the relationship. Dahomean society accepted that children should be transferred from their natal homes for extended durations, so its people readily accepted the idea of using children's bodies as collateral in conjunction with their circulation.

While the Dahomean state tried to regulate moneylending, nonstate institutions continued to operate independently to facilitate commercial activity that the state was unable or unwilling to support. Domestic pawning may have always been part of the informal economy, though it likely existed in a way that separated the financial transaction from the child transfer. Both a child transfer and a loan could have occurred within the same relationships, but because of official royal ideology about ownership of people, land, and wealth ultimately belonging to the king, these exchanges were not explicitly connected.[58] Dahomean citizens were probably not entitled to pawn any form of wealth since they only possessed it temporarily with the king's permission.[59] Business interactions, however, depended on personal trust, which often led to the development of familial and social kinship relationships. Dahomeans could loan money to friends, business partners, and family, and they could transfer their children into these people's homes, but they could not combine the two. Pawning may have been technically illicit from the monarchy's point of view, but it remained one of the few popularly accessible financial institutions. It enabled both women and nonelite men to acquire capital even if they could not do so through officially sanctioned royal channels. Moneylenders, female or male, increased their productive capacity by using the pawn's labor until the borrower paid their debt.[60] By taking pawned girls into her workforce, Agbessipé converted her economic capital into social capital and labor power.

Agbessipé was an ambitious trader who gradually acquired enough workers to expand her palm oil business from a small workshop to a large-scale palm plantation. The first step in her commercial success was to gain control over the labor of pawned individuals. Frederick Forbes, who visited the kingdom in 1849–1850, provided the first irrefutable description of pawning in the Kingdom of Dahomey in at least one hundred and twenty years. Forbes stated, "Pawns (as the fashion terms the slaves on the Gold Coast) are received and held by Englishmen indirectly and are to all intents and purposes their slaves." Forbes hinted at the exogenous nature of pawning by referencing the Gold Coast, where British traders had long encountered this practice. He explained how pawning, in his opinion, overlapped with slavery, "The plan adopted is this: the merchant takes unto himself a *femme du pays*, and she manages his establishment."[61] European trading companies prohibited their employees from directly engaging in trade for their personal profit. Many traders stationed along the Atlantic Coast of Africa supported a femme du pays, or country wife, in her endeavors. She acted as his representative, trading on his behalf to benefit both of them.[62] Forbes does not specify where this British merchant and his country wife lived, but in the Kingdom of Dahomey at this time, Europeans resided exclusively in Ouidah. Forbes claimed that the English trader did not ask how his country wife acquired workers. "Her [the country wife's] mode is to accept pawns, i.e. purchase slaves, by receiving man, woman, and child in liquidation of debt; in other words, selling goods to native merchants, who, for convenience, leave slaves in payment. These pawns are as directly slaves to their master as any slaves in the United States." Forbes described the household that had been set up by a British trader and his country wife (Agbessipé): "I myself am aware of one *femme du pays* of a British merchant being the owner of forty pawns, who perform household and other services of the master, and are, except in name, his slaves.... How far is this removed from actual slavery?"[63]

In the mid-nineteenth century, Yorùbá regarded the status of pawns as separate from that of slaves and did not conflate the two. Reverend Samuel Johnson, a Yorùbán who had been enslaved as a boy and liberated by the West African Squadron, then settled and educated in Sierra Leone, claimed that only "those [Europeans] ignorant of the legal conditions ruling the system" would confuse iwofa with slavery. Johnson described iwofa as a "system of engaging domestic servants for service." Johnson lauded iwofa as a form of apprenticeship that parents would voluntarily put their children into even "when there is no debt to pay in order to train him [or her] into habits of discipline and industry, and return the money when they feel that the child has been sufficiently trained."[64] The ideals of iwofa, he explained, aligned with entrustment arrangements with the addition of a monetary exchange. Entrusting, as it had been explained to Europeans visiting Dahomey in the 1840s–1870s, and iwofa both placed a high value on nonbiological parents training and disciplining children who lived in their houses for a temporary, though perhaps extended, period.[65]

Agbessipé may not have been the first to reintroduce pawning to Ouidah, but due to her heavy reliance on the practice, she became the most prominent lender who accepted pawned girls. The forty pawns leased to Agbessipé was a significant number for a single household. Few women were wealthy enough to lend sufficient money to be able to employ so many pawned dependents. Agbessipé's access to capital through her husband and trade partner allowed her to loan money and accept pawns as security. While Forbes does not state the gender of the pawns in the household of the British merchant and his country wife, he implied that the pawns in Dahomey were usually girls or young women: "Should the pawn become a parent, neither the parent nor the child can be forcibly expatriated."[66] Forbes used the gender-neutral *parent*, an unmarried male pawn would have had no claim of paternity to any children he fathered while bonded to a household.[67] Only female pawns would have had socially recognized evidence of their parental status.

Although there is no concrete evidence, the time period and partial clues suggest that an exogenous community, with no access to the monarchy's credit-giving system, reintroduced the practice of pawning to the city of

Ouidah. Dahomey was composed of various foreign communities, but during the early to mid-nineteenth century, the Kingdom of Dahomey absorbed a large influx of Yorùbá women, children, and men. This migrant community left its mark across generations as its offspring sought social mobility in familiar ways. Agbessipé was one prominent example of a larger phenomenon occurring in the Yorùbá community in Ouidah. As the king's ability to control or provide credit to this population declined, Yorùbá women and men looked to customary practices from their ancestral homeland, such as iwofa, to achieve their goals. Pawning fit into a larger group of dependent relationships that had long coexisted in Dahomey, and it was accepted despite its official prohibition.

"The True Wealth of the Country Is the Oil Palm": Women, Wealth, and Palm Oil in Ouidah

Agbessipé employed her pawned laborers to start or expand a business processing and selling palm oil, a newly profitable export industry in the mid-nineteenth century. Dahomeans had always produced palm oil for domestic consumption and had, since the late sixteenth century, traded limited amounts of palm oil with Europeans.[68] European demand, however, fundamentally changed with the industrialization of its economy. The high prices European traders paid for palm oil in the 1830s encouraged West Africans in the Bight of Benin to enter the trade.[69] Women like Agbessipé also took advantage of this opportunity. The country wife's forty pawned girls provided the labor power necessary to start a medium-scale enterprise of palm oil production. For centuries, women in both Dahomey and Yorùbáland had relied on artisanal techniques to produce enough edible palm oil for the domestic market. By European estimates, Dahomeans consumed "enormous" amounts of palm oil daily.[70] In the artisanal process of making palm oil fit for human consumption, men only performed the first step of harvesting the palm fruit from the tree. After the men climbed to the top of the palm trees and collected the fruit, West African societies considered the remainder of the labor "women's work."[71] Girls and women transported the palm fruit back to their residences and threw it into troughs or canoes depending on the volume harvested. They then hauled large volumes of water to the repository and submerged the palm fruit in the water to soak.[72] Next, women boiled the palm fruit in pots for three to four hours.[73] Boiling the oil over and over caused the water to evaporate and produced a clarified oil.[74] Agbessipé may have supervised the skimming and clarifying of the oil, but she relied on girls from different age groups to procure the firewood and water. Women relied on older girls to fetch the water and younger girls to gather the firewood needed for the repeated cycles of soaking and boiling.

Women carried three- to six-liter pots of palm oil on their heads to sell to local wholesalers. At coastal warehouses, a constant influx of women streamed in from morning until night. Older girls may have carried pots of several liters of palm oil on their heads, but women monitored the transaction and negotiation, watching closely as men tested the oil by heating it and then pouring it into casks and measuring it. The women kept "a sharp look out after their own interests" to ensure that wholesalers did not cheat them of any of their profit.[75] Wholesalers then resold the oil in bulk to European traders and firms.[76] Female palm oil vendors demanded imported items that differed in markedly gendered ways from what male slave traders had valued for their higher-priced human commodities. Slave traders sought gin, rum, tobacco, cloth, muskets, powder, flints, cowries, handkerchiefs, hardware, glass, and, to a lesser extent, wine, sugar, iron bars, silk, and luxury items. Plantation-owning traders continued to demand all of these articles in exchange for large volumes of palm oil. Many such traders had previously dominated the slave trade and continued to seek the same products. In addition to these goods, which were mostly consumed by men or women who did not conform to gender norms, the palm oil trade created a remarkable demand for lower-priced items intended for female consumption and usage. Arguably, men could have been purchasing these items as gifts for women or simply for resale, but if that were the case, the men who dominated the slave trade would have wanted these products. The traders who sold palm oil wanted smaller articles, such as perfumery, jewelry, and ornaments to exchange with female sellers. This demand for lower value items reflected the importance of small-scale female traders who sold several quarts of oil, which exceeded their household's consumption and tax needs.[77] Perfume, jewelry, and "ornaments" may seem like luxury items, but each of these products established a woman's status through noticeable manifestations. Women sought these status symbols because they lived in an environment where the majority of women were enslaved, of slave origin, or only one generation removed. Women selling palm oil needed to display their status to offset their vulnerability to being enslaved or mistaken for slaves.

Initially, Agbessipé's choice to acquire pawns rather than slaves to process palm oil reflected the limits of her available capital and her proximity to abolitionist ideas. Unfortunately, there is no record of the amount of money she lent to each pawn's household, but by the time she had advanced even forty small loans, she likely had enough money to purchase some slaves. Why, then, did she choose pawns over other options? Part of her hesitancy was likely due to her knowledge of British views on slavery. Growing up in cosmopolitan Ouidah where the vocabulary regarding slavery was "softened" for members of the European community, Agbessipé might have been sensitive to her husband's views or sympathetic to his position in the English community. Beyond any barriers that may have denied her ready access to alternative labor, she strategically decided to employ pawns rather than slaves.[78] Agbessipé considered lending money in exchange for pawned girls to be a more attractive option than buying slaves because it simultaneously increased her commercial productivity and indebted to her individuals seeking capital. Unlike purchasing a slave, the loaning of capital in exchange for a pawned family member created networks of dependence among free people. One of the characteristic forms of vulnerability enslaved persons experienced was their limited kinship and support networks, which negatively impacted their children to some degree. All enslaved persons and those descended from them tried to develop wide-reaching networks to replace the ones from which they had been stolen.

Agbessipé leveraged her access to capital to build networks of dependents. Individuals turned to her, the daughter of an enslaved woman, for loans. They indebted themselves to her, which solidified her rise in Ouidan society to a member of higher status and wealth. Rather than abating, her ambitions grew from this point. She continued to enlarge her household beyond the forty pawned girls. Agbessipé's ties to the "white" community of Ouidah increased her awareness of global commodity prices and her sensitivity to the rapidly changing politics of the Dahomean monarchy. These connections, along with her entrepreneurial spirit, facilitated her economic success and social mobility.

Agbessipé: From Country Wife to Palm Plantation Owner and Brothel Madame

In the last decade of Gezo's reign, from 1848 to 1858, Ouidah experienced a short-lived economic boom due to his alliance with the commercial class and favorable prices for palm oil on the international market. In the 1850s, Ouidah's population rebounded to around twenty thousand.[79] The expansion of the palm export trade affected the town's demography. During Agbessipé's lifetime, Ouidah's enslaved population increased to make up at least two-thirds and perhaps as much as nine-tenths of the total population.[80] Slave labor was the primary mode of production for legitimate trade.[81] Most of the enslaved individuals were women and girls, who made up around 75 percent of the city's population.

Even though her initial success had relied on her relationship with a European man, Agbessipé accumulated more wealth after his departure because she felt free to explore other options for acquiring workers. Before her husband's return to Europe, he gave her a sum of money, which she used to buy enslaved girls. People from all backgrounds who participated in Atlantic commerce did so with the understanding that their success depended on the enslavement of others, so they had few reservations about owning slaves.[82] Agbessipé's mother's personal history in no way challenged her acceptance of the legitimacy of slavery as an institution. She knew that her social and economic advancement within Dahomean society depended on her reliance on enslaved laborers in addition to other forms of dependents. As her wealth from palm oil increased and once she acquired enslaved girls, Agbessipé expanded her economic pursuits to include brothel keeping. The enslaved girls purchased by Agbessipé served the sexual needs of the booming port. The different businesses in which Agbessipé employed pawned girls versus enslaved ones is evidence that child pawns and slaves were not synonymous. She employed slave girls in her brothel, but because she did not control the sexuality of the girls pawned into her household, she could not prostitute them. The contractual relationship between the debtor and lender prohibited her from using pawned girls in her brothel. A slave mistress did, however, control her slaves' sexuality and reproductive capabilities.[83]

In this environment, Agbessipé continued to acquire dependents as her slaves had children who maintained ties of clientage with her as their patroness. She also acquired more pawns, purchased slaves, and attracted free individuals. Her household eventually grew to include a total of 480 dependent children, women, and men.[84] The scale of her workforce indicated the number of laborers she needed to work a palm plantation. She became one of the few female plantation operators who was not from the royal family.[85]

Agbessipé's extensive wealth eventually attracted the attention of the Dahomean monarch, who monitored the amount of riches any single merchant accrued. While Gezo may have been more lax in enforcing royally decreed economic policies, his successor King Glèlè was less so. During Glèlè's reign, the main challenge to royal authority came from Ouidah's wealthy private merchants, who could independently and directly enter the palm oil trade in competition with royal plantations.[86] Glèlè enforced commercial regulations that Gezo had allowed to lapse, including ones regarding private credit-giving.[87] In 1861, just three years after becoming king, Glèlè sent an official delegation to seize property from Ouidah's merchants and bring them to heel. This plundering of Ouidah's wealth lasted for three weeks and recurred in 1866.[88] Glèlè also actively prevented elite families in Ouidah from accumulating extensive riches by heavily taxing estates and "breaking" houses. This royal prerogative arbitrarily confiscated wealth from those who posed a threat to royal power. Glèlè penalized many Ouidan merchants because of their prosperity.[89] He "sensed danger from the fruits of Agbessipé's labor" and "broke" her household, confiscating hundreds of her dependent workers.[90] Glèlè forced Agbessipé to come to Abomey and meet with him. While there, Glèlè dictated new terms for her business activities. Agbessipé was released and allowed to take six slave girls back to Ouidah. From that day onward, she promised to pay an annual duty for her brothel commerce.

Conclusion

Yorùbá migrants had a robust cultural influence on Dahomean society during the nineteenth century due to the sizable influx of new arrivals into the kingdom at this time.[91] During Gezo's reign, the large-scale forced—and occasionally voluntary—relocation of Yorùbá peoples to Dahomey impacted all levels of society in various ways.[92] Yorùbá women, men, and children carried into slavery their culture, history, and ideas about childhood norms.[93] Yorùbá women, such as Agbessipé, adapted existing practices regarding child circulation to both offset their own vulnerability and leverage new economic opportunities to their benefit. The adoption of iwofa in Ouidah was just one example of how established structures in Dahomey flexibly responded to the demands of the global economy.[94] The Yorùbá community may have been aware of the long-standing official prohibition on forms of credit-giving, but they also accurately assessed the political environment of the time. Agbessipé and other women like her realized that Gezo did not enforce certain long-standing commercial restrictions because of his dependence on the merchant community in Ouidah for his successful usurpation of the throne from his brother Adandozan. In the 1840s, when West African women in Dahomey took on the additional business of processing palm products for export, they benefited from this permissive commercial environment. In these economic and political circumstances, Agbessipé seized a fleeting opportunity. She found creative ways to afford and attract the extra household labor that "legitimate" demanded. Her strategy succeeded only as long as the political climate remained willing to overlook her transgressions to royal decrees.

As the scale and profits from the palm oil trade eclipsed those of slave trade, the monarchy found ways to seize this profitable business from women in order to establish male control of it. The commercial and political environment that facilitated Agbessipé's meteoric success ended abruptly with Gezo's death in 1858. When King Glèlè took the throne, he felt threatened by the independent wealth and power of Ouidah's merchants.[95] Agbessipé was part of this larger phenomenon, but beyond her wealth, her status as a woman who controlled the labor of enslaved persons and pawned girls presented a challenge to the rising patriarchal foundation of monarchical power.[96] At its peak, her female-run household supported almost five hundred dependents of various statuses.[97] The mix of free and enslaved dependents reflected her social and economic advancement and was an outward expression of her wealth and position.[98]

As the story of Agbessipé shows, girls' servitude and bondage to women was not a consequence of these women's attempts to gain economic independence; rather, it was a prerequisite for it. Girls were the main source of labor that women depended on to build their economic wealth. Agbessipé's story reflects the larger strategies that women in the Atlantic World relied on. Her degree of success was exceptional, but her strategies were anything but extraordinary. Few women would amass hundreds of dependents or dozens of pawns. However, women's ability to benefit from the new opportunities provided by the export of palm products directly correlated with their ability to establish a group of female dependents who could support their business ventures and lessen the burden of household chores on themselves. Each residential compound functioned as a commercial workshop that relied on contributions from a mix of women and girls of all ages and statuses.

During the 1840s and 1850s, women had a short-lived chance to seize economic opportunities in Ouidah. As Agbessipé's story demonstrates, the economic and social successes that resulted from the large Yorùbá diaspora threatened the monarchy. Glèlè ruled with a pronounced animosity toward the Ouidah merchant community, and Agbessipé was just one of the elite whose houses were broken. Glèlè's hostility was also part of a larger disenfranchisement of women from political and economic power. Agbessipé's astounding entrepreneurial success led to her economic downfall. However, in the decades that followed, she and her descendants rebuilt their wealth. In 1917, a female-headed lineage still bore her name and controlled a palm plantation. Agbessipé's history provides a concrete example of how the monarchy became increasingly hostile to ordinary women's power in economic spheres.[99] While merchants of both genders had their houses broken by the king, subsequent generations of men navigated the Dahomean social and economic hierarchies to reach their heights. In the colonial economy before World War II, no woman seems to have had opportunities similar to those of Agbessipé. Both the Dahomean monarchs of the late nineteenth century and the French colonial administration created insurmountable barriers that prevented women from replicating Agbessipé's success for another century.

Glèlè's reign ended after a long convalescence during which he disappeared from public view. On December 28, 1889, his death was announced.[100] Prince Kondo took the reign name Béhanzin. The main threat to his power was not the merchant community in Ouidah but rather the aspirations of the French to consolidate their power in the Bight of Benin. How would Béhanzin's policies affect women and the entrusted and other dependent girls living and working with them? How did the expansion of French protectorates and the subsequent establishment of a French colony of Dahomey affect the lives of girls and women of the region?

"Servantes d'un traitant noire de Porto Novo" by Pierre Brot © Musée du Quai Branly—Jacques Chirac, Dist. RMN-Grand Palais/Art Resource, NY.

4

A Runaway Girl amid the Turmoil of Conquest

Household Economies and Colonial Transformations in the Kingdoms of Hogbonou and Dahomey, 1880s–1890s

In the photograph titled "Servants of a Black Trader of Porto Novo," an older woman stands in the back row to the right of the center. Eleven anonymous girls of various ages, ranging from toddlers to teenagers surround the older woman. A baby strapped to the back of a teen positioned on the edge of the picture to the right completes the group. As the title indicates, this image came from Porto-Novo, the capital of the Kingdom of Hogbonou, a small coastal polity to the east of Dahomey. In 1882, Hogbonou negotiated the establishment of a French protectorate over the kingdom. It became the base of French expansion in the region, and Pierre Brot, the photographer, was a French colonial administrator stationed in Porto-Novo. Brot visited the household of these girls and woman sometime between 1894 and 1900.[1] With the possible assistance of a translator, he prompted them to gather in what appears to be the courtyard of their compound. He instructed the younger girls to sit in a line in front of the older girls and woman standing behind them. He positioned the girl with the baby strapped to her back in profile, much like the positioning seen in the image of the carrier of palm kernels and her child from chapter 3. Unlike other similarly staged group photographs in the collections of the Musée du quai Branly, the title of this image identified the subjects as "servants" in the household of a wealthy male trader. The girls and woman were not identified as family or members of a particular ethnic group, as was the case with the other photos in the collections. Their servile status denied them the opportunity or ability to dress in a shared fabric or adorn themselves with finery and accessories, features of these other types of group portraits. Their servile status united these girls and woman.

The concept of "servants" encompassed various forms of dependence as expressed in local languages such as Fon and Yorùbá, but the status lost all nuance and collapsed into a singular word in European languages. The term *servants* could be applied to girls who were entrusted, dashed, or pawned. Europeans also used the term *servants* to refer to domestic slaves. For example, the older woman shown in the photograph may have been regarded in Yorùbá as an *ifolé*, or a homeborn slave—a dependent born in the household to subservient outsiders.[2] In Fon, she may have been called a *devi*, a domestic slave who, due to her long residence in the household, had become a trusted member charged with a supervisory role over the girls. This woman most likely arrived in the household decades prior to Brot's visit and the photography session. Households sought youthful laborers as new acquisitions, though they maintained long-standing servile members, such as the older woman, out of obligation. Whether an ifolé or devi, based on her age, experience, and loyalty to the household, she would have been a manager of the young workers in the household workshop, which at that time would have processed palm oil and kernels. But how did she or the household head attract, recruit, coerce, or purchase this workforce of young girls? Where did they come from? Which servile status were they?

There are no straightforward answers to these questions. Each girl likely held different statuses that incorporated them as bonded dependents in the same home. Some could have been entrusted, pawned, or enslaved; others might have been runaways looking for some control over the circumstances of their dependence and the ability to choose their own household. Girls understood that their dependence was inescapable, but they often tried to negotiate the terms of that relationship. Running away to join an unknown household was risky for entrusted and pawned girls because their dependence would not have had the same institutional limitations and safeguards. A runaway girl also lacked kin to appeal to in cases of abuse, which made her vulnerable in ways that overlapped with enslavement. Some girls rejected the dependent relationships their guardians arranged for them by running away, which liberated them from what they considered to be undesirable circumstances—but this left them susceptible to exploitation and abuse.

One of these runaway girls was Aholoupé. She was entrusted in Abomey in the 1880s and fled to Porto-Novo in the 1890s. Aholoupé, like the woman and girls in the photograph, experienced the social, economic, and political changes that accompanied the shift from independent kingdoms along the Bight of Benin to a consolidated French colony that eventually joined together Hogbonou and Dahomey to other entities. At this time, major economic transformations occurred alongside the establishment of the colonial state. The most significant of these was the processing of palm kernels for export in the 1860s.[3] By the 1880s, the export of palm kernels grew from an insignificant corollary industry of the oil trade to one that surpassed the revenue generated by palm oil. The kernel trade, unlike the oil trade, continued to be controlled by women even after the shift to plantation-style palm production. The kernel trade was a new economic opportunity for women, which greatly increased their exploitation of girls' labor and created a high demand for it that remained in place into the colonial era. In the 1860s, households consigned the burden of kernel processing to girls and older women. This chapter asks: How did such profound transformations impact girls' and women's day-to-day lives? How did these macroeconomic and global geopolitical changes impact female relationships within households? How did the hyperexploitation of young girls' labor change their experiences of girlhood as well as the norms that defined the institution of girlhood in colonial Dahomey?

Although the names of individual girls are rarely mentioned in the official documentation of the conquest era, Aholoupé was one of the few to attract the attention of officials. The colonial state noticed Aholoupé's disappearance because it occurred within the context of a larger investigation into Abomey's royal family. Recording the life of a runaway girl in the 1890s was extraordinary, but not when the girl had fled from a household of the Abomeyan royal family.[4] The colonial government investigated Kodokoué, a brother of King Béhanzin (r. 1889–1894) who also served as a government minister in both Béhanzin's court and that of his successor, Agoli-Agbo (r. 1894–1900). Aholoupé's guardian had betrothed her at a young age to Kodokoué. She entered his household as his prospective fiancée and an entrusted girl to his female relatives. This chapter investigates questions about Aholoupé's experiences and interior life. Answers to the questions are elusive because of the documentation's focus on Kodokoué and his guilt or innocence.

In addition to the scant primary source information about Aholoupé in the official investigation of the royal household, this chapter analyzes travelogues and early ethnographic-style writings to glean contextual details about the environment in which girls of the era lived. With the establishment of the French colonial state in the 1890s, the volume of available sources increased dramatically. At the turn of the twentieth century, Frenchmen stationed in the colony of Dahomey wrote and published works documenting their observations and recorded the traditions that informants recounted for them. This chapter analyzes sources on both the Kingdoms of Dahomey and Hogbonou, as these kingdoms evolved into the French-controlled colony of Dahomey.

Aholoupé's life story fits within the larger colonial phenomenon of runaway women or, more appropriately, runaway girls. Much of the historical literature on runaway girls and women in colonial Africa focuses on the period after which colonial courts were operational.[5] Colonial courts, however, concerned themselves with determining where to draw the line between "legitimate" marriage and marriage as a euphemistic device to conceal female enslavement. Aholoupé, like many runaway women, wanted to decide whom she was to marry. In 1892, Aholoupé was approaching marriageable age, and rejecting her fiancé must have been part of her motivation for running away. In the wake of France's 1892 invasion of Abomey, Aholoupé, a preteen or teenage girl, planned to escape among the masses who fled the capital when King Béhanzin set the city ablaze while retreating from French troops. In her case, this escape meant leaving the arranged marriage, fleeing to a colonial urban center, and severing her ties with kin.[6]

The late nineteenth century was a time of political division and transformation, a time when women's and children's vulnerability to enslavement increased. Studying the life histories of girls such as Aholoupé highlights the agency that girls could and did exercise despite their vulnerability. This chapter argues that Aholoupé seized the opportunity to escape amid the turmoil of the French conquest in Dahomey. With no help from colonial institutions such as the courts, she created her own path toward freedom and independence from the arranged marriage and entrustment that had been planned for her in her youth. Her actions cast doubt on the popular ideals that lauded entrustment as a positive and necessary experience of girlhood. Aholoupé's choices highlight the fact that not all situations of entrustment proved to be beneficial or even tolerable to the girl herself. Entrustment ideals diverged from some girls' lived realities.

Aholoupé: An Entrusted Girl in a Dahomean Minister's Household

Aholoupé was born in the late 1870s or early 1880s, near the end of King Glèlè's reign.[7] Aholoupé left her birth home near Zagnanado at a very young age when, in 1885, Chief Kossouhow, village chief of Banamè, gave Aholoupé as a wife to the Dahomean minister, Kodokoué.[8] The record neglected to mention why the village chief had the authority to betroth Aholoupé. It is possible that she had been born in the chief's house to enslaved persons, or perhaps her father had died and Kossouhow was the paternal relative who now had lineage rights to her.

Kodokoué's appointment as a royal minister attested to the nineteenth-century trend of consolidating power among male royals, a group who had never participated in the kingdom's political affairs. Royal men became more active and visible in court politics, especially during the prolonged struggles for succession as monarchs aged.[9] The struggle among princes for succession began in Aholoupé's youth, years before Glèlè's death at the end of 1889. During the last decade or so of his reign, Glèlè made no public appearances. The Dahomean population and European visitors believed him to be in poor health, perhaps even blind. Kodokoué was never a strong contender for the throne, but he and his household were undoubtedly involved in the political struggles among his relatives. It was a critical time to collect dependents and use their labor to produce greater wealth for the princely minister. Kossouhow would have been aware of this and likely hoped that his support at this crucial time would later be rewarded.

When she was transferred to Kodokoué's household, Aholoupé was too young to marry him, so she lived there for seven years from around 1885 to 1892 as an entrusted girl.[10] There, Kodokoué's older female relatives trained Aholoupé to be "a good spouse."[11] By the age of awareness (around seven years old), Aholoupé would have been expected to work with a certain level of autonomy. Girls of this age "already earned their keep, they carried little loads [on their heads], at times a lot heavier than their little arms could handle with an astonishing fortitude."[12] Women trained girls to do the most arduous and time-consuming work of the household, including the processing of agricultural products and preparing food for consumption or sale.

Preparation of the staple foods of the Dahomean diet required hours, if not days, of labor performed by many women and girls.[13] Grinding grains, tubers, and legumes to pastes and powders was one of "the heaviest work the women [and girls] have to perform."[14] Women and girls ground maize, cassava, yams, sorghum, millet, and beans.[15] Maize-based products provided the majority of calories consumed by average citizens. To prepare *cankie*, the "diet of the lower classes," girls first soaked the maize overnight, then began the exhausting process of grinding the maize into a coarse powder. For cankie, girls and women mixed the ground maize with boiling water and stirred the mixture to remove the husks. The cankie was boiled until it took on a thick, porridge-like consistency. After cooling and thickening the dough, women and girls formed it into orange-sized balls that they then wrapped in plantain leaves for household consumption and sale in the market. Sometimes Dahomeans ate cankie by itself; other times, women and girls served it with sauces or smoked fish.[16] Aholoupé learned to prepare all of these foods and faced harsh punishments for mistakes that ruined the final product. Much of the work involved in preparing these foods was combined with other chores, but there were times when the preparation required the girls' undivided attention. In addition to starch-based products, girls also boiled eggs, smoked fish and shrimp, roasted or boiled groundnuts, cooked meats, and stewed vegetables for sale.[17] Within the confines of the household compound, girls processed agricultural products and prepared foods to sell.

After completing the food preparation, women and girls transported their goods to market in bundles or trays balanced on their heads. Young Aholoupé built her strength gradually so that she could eventually carry a tray or basin stacked high with prepared foods weighing as much as twenty pounds atop her head.[18] Hawking goods in the streets was a physically exhausting and, at times, unpleasant or even dangerous activity for girls. Despite this, Dahomeans believed hawking was an important skill and significant part of girlhood, as is evidenced by the Fon proverb "So wae re jar, Jor gee, ah jor gee sar" ("The readiest means a sale to meet, Is to cry your goods throughout the street").[19] The experience that girls gained while hawking taught them the professional skills necessary to succeed in market trading as adults.

Living in Kodokoué's household, Aholoupé spent her days cleaning the compound, laundering clothes, processing agricultural products, and hawking goods in the streets. Like all girls regardless of status, she would have done these tasks in any household she lived in. She realized that running away would not free her of this onerous workload. She contributed to both the functioning of the household and its economic endeavors.

The war between France and Dahomey disrupted the entrustment arrangement of Aholoupé to her betrothed's household. When French troops marched on Abomey in November 1892, Aholoupé and her friends fled into the bush, the wild uncleared area beyond the settlements not used for farming or housing. Before retreating to the north on November 17, 1892, King Béhanzin set fire to Abomey, his capital. Aholoupé and her friends may have watched the flames from afar, seeing smoke and the glow of embers as the city burned in the distance from where they hid. Perhaps Aholoupé even felt the ashes stick to her skin as the capital literally drifted away.[20] Aholoupé's friends eventually returned to their homes in the days and weeks after France took control of Abomey, but she did not. With the city of Abomey in ruins behind her, Aholoupé disappeared into the countryside, never to return in the days, weeks, or years following the attack.[21]

Her parents wondered what happened to their daughter. Was she alive? Eventually, they concluded that her fiancé, Kodokoué, had sold her into slavery. Other accusations of slave trading leveled against Kodokoué likely influenced their suspicion that Aholoupé had met the same fate. The colonial state took this allegation seriously, found it plausible, and imprisoned Kodokoué. For two years, Kodokoué was jailed in Porto-Novo for trafficking Aholoupé. The royal family secured his release only when the missing girl had been found. In 1897, authorities discovered Aholoupé in Porto-Novo, the former capital of the Kingdom of Hogbonou and current capital of the newly formed colony of Dahomey. She had run away of her own volition to Porto-Novo to start her life anew.[22]

Why did Aholoupé not return to Abomey like her friends did? Why did she flee? What had transpired to make her so unhappy that running away was, in her estimation, the best option? Like other runaways, she wanted to escape a relationship that she found undesirable.[23] It is unclear whether she ran away because she was unhappy with her working conditions and the way she was treated by the female members of Kodokoué's family, Kodokoué as a prospective spouse, or perhaps both. Even if she had not been mistreated, Aholoupé could have simply wanted to assert her personhood and choose her household or partner. Because she had not married Kodokoué when she fled, Aholoupé was probably not of marriageable age; therefore, she was likely no older than thirteen in 1892. Most entrusted girls tended to run away at this age.[24] Aholoupé's young age attested to her determination to change her situation and bravery in the face of the unknown. The documents do not provide any information about her motivations or circumstances in either her entrusted household in Abomey or her chosen one in Porto-Novo. What had Aholoupé done to survive during those five years as a runaway girl? Did she go immediately to Porto-Novo? Why did she choose to settle in Porto-Novo? Who helped her along the way? How did she find a household offering protection to an unattached girl? The archival record does not contain answers to any of these questions.

Aholoupé's Life in Porto-Novo during the Conquest Era

Aholoupé walked more than ninety miles from the hinterland of Abomey to the city of Porto-Novo. In doing so, she traversed a political border in flux. She went from the Kingdom of Dahomey to the Kingdom of Hogbonou, which was under a French protectorate. In the century preceding Aholoupé's flight, the political maneuvers of the neighboring Kingdoms of Hogbonou and Dahomey were closely intertwined. Since the 1760s, Hogbonou had been a sporadic target of raids by its neighbor Dahomey.[25] Hogbonou allied with the Oyo Empire as a tributary state in exchange for its support against Dahomean aggression. When Oyo's power crumbled and the state dissolved around 1830, Hogbonou searched for a new source of protection against its powerful western neighbor. From the 1860s onward, Hogbonou courted an alliance with France to counter threats to its sovereignty. King Sodji (r. 1848–1864) appealed for the establishment of a French protectorate over his kingdom as a proactive measure against the imminent threats posed by both Great Britain and Dahomey.[26] In 1863, France agreed to a preliminary treaty with Sodji.[27] The early French protectorate of Hogbonou lapsed under Sodji's successor, King Mikpon (r. 1864–1872), but King Toffa (r. 1874–1908) renewed it in 1882 due to ongoing Dahomean attacks.[28] Despite this political turmoil, the Kingdom of Hogbonou, like Dahomey, benefited from the collapse of the Oyo Empire and the chaos of the ensuing Yorùbá Revolutionary Wars.[29] Porto-Novo rose in regional prominence as one of the new economic centers of the palm export trade from the 1870s onward.

News of these regional political changes spread among itinerant market women and migrants—voluntary and enslaved—and girl hawkers, such as Aholoupé, who listened to news and gossip during her day in the markets and streets of Dahomey. Aholoupé would have known that Dahomey and Hogbonou were bitter rivals and that Kodokoué's royal status in Dahomey did not have influence in Hogbonou. She was also aware of Porto-Novo's thriving economy. In addition, France's protectorate over Hogbonou might have made it an even more attractive locale to seek refuge from her powerful fiancé.

Aholoupé walked for at least three to four days before arriving at Porto-Novo. The duration of her trip would have depended on whether she went there directly, took a circuitous route, or stayed in places along the way before reaching her destination. She likely joined other migrants as they traveled southeast. In late 1892, travelers from Abomey to Porto-Novo would have had difficulty avoiding the destruction left behind by the Second Franco-Dahomean War of 1892–1894. Over the course of her long journey, Aholoupé might have encountered smoldering villages recently razed by either the French or the Dahomean army. Even more gruesome, Aholoupé may have crossed battlefields strewn with dead, decomposing Dahomean female and male soldiers left behind as their comrades hastily retreated from the advancing French forces.[30]

In the 1890s, Aholoupé would have been just one among thousands of newly arrived individuals seeking a household to join in Porto-Novo. Hogbonou's population swelled in the second half of the nineteenth century. In 1886–1887, the Kingdom of Hogbonou had a population of 250,000, with 10 percent of its inhabitants living in the capital of Porto-Novo.[31] The small kingdom's relatively high population density reflected the fertility of the land and the people's ability to develop more advanced methods of production.[32] Porto-Novo's population grew rapidly from 25,000 to 35,000 just five years later, a year before Aholoupé's arrival.[33] From 1892 to 1897, the population continued to expand exponentially. By the turn of the century, the city had around 50,000 residents, making it slightly larger than Abomey, which had a population of 40,000, and more than twice as large as Ouidah, which had a population of 20,000.[34] Among the new arrivals were voluntary émigrés and enslaved persons forcibly relocated to the kingdom. Hogbonou, like Dahomey, saw a rise in its enslaved population during the era of "legitimate" trade, the era when palm products replaced enslaved humans as the major export commodity from West Africa.[35] In the 1860s, Lieutenant Gellé of the French Navy noticed twice as many slaves in the Kingdom of Hogbonou compared to the previous decade, when the slave trade was still ongoing.[36] During the nineteenth century, slave labor was part of the production and trade of virtually every legitimate commodity exported from West Africa.[37] Hogbonou accepted free refugees from the Yorùbá and Franco-Dahomean wars; however, these free workers were greatly outnumbered by the influx of slave labor.

Upon arriving in Porto-Novo, Aholoupé would have needed to find a sympathetic household to take her in as quickly as possible. Her plight would have been familiar to many in the Kingdom of Hogbonou. Just two years earlier, during the First Franco-Dahomean War of 1890, many inhabitants of Porto-Novo would have faced a similar displacement when the civilian population of the Kingdom of Hogbonou bore the brunt of Dahomean raids. From the start of the conflict in February until its end, inhabitants fled their villages en masse, seeking refuge from the Dahomean armies. In October 1890, the French Resident of Porto-Novo reassured the people that it was safe for their families to return to their lands, houses, and businesses. By the first week of November, entire villages were quickly repopulated with former inhabitants.[38] The people of Porto-Novo had vivid memories of either their own or their family members' forced relocations due to war. The household that took in Aholoupé likely did not question the reasons she gave for her situation.

Aholoupé would have sought a formidable patron or patroness to bind herself to for protection. Remaining alone without a household or kin network in a strange city would have exposed her to capture and enslavement, a common fate among children in late nineteenth-century Africa.[39] Without family or a husband, her freedom and status were incredibly fragile. How did she choose a household? Did she abandon one after another until she found one that she liked? In the aftermath of the Dahomean raids on Hogbonou and a booming export trade in palm kernels, girls' labor was in high demand to rebuild the economy. Aholoupé likely had little trouble in finding a welcoming household that exploited her labor.

It was no coincidence that Porto-Novo's demographic growth corresponded to the palm oil and kernel boom.[40] Porto-Novo's labor supply expanded and allowed the kingdom to nearly double its volume of exported oil and quintuple its volume of kernels from the 1870s to the 1890s. The newly arrived men, women, and children to the Kingdom of Hogbonou made this astronomical increase in productivity possible. By 1893, one year after Aholoupé arrived, Porto-Novo exported nearly half a million francs' worth of mostly palm products. In comparison, Ouidah exported approximately one-fifth of that amount. Within a decade, Porto-Novo exported approximately four times as many palm kernels as Ouidah and one and a half times as much palm oil.[41] The Hogbonou monarchy encouraged the development of an export-based monoculture economy centered on palm products. Kings Sodji (r. 1848–1864), Mikpon (r. 1864–1872), Messi (r. 1872–1874), and Toffa (r. 1874–1908) attracted immigrant merchants who had been persecuted in Dahomey. Porto-Novo enticed dozens of Ouidan families fleeing from the Dahomean monarch's arbitrary harassment as well as other Dahomeans unhappy with the increasingly oppressive environment.[42] Sierra Leoneans settled in Porto-Novo as representatives of Lagosian trading houses' auxiliary locations in Porto-Novo.[43] The Kingdom of Hogbonou and especially its capital Porto-Novo attracted a diverse group of voluntary migrants due to a combination of a favorable political environment and abundant natural resources.

Other factors besides the number of workers assisted Hogbonou's commercial expansion. A less-pronounced gender imbalance facilitated the kingdom's ability to produce such large volumes of palm oil.[44] Unlike Dahomey, significant portions of the population were not annually drafted into military service to conduct raids on neighboring populations. No militaristic zeal dictated the patterns of agricultural labor, nor did any categories of men become exempted from agricultural labor. Both free and enslaved men in Hogbonou worked in the fields and orchards. In striking contrast to their Dahomean neighbors, Europeans in the nineteenth century praised the men in nearby Hogbonou for their hard work in agricultural pursuits.[45] Visitors described Hogbonou as being "extremely beautiful and fertile" with verdant, "magnificent" vegetation. The kingdom's landscape looked as if in certain seasons, no "corner of the earth" could "come into existence without being covered with a plant or a grass of some kind."[46] The inhabitants of the kingdom produced "all the necessaries of life in great abundance" and did not need to import items for their subsistence.[47] Farmers in the kingdom produced excess amounts of maize, manioc, potatoes, beans, and other vegetables, which they exported to the regional markets of Porto-Novo, Lagos, and Badagry.[48] The tropical climate and rich soil encouraged palm trees in the region to grow in a semiwild state.[49] Because these trees needed very little cultivation, farmers could focus on planting more trees, clearing the debris from underneath the trees, and cutting down the palm fruit when it was ready to harvest.

It is difficult to determine how exceptional Aholoupé's life story was. It seems that most girls of the time did not seize the opportunities provided by political chaos to change their circumstances. Aholoupé's parents had immediately assumed that their missing daughter had been trafficked, not that she ran away. Kodokoué's conviction confirmed that French officials believed Aholoupé's more likely fate was having been a victim of human trafficking rather than intentionally running away of her own volition. Aholoupé's escape from Kodokoué reflected her desperation and determination to get away from an unsatisfactory situation, and it proved that she recognized her value as a laborer and felt confident she would find a willing patron or patroness in Porto-Novo to take her in as a dependent.

Rebuilding Households, Reclaiming Kin

After the conquest of Abomey, the Second Franco-Dahomean War continued for another thirteen months. Béhanzin, the last independent ruler of Dahomey, surrendered to the French on January 5, 1894.[50] After the defeat of the precolonial Kingdom of Dahomey in 1894, France established the colony of the same name. France combined the former Kingdom of Dahomey with the nearby Kingdoms of Hogbonou and Ketou, the Bariba city-states, and decentralized regions to create southern Dahomey. The colony of Dahomey was a conglomeration of formerly independent entities. France marginalized Abomey, the inland capital of the Kingdom of Dahomey, by making Porto-Novo, the seat of a rival kingdom, the capital of the colony. France invested heavily in infrastructure in coastal Cotonou, which transformed it into the colony's economic center.

Once the hostilities ended, households in both former kingdoms tried to find displaced and captured family members. When Aholoupé's parents could not find her, they accused Kodokoué of slave trading, a charge influenced by the ongoing controversies surrounding the Abomeyan royal family. In the 1890s, the Dahomean palace was at the center of the ongoing slave trade, with the royal ministers and wives acting as intermediaries for the newly installed King Agoli-Agbo. Kodokoué was just one among many members of the royal household investigated for multiple instances of slave trading.[51] The French administration's June 1895 investigation stated: "The king Agoli Agbo has begun again to make commerce of slaves; he sells children that he hides out of the view of whites." Bocossa, chief of Sagon, further explained that young children fetched higher prices than men.[52] Further supporting the assertion that Kodokoué likely sold Aholoupé, the French administration uncovered conclusive evidence that he had sold at least six slaves and bought another.[53] All the slaves were identified as women or children.

Children were in high demand in Porto-Novo. The investigators alleged that King Agoli-Agbo instructed Fongni, an indigenous chief, to sell two hundred children.[54] The French Resident of Allada commented: "I know that the Dahomeans trade children for merchandise and that the Nagos [Yorùbá of Porto-Novo] certainly accept this mode of payment... it was more or less impossible to suppress these exchanges."[55] The Dahomean monarch's attempts to raise money for his bankrupt treasury by trafficking children to the Kingdom of Hogbonou were thwarted by the French colonial government. Agoli-Agbo was unable to profit from trafficking as his predecessors Gezo and Glèlè had done. Kodokoué was one of the ministers embroiled in this royal scheme and the French investigation of it. Aholoupé's parents and the colonial tribunal assumed that Kodokoué had sold Aholoupé based on the evidence of his other confirmed slave-trading activities as well as the popular use of children as a form of currency and the heightened vulnerability of girls to enslavement.

In the second half of the nineteenth century, the majority of Dahomey's population was or had been enslaved, with a significant number of slaves being women and children. The enslaved population was estimated to be between two-thirds in 1866 and four-fifths in 1871. This led to a fatalistic assumption that anyone could be enslaved at some point. Pierre Bouche, a Catholic missionary who lived in Porto-Novo, Ouidah, Lagos, and Agoué from 1866 to 1869 and 1873 to 1875, described this popular attitude in the late nineteenth-century Gulf of Guinea region: "One is a slave, not by inferiority of nature, but only by accident, because one was easy to surprise or steal, because one was too weak to resist his enemy. Everyone knows that the slave is a [wo]man like the others; that [s]he does not differ from his [or her] master only by the condition that [s]he finds himself [or herself] reduced to by happenstance, an unhappy condition, but judged necessary and authorized by custom."[56] In accordance with this view, Aholoupé's parents assumed that their daughter had found herself in such an "unhappy condition."

In 1895, the colonial tribunal convicted Kodokoué of the human trafficking of Aholoupé and others. He spent two years in a colonial prison, during which time Aholoupé's family and the royal family continued to search for the girl. They had no confirmed information on her whereabouts; however, throughout the 1890s, enslaved persons were routinely located by their families. After taking Abomey in 1892, French officials encouraged those held as captives in the palaces to return to their homes.[57] This policy prompted the family members of enslaved individuals to try to find them. From 1892 until the end of the decade, many individuals were reclaimed through officially sanctioned returns and royal search parties sent between Dahomey and Hogbonou.[58] As one example, the Dahomean army took fifteen-year-old Marie Lima captive when they attacked the town of Meko in 1882. Joaquim João Dias Lima bought her and took her as a wife. Marie's ability to have children for Lima's patrilineage integrated her more fully into the family.[59] Family tradition reported that when Marie's mother came to free her after the French conquest in 1894, Marie refused to leave.[60] She had been forced into her marriage to Joaquim, but after more than a decade, she deemed it in her best interest to stay married and live in his household with her children. Not only did she refuse to abandon her children, but she may also have grown fond of her husband and master. At the very least, she had married into a prosperous household where her status as wife, in her estimation, was preferable to being a slave. By the time France had defeated Dahomey in 1894, Marie had lived almost half of her life and her entire adult life in the Lima household in Ouidah. During the first years of colonial rule, hundreds or perhaps thousands of girls and women had to make their own choices about whether to stay where they had begun building lives or return to their natal communities.

Aholoupé, however, had not been sold by Kodokoué or anyone else. In the confusion of the war, she somehow made her way south to Porto-Novo, which was where she was found in 1897. The French administration had imprisoned several Dahomean ministers who were members of the Abomeyan royal family based on accusations of selling slaves. Kodokoué used his extensive family and business networks to find his onetime fiancée, understanding that this might be his only chance to be released from the colonial prison.[61] Kodokoué's criminal dossier does not contain any further information about these five years in Aholoupé's life or her motivations for leaving Abomey.

Conclusion

By the second half of the decade, France's defeat of Dahomey led to a surge in the repatriation of captives and the formation of search parties to find missing family members who had disappeared during the turmoil.[62] Aholoupé's story is remarkable because, while it was assumed that she had been enslaved, she actually made independent choices regarding her young life. She ran away, hoping to find a household that would free her from the entrustment arrangement and its subsequent commitment to betrothal. While all girls and women were at risk of being enslaved and behaved with a conscious understanding of this fact, not all were victims. Girls could only rarely escape servility in all its forms, but they could make decisions about their circumstances when they had the opportunity.

During this period of upheaval and transition, Porto-Novo, like other early colonial urban centers, provided a haven of anonymity and opportunity for girls seeking refuge. Aholoupé escaped the influence of Abomey's royal family by fleeing beyond its reach and blending into the masses. She made the difficult choice of risking enslavement as a lone teenager traveling to Porto-Novo instead of enduring her entrustment and betrothal to Kodokoué. There is no record of the hardships or abuse she may have experienced in Kodokoué's household that prompted her to take this chance. In the late nineteenth century, the circulation of girls remained an essential component of the household economy; their labor drove the export trade in kernels. While most girls had little to no control over where they were relocated, some recognized their value as laborers and seized this opportunity to make choices about their lives. Women and girls unhappy with their situations in Dahomey took advantage of the extreme volatility of the 1890s to shape their own destinies in nearby Hogbonou.

As the French colonial state established itself and its administrative systems, girls and their guardians had new avenues to challenge and renegotiate relationships of dependence. After an initial period of liberatory intervention for women, colonial administrators realized it was in their interest to bolster patriarchal controls over women. Colonial courts even invented crimes, such as female desertion, to control these women and their movements.[63] By the 1910s, the colonial courts began intervening in forms of de facto enslavement. Most often, these investigations focused on the pretense of marriage in concealing the trafficking of girls and women. Decades later, in the 1930s, the courts' attention shifted to examining the guise of guardianship.

"Porto-Novo—Sur Le Marché" (1908) by François-Edmond Fortier, public domain.

5

Entrusted or Enslaved?
Colonial Legal Debates about Girls' Statuses, 1900s–1930s

In 1899, a six-year-old girl named Houmé was kidnapped from her home in Abeokuta (modern-day Nigeria). She was then enslaved in Adjohoun, a village near Porto-Novo in the colony of Dahomey. The French colonial tribunal in Porto-Novo recorded her life history when she appealed to it for her freedom in 1909.[1] There are no pictures in the archive that identify Houmé by name; however, a photograph of Porto-Novo's market captured by François-Edmond Fortier in 1908 titled "Porto-Novo—In the Markets" features a girl on the cusp of womanhood at around fifteen or sixteen years, the age Houmé would have been in 1908. Looking at Fortier's photograph raises the question: How many of the women and children pictured experienced slavery at some point in their lives? Was the teenage girl kneeling behind the sugarcane in the image a victim of kidnapping and enslavement in her youth, just like Houmé? The taller child standing in front of the teenager appears to be about the same age as Houmé had been in 1899 when she was captured and taken away from her home. During exchanges like these, did Houmé think of her childhood? Did she yearn for her homeland and wonder about the people she left behind?

These questions are largely unanswerable due to the limited scope and framework of the legal records, the only source about Houmé's life. In 1903, France established a colonial legal system for French West Africa (AOF) and, in 1905, outlawed slavery and human trafficking.[2] With the establishment of colonial tribunals, girls had more opportunities to challenge the conditions of their dependence—if they had an adult's support. These colonial institutions recorded girls' accounts with varying degrees of latitude in terms of what they believed relevant in the context of the case.[3] Across West Africa, colonial courts only heard a limited selection of slave trading cases, and they often only left cursory records.[4] This chapter presents an in-depth study of three cases, each highlighting a detailed *procès-verbal*, or a transcribed and translated record of a girl's oral deposition in front of legal authorities. In the procès-verbaux, girls variously described their experiences as enslavement, entrustment, pawning, and servitude. These documents provide some of the only firsthand accounts of Dahomean girls' experiences of transfer among households. In their testimonies, the girls describe how they were incorporated into their master's or mistress's household, their experiences of care or abuse in the household, and how they understood their status. Each girl also provides a brief account of her life over the course of several years. In her testimony, Houmé discusses her life story from 1899 to 1909. A second girl, Fovi, describes her experiences from 1926 to 1932 as an entrusted girl in Fohoumbo's household. The third case concerns Mahoun's life from 1930 to 1935 when she lived in Aledjessi's house with six other girls, each of whom described their dependence in various ways.

In addition to individual case records, this chapter relies on critical interpretations regarding how the 1912, 1924, and 1931 reorganizations of the French colonial legal system in West Africa. In each of these reorganizations, the administration scrutinized the underlying logic of the proper jurisdiction and procedures for prosecuting the crime of human trafficking, which fluctuated among numerous levels of the tribunals. These debates reflected the high political volatility of this particular crime in the twentieth century in the international context of imperial humanitarianism. The label of slavery had tremendous power in this context.[5] Throughout the first four decades of the twentieth century, colonial officials engaged in ongoing discussions about what constituted de facto forms of domestic slavery and if any of these forms could be considered benign or acceptable.

Houmé's case and others like it created an archetype that established both gendered and age-based criteria as factors that affected how colonial powers defined victims and perpetrators of human trafficking.[6] In this model, adult men trafficked girls and young women. Framing slavery in this way made it difficult for colonial authorities to distinguish slavery from marriage, two distinct institutions from the French point of view. However, the two could overlap in West African indigenous practices.[7] In the 1910s, the French colonial state concluded that based on this, marriage in West Africa often functioned as a guise for slave trafficking.⁸ This framing excluded women from acting as the enslavers and owners of girls.

In Dahomey, this operational designation went unquestioned for a generation until the 1920s and 1930s when international humanitarian activism focused on the issue of child pawning. Pawning was an institutionalized form of debt bondage in which an individual, often a girl, was temporarily transferred to another household in exchange for a loan given to one of her family members. The girl pawn resided in the credit-giving household until her guardian repaid the loan. While there, she worked for the lender or his wives. The pawn could be exploited but not sold or mistreated.⁹ During the era of the slave trade, Europeans trading in Atlantic Africa accepted human pawns from African traders in exchange for trade goods that these traders then took to the interior and purchased slaves. Upon their return to the coast with human cargo, European traders returned pawned individuals to these African traders. The history of pawnship was complex in the Kingdom of Dahomey because the monarchy tried to centralize control over credit-giving mechanism. From the early eighteenth until the mid-nineteenth century, Dahomean monarchs had enforced a prohibition on human pawning in the Atlantic trade. In the mid-nineteenth century, women, such as Agbessipé featured in chapter 3, relied on pawned girls to expand their entrepreneurial endeavors in hawking food and processing palm products. Pawning became an issue of French concern in the 1920s and 1930s, when African children's welfare in colonies under European rule and slavery in all its forms became highly publicized international issues.¹⁰

After the League of Nations recognized pawning as a form of de facto enslavement, international activism prompted colonial authorities to examine all forms of child transfer and circulation. In theory, entrustment, pawning, and slavery existed as distinct practices governed by well-defined cultural expectations, but in the early twentieth century, this was not always the case in practice.¹¹ In the history of entrusted girls in Dahomey, the controversies surrounding pawning sparked intense debate in the mid-1930s. The entrusting of girls became part of larger controversies regarding human trafficking and girl pawning. French authorities scrutinized the transfers of girls to unrelated households as suspected cases of trafficking and therefore a form of de facto enslavement. Court cases raised the question: Was entrusting synonymous with enslavement?

Houmé, A Girl from Abeokuta: A Colonial Consensus of a Definition of Human Trafficking

In 1899, six-year-old Houmé accompanied her mother or another kinswoman to work in the fields near her home in Abeokuta, a city in modern-day southwest Nigeria. Abeokuta was a city with a decades-long history of Dahomean slave raids. Famously, in 1848–49, Abeokuta successfully repelled a Dahomean attack that resulted in devastating losses for the agojie. Since the 1894 French defeat of the kingdom of Dahomey, these organized onslaughts had ceased.[12] Throughout Africa, the late nineteenth century, though, was an era of increased risk of opportunistic capture of individual children.[13] When women and children left their homes to work plots of land for their subsistence, they were vulnerable to kidnapping. At her age, depending on the season, Houmé would have helped pull weeds, gather produce, or search nearby for firewood. As she was performing these mundane tasks, two men abducted her. They sold her to another man who then resold her to Bouou Noukoué in Adjohoun, a village on the banks of the Oumé River near Porto-Novo in the Atlantic coastal region of the colony of Dahomey, some ninety miles to the southwest from where the abduction occurred.[14] Due to the violent nature of her abduction, the isolation she experienced during her forced relocation, and being forced to perform unpaid labor, there was little doubt that Houmé was in fact Bouou's slave. Houmé's enslavement was typical of nineteenth-century opportunistic abductions of children, a widespread phenomenon following the successful suppression of large-scale slaving operations.[15]

Houmé grew up in Bouou's household as his slave. In 1906, at the age of thirteen or fourteen, her status changed when she became Bouou's wife.[16] French colonial authorities, however, refused to recognize her as a legitimate wife because no legal, customary, or religious ceremony had been performed. From the French perspective, Houmé was Bouou's concubine. Houmé's life story was the typical example of how French colonial authorities regarded African slavery in the early twentieth century: as a teenage girl's fictitious "betrothal" to an older man. Bouou, in his forties, was indeed thirty years Houmé's senior. Regarding these marriages between slaves and their masters, colonial officials euphemistically referred to the girls or women as "wives of circumstance."[17] From the Dahomean perspective, Houmé's transition from enslaved girl to wife was part of the natural progression of how open slave societies should incorporate enslaved girls into households.

In 1908, Houmé brought charges against Bouou, her master/husband/guardian, when he betrothed her against her will to Sessou, a fifty-four-year-old man.[18] Houmé's case was one of the earliest tests of the newly established colonial tribunals' willingness to apply France's abolition decree in Dahomey. A November 10, 1903, decree established a native court system for France's West African colonies, including Dahomey, but there was a delay of several years in getting these courts operational. Among the earliest litigants who brought their cases to these new colonial courts were enslaved women whose masters claimed to be their husbands. After the 1905 abolition of slavery in AOF, these women wanted to divorce and be freed from their masters-cum-husbands.[19]

The identities of slave and wife were distinct categories with different status entitlements, but a woman could hold both statuses, either at the same time or one after the other.[20] From 1905 to 1910, French colonial courts favored granting divorces to women who had been acquired by their husbands as slaves.[21] These cases profiled the victim as a youthful female trafficked by men and then sold to an older master and "husband." Houmé's life story exemplified this paradigm of turn-of-the-century colonial slavery in AOF. Was the marriage, as Bouou claimed, a legitimate betrothal of his household dependent? Significantly, the December 12, 1905, abolition decree stated that colonial authorities would not interfere in patriarchs' legitimate exercise of authority over their household dependents. This stipulation created ambiguity for enslaved women and children in Houmé's situation. Bouou was the only man in the household who could claim patriarchal authority over Houmé; she had lived in his house for most of her young life. A key element to this typical case was the pretext of marriage. If Bouou had not resold Houmé to a new husband/master, the French administration might not have intervened and liberated her.

On January 25, 1909, the colonial tribunal in Porto-Novo judged that Bouou's actions of betrothing Houmé against her will constituted an act of human trafficking. The tribunal ignored Bouou's actions from a decade earlier when he purchased Houmé as a young girl, focusing instead on the more recent attempted trafficking of Houmé to Sessou. The colonial authorities believed both greed and anger, not concern for the well-being of a dependent, motivated Bouou. Authorities came to this conclusion after discovering that

Bouou sold Houmé to Sessou when he realized that his enslaved concubine, or "wife of circumstance," had slept with three other men. This salacious detail demonstrates how sixteen-year-old Houmé tried to make her own choices, defy her master, and embrace a sense of freedom in whatever ways she could. Perhaps she wanted to find a partner she liked or a different type of patriarchal protector who might support an attempt to flee Bouou or even purchase her freedom for her.[22] Or she may have simply wanted to find a man who fulfilled her sexual desires.

The tribunal of Porto-Novo condemned Bouou and Sessou to three years of imprisonment and one thousand francs each.[23] The tribunal cited the conviction of the two men in a subsequent 1909 case, justifying the harsh penalties based on its knowledge of the defenses and sanctions in Bouou's case. The report summarized: "The case submitted to the Tribunal de Cercle could be considered as the typical case of trafficking that still occurs, too often unfortunately under the pretext of marriage. The sold person: a girl—soon to be adolescent, does not have at the [time of the] trial only vague memories and explains herself in an unclear manner in a language that she however speaks fluently. It is the likely result of a long enough submission to different masters."[24] This account emphasizes the alienation experienced by the enslaved girl who has been taken from her natal family and culture. It also stresses the adaptability of captured girls through mastery of new languages and multiple relocations to other masters' households. Houmé did not suffer the fate of being resold to another master for the first decade of her enslavement.

Houmé's experience represents the extreme point of a continuum of degrees of unfreedom. She was taken as a young girl from her family and had very little memory of her free life. Her capture alienated her from kin, leaving her vulnerable to the whims of her purchaser/husband.[25] The court records silence her voice, but her actions speak to the fact that she was unhappy with her life with Bouou. Her bold choice of taking control of her sexuality indicates her desire to change her circumstances and secure a marriage where she had more agency or, at the very least, to protest her master's control of her body and sexuality.

The Jurisdictional Dynamism of Human Trafficking in the French West African Federation (1912–1931)

The continual revisions to directives on how to handle cases of human trafficking in colonial tribunals reflected France's ongoing struggle with addressing slavery and slave trading in AOF. In every major judicial reorganization, the governor-general issued new dictates regarding the management of cases involving slaves. In 1912, several years after the French tribunal convicted Bouou and described Houmé's enslavement as "typical," AOF administration reorganized the judicial system. One of the key issues this restructuring focused on was the jurisdiction and procedures involving human trafficking cases. The 1912 decree expressly designated acts of human trafficking (*faits de traite*) as part of the responsibility of the district tribunal.[26]

In November 1913, just over a year after the reorganization took effect, the Ministry of the Colonies sent chief clerk E. Beurdeley on an official tour of AOF to determine the effects of the decree on indigenous justice.[27] Beurdeley hailed the 1912 reorganization as an admirable accomplishment of French imperialism. In his opinion, the decree reflected the progress colonial rule had already realized in West Africa, as well as the early stages of a successful evolution of indigenous life.[28] Beurdeley explained that due to the early involvement of indigenous assessors in this development, human trafficking should be reserved for the district tribunal, the third level in the court hierarchy after 1912. By classifying human trafficking as a felony exclusive to this level court, French authorities adjudicated these cases with the option of asking indigenous assessors to consult. The architects of the reorganization justified the inclusion of human trafficking in this category of felonies because the "as yet primitive morals of the indigenous judges do not permit them to always appreciate the full gravity" of human trafficking with impartiality.[29] French authorities doubted African assessors' abilities to decide these matters in a way that aligned with France's self-professed civilizing mission. They deemed it necessary to handle human trafficking along with other felonies under the supervision of a French district commandant as the presiding judge.[30]

In March 1924, the French administration once again overhauled the indigenous court system of AOF, and human trafficking proved to be a controversial issue in need of procedural change. Governor-General Jules Carde bluntly pointed out that the shortcomings of the previous colonial legal regimes necessitated further reform. Carde admitted that the errors proven by two decades of experience had revealed the system's shortcomings and pointed to the difficulties in applying the procedures and laws outlined in the 1912 decree.[31] The major modification the 1924 decree introduced in trafficking cases was the amount of oversight these cases had beyond the district tribunal. Despite Carde's priority of eliminating this "most revolting" form of barbarism in West Africa, he refused to allow the superior tribunal (called the *chambre d'homologation*, or court of validation) to review cases of human trafficking.[32] Ernst Roume, the architect of the 1903 colonial legal system, had added the chambre d'homolgation to the apex of the native court structure. It oversaw the political administrators, who lacked legal training but still acted in legal capacities in lower and midlevel colonial tribunals. Professionally trained French magistrates staffed the chambre d'homolgation in Dakar to ensure an impartial assessment of the colonial administrators acting in legal capacities.[33] These magistrates validated or annulled the judgments decreed by political functionaries. Circumventing the chambre d'homolgation in trafficking cases meant that disctrict-level French administrators alone would decide these cases, unencumbered by procedural safeguards. Carde justified his denial of surveilling trafficking cases with the claim that the chambre d'homologation would not judge these cases "with the same celerity of a local tribunal."[34] Carde trusted neither the first-degree tribunals nor the French magistrates to decide cases of human trafficking. Indigenous assessors had not yet mastered and internalized the French civilizing mission, whereas the trained magistrates in the federation's capital lacked local-level knowledge of institutions of dependence. In his circular, Carde admitted that no singular idea or definition of slavery existed among the societies of AOF. He indirectly acknowledged the diversity of dependent relationships and the degrees of enslavement that each entailed.

Both the evolution of the colonial court system and the jurisdictional and procedural dynamism of the crime of human trafficking continued with the judicial reorganization of 1931. The December 3, 1931, decree established a reversal of official policy concerning the role of indigenous assessors in the colonial legal systems. The reform increased the powers of these Dahomean members of the tribunal through allowing them to participate fully in the judicial processes of felony criminal cases. Article 3 of the decree emphatically stated this reorientation: "The European and indigenous members of [all] jurisdiction[s] have, always and in every matter a deliberative voice."[35] This theoretical recognition of parity among French and indigenous assessors radically transformed a foundational element of the colonial legal system. Ironically, upon the enactment of the December 3, 1931, judicial reorganization, colonial tribunals no longer considered the crime of human trafficking to be a felony charge. The 1931 decree recategorized it as a *délit*, or misdemeanor charge, that only indigenous authorities could decide on, with no input or oversight from French officials. This change almost entirely purged human trafficking charges from the colonial judicial record, with the indigenous assessors choosing to hear and issue judgments on very few of these cases.

Over the decades, these reforms led to a sudden decrease in the relative importance of human trafficking cases in colonial tribunals in Dahomey. On one hand, Dahomeans may have accused their countrymen of declining frequency of trafficking as the political weight of this crime and the volatility of its meaning increased. On the other hand, Dahomeans found colonial tribunals more useful and predictable in adjudicating other matters. During the first decade of the twentieth century, human trafficking charges represented approximately 10 percent of all crimes against persons in Dahomey. In the 1920s, the charges declined to 1 percent and by the 1930s to just 0.1 percent.[36] These figures demonstrate that human trafficking accusations had all but disappeared from colonial tribunals by the 1930s. This shows that in Dahomey, like in other parts of AOF, women had initially received limited support from French colonial tribunals when they sought liberation; however, due to a conservative backlash, they became hesitant to seek help from colonial authorities in their pursuit of freedom from enslavement.[37] The decline in human trafficking charges showed that both Dahomean assessors and the population at large wanted to hide questionable practices involving the acquisition of household dependents. It also showed that the French administration in Dahomey did not want to interfere with the various practices of domestic servitude.

Fovi and Fohoumbo: The Entangled Histories of Girl Transfers, Monetary Exchanges, and Affective Bonds

Judicial statistics are incomplete because they omit cases in which trafficking was not the official charge. Tribunal authorities expressed concerns about other types of cases that involved girl circulation, which they believed could be trafficking. The new international pressures emanating from the League of Nations forced France to reassess its stance on both girl pawning and entrusting. In rapid succession, the league adopted the 1921 International Convention on the Suppression of Traffic in Women and Children and the 1924 Geneva Declaration of the Rights of the Child, and then, in 1926, the League of Nations' Advisory Committee of Experts on Slavery issued its Convention to Suppress Slavery and the Slave Trade, which in 1930 resulted in the addition of pawning to its list of de facto slavery.[38] The Global Depression of 1929–1939 intensified the issue, as girls' vulnerability increased due to widespread financial desperation in Dahomean households. The situation was further worsened by colonial taxation policies. Despite France's official reticence to intervene, Dahomean plaintiffs dictated what social issues the tribunals could adjudicate. While French officials did not actively seek out cases of entrustment, Dahomeans did choose to arbitrate some disputes about girls' guardianship and dependence within the colonial courtroom. In the 1930s, two basic scenarios brought these cases to the attention of legal authorities. In the first, a parent or male guardian complained about the violation of a contractual arrangement of dependence that deviated from traditionally accepted social norms. In these cases, the complainant usually had managed to maintain limited contact with the girl or girls in question. This individual claimed that the woman to whom their daughter or other female relative had been entrusted overstepped their authority or rights. In the second scenario, the social mother, a woman who has accepted the responsibility of acting as the guardian of a girl who was not the girl's biological mother, brought a complaint against a man whom she alleged had kidnapped the entrusted girl from her household. The charges outlined in the written and oral complaints that initiated cases involving entrusted girls varied, but they all led to human trafficking investigations and the use of terms such as *sale of children*, *pawning*, or *human trafficking* in the official correspondence.

In 1932, Fohoumbo, a thirty-something female seller of maize, lodged a complaint against Kadja Boco for kidnapping eleven-year-old Fovi. Fohoumbo explained in her testimony to the district commandant that Fovi had been entrusted to her six years previously. In 1926, Fohoumbo had mentioned to Kadja, a business associate whose maize she resold in the market, that she planned to look for an entrusted child in Abomey. Kadja offered to go on her behalf. He returned six days later with the then-five-year-old Fovi.[39] The official charge in this case was kidnapping, but the transcribed testimony shows that Charles Marcadé, district commandant of Ouidah, was more interested in whether Kadja, the accused kidnapper, had trafficked Fovi and then whether Fohoumbo had bought the girl and treated her as a slave.[40]

The tribunal's questions to Fohoumbo reveal its suspicions of trafficking. Fohoumbo admitted that she knew as early as 1930 that colonial law forbade buying children; however, she was probably referring not to slavery but to pawning, a recently condemned form of child transfer.[41] French views on pawning changed during the 1920s and 1930s when the League of Nations' Temporary Slavery Committee and then its permanent successor, the Committee of Experts on Slavery, reexamined which forms of dependence constituted "modern" slavery.[42] Fohoumbo explained that in 1931, "Kadja came and told me that the Whites do not permit the purchasing of children."[43] Fohoumbo nonetheless approached French authorities for the return of Fovi, vehemently denying that she had bought the girl. Fohoumbo supported this assertion by stating that Kadja had requested two hundred francs to find an entrusted girl, but she stressed that she gave him no money.[44] Fohoumbo's testimony shows that Dahomeans developed real-time awareness of changing international views of child circulation and that they participated in discussions regarding these topics.

Fohoumbo's and Kadja's interpretations of the girl's status differed greatly. Kadja, unlike Fohoumbo, feared being prosecuted for brokering the deal. His evasive answers about money contrasted with Fohoumbo's forthright recounting of her expenditures. Kadja probably paid or loaned some amount of money or goods to Fovi's parents, which he refused to admit to Marcadé. Monetary exchanges often solidified patronage and dependency ties, with the transferring of girls further strengthening these relationships. The two matters involved the same parties, but these two exchanges—monetary and human—remained distinct manifestations of an unequal relationship of mutual obligations. Fohoumbo was not involved in any sort of financial transaction that accompanied Fovi's transfer to her. Kadja, however, may have engaged in a monetary exchange.

Commandant Marcadé repeatedly asked Fovi what she remembered about her parents and her transfer to Kadja and Fohoumbo in 1926. One of his questions was: "Did you not ask why your parents entrusted you to a stranger?" Rather than answering the question directly, Fovi responded that Kadja was not a stranger because he came to her village frequently. Both Fohoumbo and Kadja mentioned traveling regularly to Abomey several times in their testimonies.[45] Kadja likely bought agricultural produce wholesale from Fovi's parents in Abomey, transported it to Ouidah, and then resold it to Fohoumbo and other women, who marketed it in small quantities.[46]

The commandant's next question was: "Did your parents mistreat you?" Fovi's response left much unexplained. She answered that they did not mistreat her and supported this assertion by saying, "It was my mother who entrusted me to Kadja."[47] This comment indicates that Fovi viewed her mother's decision to entrust her to Kadja as a form of maternal care. Fovi believed that her mother had acted in Fovi's best interests when choosing

Kadja to find a guardian for her. The commandant's questioning of Fovi continued. Marcadé wanted to know how the child's mother had explained the entrusting arrangement to her:

> COMMANDANT: What did your mother say to Kadja and to you?
>
> FOVI: My mother said that I would stay in the house of Kadja and when I would be grown, she would come and look for me.
>
> COMMANDANT: And she came to look for you in Ouidah?
>
> FOVI: She came to Ouidah two months ago and she stayed three days in the household of Kadja with me and she left again. She said to me in parting that she would return soon to look for me.[48]

Fovi and her mother both understood the entrustment arrangement as temporary, but when Fovi left her natal home at five years old, she had only a vague idea of how long it might last. It was unclear from Fovi's testimony, how often her mother visited her. Was the visit mentioned in her testimony the first one? Or did her mother see her regularly? The mother's visit does make it clear that this arrangement was fundamentally different from one of enslavement, which would have resulted in completely separating the slave from her family. The ongoing relationships that developed between natal lineages and social mothers further complicated the dynamics of these arrangements. Much like the betrothal of future spouses, representatives of two households negotiated the details of the entrustment relationship over an extended period. Entrusting ideally expressed the evolution of an existing relationship between two adults as well as the investing of resources in the further development of that relationship. Social motherhood split physiological motherhood, the bearing and begetting of children, apart from the socialization functions female parents performed during crucial stages of girls' youthful maturation.[49] This division though did not erase or replace the biological bonds of birth mothers. Entrusting divided and redistributed parental responsibilities but left parental ties intact. Entrusting one's daughters created networks based on ongoing and long-standing relationships, albeit oftentimes hierarchical ones.

Furthermore, the fact that Fovi was staying in Kadja's house raised questions about his relationship with Fohoumbo. It is possible, however, that the translator accidentally recorded Kadja's name rather than Fohoumbo's in the transcription or that Fohoumbo was related to or a dependent of Kadja. The records do not indicate whether the two were spouses, but if the transcription is correct and Fohoumbo lived with Fovi in Kadja's house, then it is clear that they were more than just trading associates. Neither Fohoumbo nor Kadja claimed to be kin, so the two were most likely engaged in a servile or sexual relationship. Fohoumbo could have been Kadja's concubine or the descendant of a line of enslaved persons continuing the tradition of dependence in his household. It is also possible that Fohoumbo, who was born around 1894, had been enslaved in a fashion similar to Houmé and continued to live in her master's compound.

Fohoumbo seemed genuinely shocked that Fovi's mother decided to reclaim her daughter when she did. Fohoumbo likely anticipated that Fovi would stay with her for several more years, at least until she was closer to fourteen or fifteen. Fohoumbo emphasized the emotional bonds that had formed during the six years Fovi had lived with her: "I raised the child, I fed and clothed her." Fohoumbo said she did not understand why Fovi had been taken from her at that time, since she had been responsible for Fovi's welfare for years.[50]

Female defendants such as Fohoumbo insisted that the girls in their households were "entrusted" to them and denied any involvement with human trafficking. Dahomeans differentiated between entrusting and slavery, women tried to explain this to French authorities.[51] Neither Fohoumbo nor Fovi described their relationship as one of mistress and enslaved girl. The enduring relationship between Fovi and her kin also undermined the supposition that she had been trafficked. Dependent relationships involving girls in colonial Dahomey proved Carde's earlier point that French tribunal members could not understand these nuanced and complex statuses as clearly as Dahomeans.

Mahoun and Aledjessi: The Colonial Evolution of the Crime of Trafficking in the 1930s

In the early to mid-1930s, colonial authorities conducted several in-depth investigations concerning market women's custody of girls who worked for them. One of the most detailed and well-documented cases involved Aledjessi, a woman who employed and housed six girls who were not related to her. In 1935, Sodekandji, the father of one of the girls, brought charges against Aledjessi, to whom he had entrusted his daughter Mahoun five years earlier. Sodekandji admitted to having pawned his daughter in exchange for a loan to pay his taxes, a common problem in AOF during the Great Depression.[52] No record remains of Aledjessi's testimony or how she defended herself. The first-degree tribunal, the lowest-level colonial court, acquitted Aledjessi of human trafficking charges, but she was obligated to return Mahoun to her parents.

Aledjessi's case took a long time to fully resolve because her husband, Pierre Johnson, a wealthy, European-educated, elite landowner, politician, and activist, appealed the court's initial verdict.[53] Despite Aledjessi's acquittal on all charges, Johnson was dissatisfied because of the significant impact this legal decision would have on his and his wife's networks of dependents. His frustration with the resolution stemmed from his inability to force Sodekandji to repay the original loan that had prompted Mahoun's transfer to Aledjessi five years previously. The extended duration of the girl's stay indicated that Sodekandji was unable to repay the loan promptly, a common plight among families during the 1930s.[54] Returning Mahoun to her family did not release Sodekandji from that obligation, but Mahoun's removal from the Aledjessi and Johnson household removed the accepted form of accountability in the pawnship relationship.

Although the first-degree tribunal handled Aledjessi's case and acquitted her, the appeal went before the criminal tribunal for consideration. Johnson's petition prompted the involvement of Camille Bienvenu, the district commandant of Athiémé, who zealously investigated the case. In the process, he recorded a detailed account of the daily lives of the girls transferred to Aledjessi. On October 27, 1935, as part of the ongoing inquiry, Bienvenu; Jean Not, president of the tribunal of Athiémé; and Etienne Zitti Houhokinton, the court's indigenous clerk who acted as the interpreter and translator during the proceedings, searched a property in Athiémé owned by Johnson and inhabited by his wife, Aledjessi.[55] Authorities found five girls between eight and fifteen, all of whom were unrelated to Aledjessi or Johnson.[56] Danssivi, Agossivi, Lissassi, Tchotchovi, and Hounsi all worked for Aledjessi in food preparation and marketing. These girls shared similar stories about their daily lives in Aledjessi's household. Danssivi described her typical routine and treatment in detail: "I prepare *ablo* [steamed corn bread], I sweep the courtyard. I wash myself, and next I go sell the ablo in the village. I am not paid. When my pagne [length of cloth wrapped around the body] would become old Aledjessi gave me another. I am in the service of Aledjessi." Other girls described rising with the cock's crow to do household chores before leaving to hawk the foods they prepared in the town's streets and markets. They all agreed that they worked long hours for no pay. They confirmed that Aledjessi provided them with the necessities of life.

The girls' opinions about their treatment and status in Aledjessi's home varied. The Excerpt of the Register of Judgments for Judgment number 201 of November 4, 1935, documented each girl's statement in turn. The depositions showed that the girls had different understandings of their statuses, although none mentioned slavery. The court recorder wrote in French a variety of phrases the girls used to describe their dependent statuses in the Johnson household. The girls' choice of terminology, along with the recorder's translation of the terms, had significant legal ramifications and social meaning in the 1930s. The youngest girl, eight-year-old Agossivi, said she "was entrusted" to the Johnson household; Danssivi, ten, stated that she was the "servant of Aledjessi"; while Tchotchovi, nine, claimed that she was held in pawnship.[57] Each child emphasized different and varied elements of their shared experiences. Agossivi's choice of the term *entrusted* characterized her servitude and dependence in a historically valued, socially acceptable manner, which included an element of subservient labor. Danssivi's use of *servant* emphasized her value as a worker. Tchotchovi stressed the monetary exchange that preceded her placement in Aledjessi's house. Tchotchovi chose to describe her status in a way that challenged her situation since pawnship was a newly illicit form of child transfer. If market women, such as Fohoumbo, were aware of the shift in colonial attitudes toward pawning, then so were their juvenile dependents, who heard the talk circulating in markets while they worked. The tribunal's recent dictate that Aledjessi return Mahoun, her former coworker and coresident, likely emboldened Tchotchovi to use this word in her deposition.

The girls' discursive choices also reflect the degrees of vulnerability they experienced and their family situations. The statements of Lissassi, Agossivi, and Hounsi were stoically neutral. None claimed to be happy with their situations. Hounsi and Agossivi avoided elaboration, and Lissassi kept her language more neutral than did Tchotchovi or Danssivi. Hounsi, the oldest at fifteen, gave the simplest statement: "I have lived in the Johnson house since my earliest childhood. I am not unhappy there." Agossivi, the youngest at eight, echoed this sentiment but expanded on her personal situation, stating that her father had died long ago, and her paternal uncle had entrusted her to Aledjessi. Two of the girls stated explicitly that they were not mistreated or unhappy in Aledjessi's household. One complained that Johnson and Aledjessi had denied her permission to visit the dispensary when she had a fever. Only one girl admitted that she wished her father would come for her and take her back to her natal home.[58]

By the 1930s, the entrusting of girls had become a fundamental part of the colonial household, economy, and society. Pierre Johnson would not have spent the time, energy, and money that he did to modify the terms of his wife's acquittal if the return of a single girl did not shake the very foundations of both his and Aledjessi's fortunes and prestige.[59] Transactions in rights-in-persons, including children, formed an integral component of kinship systems and moneylending procedures, with the two sometimes overlapping. As the testimonies of Danssivi, Agossivi, Lissassi, Tchotchovi, Hounsi, and Mahoun reveal, the exact relationship between a girl's relocation and the monetary exchange varied depending on the existing relationships between the two adult parties arranging the child's circulation. All six girls talked about their circumstances and day-to-day lives similarly, but they used different terms to describe their dependence—or it is possible that the translator imposed different French terms of dependence on each girl's description. Despite his wife's acquittal, Johnson felt the need to appeal to a higher court to ensure the legitimacy and protection of the systems they had established to build their networks of dependents, which were responsible for the profits of their enterprises.

Women's Independence and Girls' Dependence

Confusion among French colonial administrators stopped them from directly condemning the entrusting of children to Fohoumbo in 1932 and Aledjessi in 1935, but they sought to learn more about West African households and children's roles within them. In October 1937, Marcel de Coppet, governor-general of AOF, commissioned Denise Savineau of the Colonial Education Service to tour France's West African colonies and report on women and families in each colony.[60] Savineau proved particularly adept at observing households and questioning West Africans about the children living there. In her field notes from Dahomey, she observed that entrusted children were "a widespread phenomenon of free domestic staff found again and again throughout southern Dahomey."[61] Savineau described many households with transferred children—some with only one child, like that of

Fohoumbo, and some with many, like that of Aledjessi. She claimed that even households of limited means relied on young domestic servants. Savineau went so far as to state: "The domestic staff of children is the consequence of women's independence."[62] She recognized that girls' labor allowed women to be economically productive in colonial society because these girls performed domestic labor and freed women from it. The colonial government acknowledged that for the colony to thrive economically, women were required to exploit the labor of girls, thereby legitimizing the practice of girl entrustment.

The growth of Cotonou as Benin's commercial center and Porto-Novo as the colonial capital, along with the decline of both Abomey and Athiémé, influenced the patterns of girl circulation. The introduction of policies that exempted children from being taxed in the mixed communities of Porto-Novo, Cotonou, and Ouidah made these coastal centers appealing sites for entrusting children.[63] Families in the interior could avoid paying head taxes on their children by sending them to households in one of these urban centers. As the mixed coastal communities grew spatially, hawking or selling goods door-to-door increased in volume and importance, which in turn increased the demand for girls. These economic and social factors influenced families from the plateau to entrust their daughters, such as Fovi, to women in Porto-Novo, Cotonou, and Ouidah.

The legal issues raised in cases of entrusted girls involved three overlapping policy objectives: human trafficking, underage marriage, and child labor.[64] The colonial legal system believed that the danger of "entrusting" girls to market women was insignificant, as its main concern with trafficking was sexual exploitation. Colonial authorities were ambivalent toward girls' entrustment to women and, more generally, African children's labor because the administration desperately needed the tax revenue generated by the transfer of these girls. After all, the French colonial state implemented child labor laws in 1936, but the archives only documented a single instance of their enforcement in the colony of Dahomey. With the exception of the most egregious cases, there was no will on the ground to enforce these laws because the colonial economy relied on child labor.

By 1938, the French administration agreed with market women's assessment that entrusting was not enslaving. Berthet, director of administrative and political affairs in Dahomey, responded to Savineau's report on the colony: "The acts 'of alienation of children [from their families]' camouflaged as a form of adoption (notably in Cotonou) which constitutes in the spirit of custom, as a sort of transitory stage, a type of apprenticeship in life skills." He assured Governor-General Jules De Coppet that "[the customary practice of entrustment] does not damage in the least our conceptions of the liberty of the human being."[65] Berthet supported the views of Dahomean women who defended the practice of entrusting children. Like Fohoumbo, he claimed that entrusting was neither trafficking nor a form of enslavement. In 1938, the Savineau report on Dahomey and the administrative correspondence it generated provided a final summation of the debates and clarified, for the time being, that entrustment was not enslavement.

Conclusion

In the early to mid-twentieth century, Africans and colonial authorities struggled to determine which forms of circulation, exploitation, restrictions on individual liberties, and moneylending constituted an illegal type of human trafficking.[66] Both popular perception and official colonial policy designated certain forms of bonded dependence as criminal while others were deemed acceptable. French tribunals examined the lives of Houmé in 1909, Fovi in 1932, and Mahoun in 1935. The life circumstances of Fovi and Mahoun bore little resemblance to Houmé's situation two and a half decades earlier.

The cases of child trafficking brought to colonial tribunals during the 1930s involved adolescent girls who left their familial homes between the ages of five and twelve. Women needed these girls to work in the household and various business ventures. Unlike Houmé, the girls suspected of being trafficked in the 1930s experienced neither violent abductions nor coerced sexual relationships. In addition, their parents or guardians arranged for the girls to be entrusted to households of the parents' choosing and successfully maintained limited contact with their daughters and nieces. The cases investigating the statuses of Houmé, Fovi, and Mahoun highlighted the conflicting agendas of the colonial state regarding female dependence and the family. The French colonial state told the international community that it had liberated women, but at the same time, it needed stable families with sufficient household dependents to ensure economic profitability for the colonial economy. Colonial legal authorities were reluctant to interfere in the entrusting arrangements of girls sent to live with social mothers because they understood the crucial role these girls played in the colonial economy.

Market women relied on the labor of girls entrusted to them by households within their familial, social, and commercial networks. Entrusted girls lived for years in these women's households and worked for their guardians. Families expected these women to act as social mothers and teach their charges business skills and appropriate behavior while also enforcing proper discipline. Entrusted girls and social mothers overwhelmingly insisted that entrustment was not enslavement. They based their defenses on their understanding of the precolonial custom of entrustment and the established colonial definition of human trafficking. The question of whether entrustment overlapped with enslavement was irrelevant to these girls and women, and the answer was straightforward: no, entrustment was not enslavement.

Colonial legal authorities tried to unravel and ascertain the causes behind the girls' transfers and determine whether a case of entrustment was motivated by monetary factors, affection, charity, or something else. The cases discussed in this chapter show how various forms of girl transfers, including pawning and entrusting, played a crucial role in acquiring family wealth.[67] Colonial authorities established the monetary loan as the defining factor in what Dahomeans regarded as a more complex, hierarchical relationship of reciprocal exchanges.[68] Court cases have brought to light instances where one party in an exchange accused the other of violating the agreed-upon terms, thereby destroying the trust between the parties.

When international organizations reclassified pawning as a form of illicit human trafficking, child entrustment became increasingly conflated with slavery in the eyes of both colonial administrators and international activists. Dahomeans, however, disagreed with this consensus. Women played key roles in cases involving entrusted girls. Social mothers actively engaged with other Africans and European officials in colonial legal institutions to safeguard their economic interests. Social mothers tried to control the development of the conversations around girls' dependence in Dahomey. Entrusted girls, such as Fovi, and social mothers, such as Fohoumbo, emphasized caretaking responsibilities when they defended the practice of entrusting. Dahomean women could not afford to lose this fight because their livelihoods depended on entrusted girls as unpaid laborers. Dahomean women successfully defended entrusting female children to social mothers as an acceptable colonial practice. The legal decisions regarding entrusted girls in the mid-1930s resulted in a lack of official determination to enforce the subsequent laws regulating child labor. The traditional practice of entrusting girls was unofficially sanctioned within an extralegal sphere where child protection laws would not apply. The French administration eventually agreed with the social mothers who claimed that any form of entrusting a girl to a woman did not constitute trafficking, at least not on the part of the accused woman.

None of the Dahomean women to whom these young girls were entrusted used the term *pawn* to describe their wards. The defendants insisted that they did not restrict the girls' freedom and that there had been no exchange of money or goods for them—both elements that defined the act of enslavement, according to Dahomean women. Social mothers separated the financial transactions that often accompanied the transfer of a girl from the consequent relationship. These women's successes resulted in legal and popular recognition of the legitimacy of girls' servitude to them in the form of an extended residential apprenticeship. "A child entrusted to me" was a popular and legally sanctioned phrase that women used to attract dependents. After a brief examination of pawnship practices in Dahomey between 1932 and 1936, the French administration decided against taking a hard stand against girl transfers of any kind. The prevalence of entrusted girls forced the colonial state to act cautiously to avoid destabilizing either the African family or the colonial economy. Neither Dahomean legal authorities nor French officials found the living and working conditions of entrusted girls compelling enough to intervene in the Dahomean household economy.

Twentieth-century colonial legal records provided insights into the relationships social mothers developed with their wards. Accusations of trafficking were not the only types of criminal cases that documented women's and girls' lives within the private sphere of the household. During the 1920s and 1930s, social mothers described their most intimate acts of caregiving to entrusted girls when they testified in rape cases. These actions further supported claims, like those in Fohoumbo's testimony, that social mothers had care responsibilities toward the girls entrusted to them.

Dahomey, "Porto Novo, Rue dans le Quartier indigene" (1930) by Frédéric Gadmer. The Musée Albert Kahn allows this image to be freely reusable by a creative commons license CC-BY-4.0.

6

"Why Did You Not Cry Out . . . ?"

Sexual Assaults of Entrusted Girls in Colonial Dahomey, 1917–1941

On June 1, 1929, eight-year-old Akouéle hawked prepared food in the streets of Athiémé. Akouéle was roughly the size and stature of the girl in Frédéric Gadmer's photograph titled "A Street in the Indigenous Quarter of Porto-Novo" (1930). The subject of the photograph—the street—features two individuals in the foreground: a finely dressed adult man and a young girl wearing a pagne around her waist and a fabric wrap tied around her head. The man displays his elite status through his attire and sandals. He wears a pristine white shirt underneath a sumptuous, brightly colored, high-quality batik ensemble of pants and a wrap with a stylishly pleated hat on his head. The young girl would have been taught to be respectful to this man; perhaps the girl in the picture even knew him—maybe the two lived in the same neighborhood. In the moment captured in the photograph, he makes eye contact with her and inclines his head toward her with his mouth open as if speaking to her. She listens to him and accepts what he is handing to her. Is he asking her to run an errand for him? Or bring produce to his door? Was she negotiating the price of her services to grind his corn or process palm kernels? The girl pictured and Akouéle both had done such tasks countless times for many people in exchange for a fee. Girls' days consisted of innumerable exchanges such as these.

This image shows the contrast in working conditions for girls in the bustling market of Porto-Novo pictured in chapter 5 and some of the quiet side streets of Porto-Novo. In residential areas, girls worked in relative isolation and interacted one-on-one with customers with little to no direct supervision.

The girl and man though were not entirely alone. In the background stands a younger child, and farther back three adults, two men and a woman with a child on her back, mull around. The presence of these four individuals reassured the girl of her safety because they would hear her cry out if anything went awry. The adults' distant oversight also policed the behavior of the man as he interacted with the girl. On that fateful Saturday in June 1929, Akouéle felt at ease hawking goods near her home in Athiéme since she knew most of the people by sight or name. Hamé, a prospective customer whom she knew, asked her to come to his door so he could inspect her merchandise. When Akouéle agreed, male and female household members whom she knew gathered around. One of them brought her a plate, and she put five servings of food on it. Hamé then left to find some money. The others went to the river to wash.[1]

Upon the departure of Hamé and the others, Akouéle found herself alone with a young man whose name she did not know. The man invited Akouéle farther into the compound. She stated: "I categorically refused [to go with him]." She knew that entering a private space posed a risk to her safety. The man did not accept her rejection. He grabbed her left arm, stuffed a handkerchief in her mouth, dragged her to his room, threw her on the floor, and raped her.[2] In Dahomey, during the early twentieth century, girls who worked various jobs—hawking, running errands, or processing agricultural products—comprised the majority of rape victims who brought their cases to colonial tribunals.[3] Akouéle was just one victim who was assaulted while she sold her goods. Girls, like Akouéle and the one shown in Gadmer's image, had no way of knowing which men meant them harm. They could not always anticipate how quickly a situation could change from one of safety to danger.

On June 19, 1929, three weeks after the assault took place, Akouéle gave her deposition to Rogneau Lucien, chief of the post of Athiémé in southwestern Dahomey, and Zitti Etienne, an indigenous civil servant who acted as translator. After listening to her very brief, stark recounting of the traumatic events of nineteen days earlier, Lucien and Etienne asked a series of jarring questions to uncover more details: "Why did you not cry out the moment when the young man raped you?" Akouéle stated that she could not and reminded them that the rapist had gagged her by stuffing a handkerchief in her mouth. The officials asked: "After leaving the domicile of the young man, did you immediately go back to your house?" She stated: "No, I continued to hawk my merchandise in the neighborhood.... Then [after finishing selling my goods] I returned home. The following day, I felt pain in my lower belly, and I told my mistress about it [the pain] at that time and I stayed home [that day ill] but I kept my silence."⁴ This exchange between the rape victim and the colonial authorities reveals several common occurrences in colonial investigations of rape. Akouéle and many other girls experienced physical and psychological aftereffects from sexual assaults, but they refused to immediately disclose the source of their affliction. Only after weeks of suffering did she admit to her mistress Ahoussi that a customer's sexual assault had caused her maladies over the last three weeks. Akouéle did so only after another entrusted girl alerted Ahoussi to Akouéle's ongoing physical symptoms. Often after a significant lapse in time from the traumatic event, entrusted girls' guardians eventually learned of the sexual assaults of their wards. These women then promptly reported the perpetrators to colonial authorities, who questioned these girls extensively to ensure that a "real" rape had occurred. All of these elements made Akouéle's case a typical one of the era.

Due to girls' reliance on an adult ally to approach colonial tribunals, their complaints of rape often included many rich details about their relationships and daily interactions with older female household members. In the course of investigating cases of sexual assault, the tribunals often found that girl hawkers lived with social mothers, female guardians to whom they had been entrusted. Social mothers were women selected by a girl's biological parents to fulfill certain parental roles over an extended period. Social mothers performed the parental responsibilities of nurturing, training, and sponsoring into adulthood.⁵ Many of these social mothers believed it was their duty to seek justice when their wards were sexually assaulted. Social mothers often played an important part in transforming entrusted girls' experiences of sexual assault into formal criminal complaints.

In the 1910s and 1920s, social mothers, through caring for entrusted girls after assaults and reporting these traumatic events to colonial authorities, determined that it was their responsibility to seek redress for the girls entrusted to them. After the implementation of the December 3, 1931, decree reorganizing the colonial judicial system, social mothers' self-proclaimed responsibility was used against them and their wards. From April 1932 until the subsequent reorganization in 1941, tribunals changed this sense of responsibility to culpability. Tribunal authorities alleged that if entrusted girls were properly trained by their social mothers regarding hawking and their sexuality, sexual assaults would be nonexistent or extremely rare. Tribunals blamed teenage—and sometimes preteen—hawkers and, by extension, their social mothers for the sexual assaults they suffered while selling goods door to door. Rather than condemning the men who attacked these girls, the authorities blamed the supposed promiscuity and careless actions of the girls themselves. The tribunals, by extension, condemned social mothers for their alleged improper training of these girls.

The first section of this chapter examines entrusted girls and their social mothers' lived experiences of relatedness. From 1917 to 1931, it focuses on the emotional dimensions of these relationships. The information on this is limited, however, because the girls' statements about their relationships were made during the legal process of investigating sexual assaults. This type of information became less available among the juridical records after the December 3, 1931, decree took effect in April 1932. Before 1932, women and girls recounted the trauma of sexual assaults, the intergenerational acts of witnessing and caregiving, and the relationships between entrusted girls and their social mothers. The second section of this chapter focuses on victim blaming and the logic that underpinned it. While girls continued to report sexual assaults after 1932, few of the details about household relationships were included in the records. Documentation instead focused on uncovering the culpability of girl hawkers for their own sexual assaults.

The judicial records of the National Archives of Benin contained more than two hundred cases of rape during the colonial period up until 1941.[6] This chapter examines in detail a subset of these cases that occurred from 1917 to 1941 in which the victim was an entrusted girl under fourteen who was working when she was assaulted.[7] Most cases before 1932 included information about the guardians who reported the assault, but after 1932, this sort of information on interpersonal relationships is more limited. These latter records do not provide any details about the girls' guardians or households of residence. Collective memory, however, insisted that the majority of girls during this era were entrusted. The earlier records from the 1910s and 1920s confirmed that this was especially common among hawkers.

Intergenerational Witnessing of the Aftereffects of Sexual Assaults

In the course of investigating sexual assaults, colonial tribunals documented the routine work performed by entrusted girls. The girls' detailed reports submitted to the courts consistently began with a description of a typical day, which might include street hawking, processing agricultural products, or running errands. The reports also described the social mothers' concern for these girls' health and safety while doing their work. Social mothers testified that they immediately reported sexual assaults to authorities as soon as girls disclosed their traumatic experiences.

Social mothers witnessed the painful aftereffects of these violent sexual attacks. Women who lived with entrusted girls observed bruises, abrasions, inflammation of the labia, abnormal genital secretions, symptoms of sexually transmitted diseases, and many other indications of harm to these girls.[8] Girls revealed, intentionally or not, these visible signs of assault on their most intimate body parts to women when they bathed together. When Akouéle "bathed in the light of day" with Alougba, a sixteen-year-old friend and coworker, her friend saw the physical evidence of the sexual assault on Akouéle's young body in the form of purulent secretions on her genitals. Akouéle had suffered for weeks without treatment. Alougba notified Ahoussi, the girls' social mother, who told Alougba to take Akouéle to a nurse. Akouéle still refused to explain the cause of her maladies to the nurse. Only when Ahoussi questioned her after the visit did Akouéle reveal that a customer had assaulted her.[9] The morning after Akouéle was attacked, she complained of abdominal pain; however, it was not until several weeks later after multiple people questioning her that she admitted the assault to anyone. Social mothers and older entrusted girls monitored younger girls' bodies.[10] In Akouéle's case, communal bathing enabled Alougba to notice bodily trauma.

In other cases, the evidence of the assault was apparent to household members even without the girls disrobing. Social mothers cared for girls who suffered from symptoms like vomiting, bleeding, pain in the lower abdomen, and an inability to sleep or eat.[11] In November 1924, sixty-year-old Natala observed that ten-year-old Saba was sick, but when she questioned her, the girl offered no explanation. Natala treated Saba's symptoms for six days with no improvement. Natala, not Saba, described the girl's ongoing suffering for the tribunal: "When she would eat, she would vomit; in examining her I observed that her sexual organs were inflamed, so I cleaned them with water. I kept soothing them, but she was always sick."[12] Natala's testimony revealed that Saba, like Akouéle, was reticent to explain the cause of her suffering to her mistress. Social mothers cared for all ailments that afflicted the girls entrusted to them regardless of the cause. They repeatedly questioned the girls and tenaciously sought answers when they suspected assault.

In addition to symptoms of physical suffering, social mothers attentively observed the psychological trauma experienced by girls following a sexual assault. Girls could not always maintain their normal activities after an assault, a disruption that caused social mothers to investigate the change in their wards' behaviors. Despite her youthfulness, Saba had always been responsible with the money she earned selling soap in the market. The trauma of being assaulted affected her mental state and made it impossible for her to conduct business as usual. When Saba returned home without the expected payment for her soap, Natala was frustrated. Saba's abrupt change in demeanor prompted Natala to question her. Eventually, Saba disclosed that Adamon, one of her regular customers, had assaulted her.[13] If girls could not trust regular customers who were known to them, whom could they trust? After the assault, Saba's world became a terrifying place where danger lurked in her everyday interactions. This affected her personality and contributed to her altered mental state. Her assailant was not a stranger. Natala may have warned Saba of the dangers, but she likely thought this warning did not apply to a known and friendly customer like Adamon. Saba's frequent interactions with Adamon made her relax her guard around him.

The danger of sexual assault was usually greatest if girls left public spaces or became isolated. Akouéle and other girl hawkers testified that they had refused to enter the private residences of their attackers, yet in the end, their attackers overpowered them, forced them inside, and assaulted them. Others, such as Salatou—estimated by the court to be around seven—were either too naive or ignored the warnings to stay out of customers' homes. Boco Cossi called Salatou into his room to buy the cakes that she was hawking. Upon isolating her, he raped her.[14] Did he cajole her into abandoning public spaces? Was Salatou simply too young to comprehend the danger of entering a man's room? How did Akouéle, who was only eight, know to avoid the private rooms of customers, and Salatou, only a year younger, did not? Who warned them to remain in public spaces? At what age were young girls cautioned about this? How did girls of seven or eight understand the risk of sexual assault? Were some girls considered mature enough to hawk, process agricultural goods, and run errands, yet also too young to be properly warned about dangerous situations and sexual assaults? Girls worked until they sold all of their goods, which motivated them to pursue every interested buyer. They feared punishment if they returned home to their mistresses without the expected money. Given the highly competitive nature of hawking, girls either risked their personal safety to make a sale or did not anticipate the danger in a particular situation.[15] How many times had girls entered regular customers' houses with no incident? Many rape victims testified that they had entered private spaces to sell goods. Despite risks, hawkers commonly felt that they must in certain instances enter private spaces to sell their goods. Girls may have known of the danger, but they let their guard down because it was impractical to avoid going inside a customer's home to make a sale.

For entrusted girls, the danger of sexual assault was not exclusively limited to customers. Such attacks could also take place in their foster homes. Salamaton's parents entrusted her to Yatossou, a long-distance market trader who traveled frequently. In Ouidah, Yatossou and Salamaton lived in a household with Boco Maclodémé. Boco's relationship with Yatossou is unclear. He might have been a boarder or related to someone in the household. The discovery of the assault was strangely similar to that of Akouéle's. After returning to Ouidah from one of her trips, Yatossou bathed with nine-year-old Salamaton. She observed pus on Salamaton's genitals. Yatossou questioned Salamaton, who admitted that every time Yatossou left the house, Boco "benefited" from Salamaton's absences and repeatedly raped her. Yatossou took immediate action. She had a doctor examine Salamaton and then reported the assaults to the colonial authorities in Ouidah at the end of May 1930.[16] Many girls knew their assailants and named them. Rapists were customers, coresidents, or neighbors.

It was rare that male coresidents witnessed the effects of rape on girls. This does not necessarily reflect a lack of concern on the part of male coresidents; it is simply the reality that men had much more limited contact with girls. In late June 1917, Donkondé asked six-year-old Bodjo, a girl entrusted to his wife, Yossago, to take a plate of food to their neighbor Ahosso. Ahosso's house abutted the back of Donkondé's house, so Donkondé assumed that Bodjo could deliver the food without incident. How many times had she done so successfully? Bodjo stated that on her way to Ahosso's house, she encountered Houmpatin, who took her by the hand and led her away to his house.[17] She followed him silently because he threatened to kill her if she cried out. Houmpatin's teenage nephew Amoussou awaited them at Houmpatin's house. Bodjo asserted that Houmpatin and Amoussou took turns raping her. When she returned home, Bodjo said nothing about what had happened. Donkondé suspected something was amiss when he learned that she had never delivered the food and that she had returned very late—nearly 11:00

p.m. He questioned her, but she remained silent that first night and day. However, when Bodjo complained of stomach pains the following evening, Donkondé took her to her biological parents to have them question her. After Bodjo admitted the rape to her father, he had an adult sister examine her. The sister confirmed physical evidence of sexual assault on the six-year-old's body.[18]

This account shows that biological parents and foster parents could care for their children in a collaborative manner that allowed biological parents to continue to have a strong relationship with an entrusted daughter. In this instance, both the biological father and the foster family lived in the same village. Living in proximity allowed regular and ongoing interactions between Bodjo and her biological family while also expanding her kin network through her foster household. Donkondé's immediate notification of Bodjo's father about the suspected assault also shows that a foster household did not have a claim to an entrusted girl's sexuality. Donkondé believed the assault might jeopardize the relationship if the circumstances were not disclosed promptly. While Donkondé did not report any evident trauma on Bodjo's body, her behavior led him to suspect that she had been assaulted. With Bodjo's social mother absent, he still chose to take action rather than ignore his intuition.

Female guardians cared about the well-being and safety of entrusted girls while they were working. Once social mothers became aware of a sexual assault, they promptly approached the commandant and filed an oral complaint against the perpetrator. Not all recorded cases of assault included details about the women's decision-making process before reporting a crime, but many described girls' hesitance to report sexual assaults to anyone. Once older women such as Ahoussi, Natala, and Yatossou discovered the assault, they reported to French administrators the physical evidence they had observed and what the girls had told them. Social mothers turned incidences of sexual assault into formal grievances presented to the colonial administration. They assigned meaning to entrusted girls' experiences and, in the process, named the crime, blamed the assailant, and claimed wrongdoing on behalf of the girl.[19]

Social mothers were dedicated to their duties of caring for entrusted girls. They became aware of changes in the girls' bodies and behaviors through their daily interactions. Additionally, they investigated and reported the physical symptoms and changes in the girls' demeanors. Due to their proximity to other household members, these girls could not entirely conceal evidence of the assaults. By vigilantly reporting these sexual assaults to authorities—sometimes with their husbands—social mothers were trying to create a safe environment in the streets and marketplaces for girls to work. The preceding examples are from the period before the enactment of the December 3, 1931, decree, which reorganized the colonial tribunal system in French West Africa.[20] After the decree, women's testimonies about the sexual assaults of entrusted girls became much more scarce in the tribunal records. The acts of witnessing the consequences of assaults likely continued, but interpreters deemed reports of such attacks to be insignificant or irrelevant to document. In colonial legal forums, the operational norms changed, and personal accounts were no longer admitted. Instead, the preference was to include clinical and official medicolegal certificates with case files. From April 1932 onward, the records disclosed fewer and fewer details about the mundane interactions between entrusted girls and social mothers. In fact, any mention of social mothers essentially disappeared from rape prosecutions. This devaluation and disregard of women's testimony extended to teenage and sometimes preteen girls' firsthand testimony about their assaults.

Victim Blaming in Colonial Tribunals after 1931: Precocious Girls or Mendacious Prostitutes?

This chapter opened with the photograph "A Street in the Indigenous Quarter of Porto-Novo" by Frédéric Gadmer, showing a man approaching a young girl in the indigenous quarter of Porto-Novo. In the image shown on the next page, the same man appears again in "Africa Scene of Commerce in the Street," another of Gadmer's photos from his 1930 trip to Dahomey. The girl in this photograph is markedly older, a teenager rather than a girl of approximately eight years old. The scenes are similar in that both girls are relatively secluded on nearly deserted residential streets while they each engage in a transaction with this man. In "Africa Scene of Commerce in the Street," the girl has her wares—various toiletry items including soap and rolls of toilet paper—displayed on a tray perched on a pedestal of a basket stacked on a crate. He is holding one of her products closely examining it. She is also offering him other items that might interest him. After the December 3, 1931, decree took effect in April 1932, tribunals' perception of this scene changed. In addition to the commerce in toiletries, tribunals imposed a subtext and secondary

Porto-Novo, Dahomey (actuel Bénin), "Afrique Scène de commerce dans la rue" by Frédéric Gadmer (1930). The Musée Albert Kahn allows this image to be freely reusable by a creative commons license CC-BY-4.0.

exchange on this interaction. They alleged that hawkers also sold sex to the men who approached them. No longer did authorities see an innocent young girl in the street engaging in a simple commercial exchange with a man. They perceived hawkers as mature, mendacious prostitutes who negotiated transactional sex with their customers.

After the judicial reorganization, tribunal members were intent on determining the "real" age of girls who were accusing men of rape so that they could determine which of the girls in Gadmer's image the hawker was—innocent girl or mature prostitute. In 1932, when Ahoudjo accused Comlan Gaudens of rape, she told the tribunal that she was nine years old. The tribunal rejected her statement and demanded that her body "speak" in her stead. In a July 1932 report submitted to the *chambre d'accusation* (indictment chamber), the five-person criminal tribunal of Cotonou evaluated the criminal charges against Gaudens. The court recorder summarized the evidence, starting with the proof offered by Ahoudjo's body: "Considering that the medical certificate concluded that the disappearance of the hymen seemed old, ... one could suppose that the girl had already had sexual encounters before the act executed by Gaudens."[21] This caused doubt among the tribunal that Ahoudjo was only nine. The presupposition that Ahoudjo had a history of sexual experience prejudiced the remainder of the deliberation and biased the tribunal's opinion in favor of Gaudens's claim that the sexual act had been transactional. The indictment continued: "Considering that in this case there is doubt about the actual age of the victim—and it does seem that the already deflowered girl consented for a fee to have sexual relations—[Ahoudjo] must be pubescent and older than nine years of age." Girls' bodies conveyed visual clues about their sexual encounters and the development of their sexuality, but these clues were interpreted to align with the prevailing belief that hawkers were at fault for their own rapes.

The tribunal reasoned that nonvirgin girls older than nine would conceivably agree to transactional sex. Before the 1931 decree, there was a conspicuous absence in the records of any reference to age. This contrasted with authorities' efforts to determine the "real [chronological] age" of the claimants after the decree took effect.[22] The tribunal concluded: "Considering [all of the above] it is important before ruling on this matter to know the real age of the victim [Ahoudjo]."[23] The tribunal refused to issue a verdict until investigators had verified Ahoudjo's age and suggested an age that supported the evidence and their narrative of events. Colonial officials wanted Ahoudjo's case to conform to their belief that girls' apprenticeship to market women exposed them to transactional sexual encounters as they sold their goods at markets and in the streets.[24]

Tribunal authorities were suspicious of hawkers' narratives even before the decree, as evidenced by the unrelenting questioning of Akouéle, but this distrust had been surmountable. Before 1932, there was a greater likelihood that the tribunals would punish the accused men. After April 1932, tribunals often uncritically accepted male rapists' defense that hawkers engaged in transactional sex with their customers and then lied about it for various reasons. The alleged plausibility of this justification for men's aggressive sexual behavior shaped tribunals' inaction concerning older or sexually experienced girls. The majority of girls who were judged to be preteens or teenagers were blamed by tribunals for their assaults.[25] One example of the perceived culpability of hawkers was the 1939 case of rape involving fourteen-year-old Lokossi. On July 25, 1939, in the village of Ganvié, Lokossi traveled by pirogue, a small canoe-like boat used to navigate the coastal waters of the colony. Once ashore, she approached four young men aged seventeen to twenty with the intention of selling them food. When she entered the building, they threw her to the floor and took turns sexually assaulting her. Lokossi's cries were heard by a neighbor, who tried to stop the assaults. Although he was too late, his intervention enabled her to escape and provided her with a witness to the attacks. Perhaps this corroboration of her resistance gave her confidence to approach the authorities. The medical exam ordered by the authorities confirmed that Lokossi had been a virgin before the men's assault. The doctor's report stated with "absolute certainty" that a rape had occurred. Despite a witness and a medical certificate that confirmed Lokossi's testimony, the tribunal dismissed the case based on the four men's unsubstantiated claims that the sexual encounters were consensual. The four men disagreed with the doctor's assertion that Lokossi had been a virgin and stated that this was not the first time they had had sexual relations with her.[26] Seemingly, Lokossi's consent was assumed or irrelevant.

The logic used by colonial tribunals was more transparent in other cases. Authorities assumed that older girls should know what would happen if they followed men into their homes. The tribunal regarded these private areas as places of potential sexual activity where girls, just by entering them, were proposing to have sexual encounters with their customers. Eighteen-year-old Attakpa Koumolo Dossou Yovo was asked by her cousin to go to the house of his friend Hounnou Chémagnan to sell him meat. She did so and waited there for payment. When Chémagnan got her alone in his room, he attempted to rape her and in the process tore her clothes. Dossou Yovo managed to bite him and escape, although he did violate her by penetrating her with his fingers. This, in her definition, was rape. She stated that before this forced attack, she had never had sexual relations with a man. The medical exam confirmed that she had been a virgin before Chémagnan's assault, and so the tribunal convicted him. However, the members of the tribunal also admonished the victim through their commentary in the judgment. After acknowledging that the rape had been medically confirmed, they continued: "Considering that the girl Attakpa aged eighteen years old was due to the maturity of her age adequately warned of the possible consequences for her of following a young boy of twenty-two years into his rooms."[27]

It is unclear, however, at what age girls should be adequately warned. The tribunal also emphasized that young "boys" posed the greatest risk to hawkers. From the evidence in the juridical records, this was true only for teenage hawkers who more frequently reported rapes perpetrated by younger men in their teens or twenties. Men over twenty posed the greatest risk for younger girls. The tribunal condemned Dossou Yovo for misplacing her trust in the character of her assailant. They blamed her despite convicting him.

Undoubtedly, the evidence of "slight" violence in the form of torn clothes supported Dossou Yovo's claims that she had resisted Chémagnan's attempts to have sex with her. However, evidence of violence was not always sufficient to bolster an older girl's accusation of sexual assault. In other cases, the violence was so extreme that even a man's claims that the girl had consented were insufficient for an acquittal. In June 1935, ten-year-old Adotevi sold Agbavo tobacco and matches on credit. She likely trusted the man because he was a respected elder of sixty. Several days after the sale, on June 14, 1935, Adotevi went to Agbavo's house to collect the money he owed her. Agbavo threw thirty centimes on the floor, and when Adotevi bent over to pick it up, he brutally raped her. After the assault, she fled to the market of Grand Popo where she took refuge. Witnesses found her in the market and took her to the hospital immediately. Agbavo had so viciously assaulted her that she lost "an abundance of blood" that the medical exam speculated could have resulted in her death.[28] Since her injuries spoke in her stead, Adotevi did not disclose whom she was living with or if she was entrusted. She also does not have an older female; rather the witnesses who took her to the hospital testified to her physical state. Agbavo's only defense was that allegedly "*la petite* offered herself to me." In this case, the physical evidence of extreme violence confirmed by a certified colonial male expert in the indigenous medical service disproved the spurious claim of consensual sex.[29]

There was hostility toward teenage girls' claims of sexual assault even before the December 3, 1931, decree. However, this hostility intensified significantly once the decree was implemented. At this point, the accused men's defenses confirmed French authorities' suspicions that hawkers did sell their bodies along with the goods they balanced on their heads. The presumption that girl hawkers were profiting from sexual encounters in addition to selling goods cast doubt on the veracity of their claims of rape. This doubt extended to the social mothers who allegedly taught the girls about transactional sex. Tribunals presumed that both the girls and the women who supported them lied about the circumstances of the sexual encounters with their customers.

The tribunals portrayed girl hawkers as promiscuous liars. By extension, the women who supported them were also considered to be suspicious characters. The alleged tendency of girls and women to lie about sexual encounters undermined even the most basic statements made by female plaintiffs, witnesses, and victims. As a result, tribunals overlooked the significance of intergenerational witnessing of physical trauma, which had been crucial to the prosecution of rape cases.

Conclusion

Girl hawkers shared their stories of experiencing sexual assault, highlighting the constant threat they faced every day. Their profession rendered them uniquely vulnerable to the unwanted sexual advances of their customers. Entrusted girls had to continually assess and reassess their personal risk of sexual assault while they hawked goods, ran errands, or processed agricultural products. Many times, girls knew their attackers or had some previous interaction with them. This might explain why they sometimes lowered their defenses and entered private spaces or agreed to be alone with these men.

After an assault, girls returned to their households where older girls and women witnessed evidence of their suffering. When a social mother noticed the physical consequences of an attack, she often questioned the girl and reported the assault to the tribunals. This intergenerational act was performed frequently before April 1932, and it most likely continued after the decree, even though tribunals stopped recording this type of information. Social mothers showed their concern for the girls in their employ by treating their injuries, questioning them for explanations, and seeking recourse. Female guardians advocated for safe working conditions in colonial streets and marketplaces for their youthful employees, and they held the colonial state responsible for the safety of hawkers in the expanding economic centers in the southern region of the colony.[30] In the cases studied here from 1917 to 1932, female guardians of entrusted girls chose to make their claims for recompense through colonial courts. These cases certainly represent only a small fraction of the sexual assaults experienced by girl hawkers. Although there were undoubtedly other options in Dahomey, many women believed the colonial tribunal to be the most suitable, or perhaps the only, place to seek justice for the rapists of girl hawkers.[31]

After 1932, social mothers disappeared from the official records, but these women undoubtedly continued in their caretaking and encouraged girls to testify before the tribunals. Social mothers advocated for the girls' well-being, even though their accounts of the impact of rape on girls' bodies, minds, and behaviors were overshadowed by the male colonial medical officers who focused on using technoscientific methods to examine girls' bodies for "evidence."[32] The Dahomean women who testified in the 1920s documented girls' physical and mental suffering in the days and weeks following sexual assaults much more thoroughly than the European doctors who examined them. After the December 3, 1931, decree took effect, indigenous and French men evaluated the evidence women and girls presented to tribunals differently than before the decree. Male legal authorities increasingly ignored social mothers' assessments of entrusted girls' bodies and minds. These women's authority as witnesses in rape cases was undermined by male tribunal members who prioritized the certified medical examinations performed by colonial doctors. After 1932, the documentation of rape cases during the colonial era shifted from focusing on the daily lives and support systems within households to portraying victims as the ones at fault for the attacks they suffered.

In the 1930s, entrusted girls became more vulnerable to labor exploitation and sexual assault as older safeguards deteriorated. Despite this, girls continued to be transferred from their natal homes. Chapter 7 shows how, in the 1930s, the practice of entrustment was changed into one of borrowing girls. This form of girl transfer took place under conditions prompted by economic hardship. In many cases, parents were unable to maintain relationships with their daughters. The sense of responsibility and accountability of the entrustment relationship had disappeared. Chapter 7 connects the anxieties about girls' vulnerabilities in such situations to another more outlandish risk—human sacrifice.

Abomey, Dahomey (actuel Bénin), "Afrique Une allée près du mur d' enceinte du palais de Guézo" (1930) by Frédéric Gadmer. The Musée Albert Kahn allows this image to be freely reusable by a creative commons license CC-BY-4.0.

7

The Télé Affair (1936–1938)

Anxieties about Transformations in Girlhood in Colonial Abomey

A lone figure, a preteen or teenage girl, stands on a dirt path lined with trees and decorative grasses. The thoroughfare itself is empty except for her. She wears a simple white pagne tied around her neck without any other accessories. She is empty handed with nothing balanced atop her head. She stares out into the distance at something beyond the frame of Frederic Gadmer's photograph. The caption accompanying the image, "A path near the outer wall of Gezo's Palace," explains that the reddish clay wall behind her is actually the remains of the outer perimeter of a nineteenth-century palace of the monarch Gezo, who reigned from 1818 to 1859. This 1930 photograph shows that Abomeyans lived in the shadow of the former glory of the kingdom, which had been reduced to rubble when the Dahomean armies retreated from French forces in 1892. The caption's emphasis on the crumbling architecture in the background occludes the girl entirely. While the girl may have turned her back on the palace, she lived within a society where the former royal family was in the process of reclaiming its historic authority within colonial power structures. Both the caption and the image highlight the ongoing relevance of political epistemologies rooted in the precolonial past. For the four decades from the 1890s until the 1930s, the French colonial government had purposefully dismantled the power of the Abomeyan royal family, destroyed its sources of income, and left its authority in ruins much like Gezo's palace. In the 1930s, a political shift occurred. French administrators wanted to restore select members of the royal family to positions of power in the colonial government. How though would these individuals legitimate their authority? Would these descendants of the kings of Dahomey rely on precolonial methods, many of which relied on girls as fundamental resources? Abomeyans believed that Chief Justin Aho, the great grandson of King Gezo and a chief in the French colonial administration, used thirteen-year-old Télé Acapovi to restore the stature of the royal family.

On the night of Saturday, April 11, 1936, Télé walked along an isolated road such as the one shown in the picture. By the time Télé left the city center, at around seven that April night, the sun was setting, and the streets of Abomey had emptied, due to the approaching holidays. Many *vodunsi* (initiated practitioners of the indigenous vodun religion) and Christians had already headed home to prepare for the festivities associated with the end of the dry season and Easter, the respective high holidays for each faith. Ayoko, a fellow market trader and hawker, accompanied Télé for a time until she reached her own house. Télé, she initially said, continued on the path toward the Lawson home alone, or, as she later claimed in a subsequent interrogation, Télé followed a man with a lantern down the darkening road. Télé never reached her destination. She had seemingly disappeared into thin air that night.

Télé's guardians William and Mathilde Lawson reported her missing to the district commandant after the end of the Easter holiday on April 14, 1936, three days after her disappearance. The negligible physical evidence prompted conjecture, which produced two hypotheses: a royal and a popular one.[1] The royal family of Abomey speculated that Télé simply escaped from her abusive guardian and employer Mathilde Lawson, alleging that Mathilde beat Télé on multiple occasions for relatively minor offenses. According to the royal family, after Télé lost a small portion of her earnings, she fled the city, too afraid to return to the Lawson household with a loss in profits. However, Abomeyans not connected with the royal family asserted that Aho ritually murdered Télé in a human sacrifice ceremony associated with the *nεsúxwê* cult dedicated to the royal family's ancestors. *Nεsúxwê* deified deceased members of the royal family whose descendants worshipped them and performed ritual ceremonies to propitiate their ancestral members. When the living appeased these deities, they in turn granted favor on their living descendants. Aho was rumored to have "watered the graves" of his ancestors with human blood, historically a key component of worshipping the *nεsúxwê* cult.[2] He allegedly performed this ritual sacrifice to reclaim the lost power and prestige of the Abomeyan royal family.

Whether Télé ran away from a cruel mistress or fell victim to a human sacrifice ritual, Abomeyans believed some tragedy had befallen the girl. The photograph of the girl standing in the middle of the roadway outside of Abomey captures this uncertainty. She is not facing the road in either direction; she simply stares into the distance, looking at something beyond the trees. She remains stuck, not moving in any direction. The photo, taken several years before Télé's disappearance, seems to foreshadow the ambiguity surrounding her fate. After her last known interaction with Ayoko, which way did Télé go? Was either the royal or popular version what actually happened to her? Or what were the other possibilities?

To this day, there is no consensus as to what actually happened to Télé. Abomeyans remain divided over which version of history is true. This chapter explores the rumors but does not try to prove their veracity. From the perspective of a history of girlhood, the actual outcome of the Télé Affair is in some ways less important than the controversies that emerged from the speculation about this girl's fate. As historian Luise White points out, true and false are not binary opposites that can never meet. Rumors that are credible and seem reasonable have a certain power.[3] Abomeyans' belief in the rumors made them potentially damaging to the French administration since they implicated one of the most powerful indigenous chiefs that France had installed to act on its behalf. This chapter argues that the rumors about Télé's disappearance revealed anxieties about the evolution of traditional norms of girl transfer in the colonial context. The anxieties documented while recording speculation about Télé's fate showed that in the 1930s girlhood norms were changing in ways that heightened girls' vulnerability to both mundane and exceptional forms of abuse, exploitation, and violence.

Télé's life is perhaps the most extensively documented of any girl in colonial Dahomey. Unfortunately, all the details about her come from secondhand sources rather than Télé herself. For over two years after Télé's disappearance, the colonial state compiled hundreds of pages of documentation about the young girl's life. Most sources speculated on her relationships with family members, her mistress, and an alleged unnamed lover. Colonial administrators at all levels shared their views on Télé's fate. The governor-general in Dakar dispatched investigators to Abomey multiple times. These investigators recorded the rumors and suspicions expressed to them by Abomeyans. In addition to contemporary documents, older Abomeyans still recall the so-called Télé Affair. In particular, interviews with Dr. Romuald Michozounnou,

Gabin Djimasse, and Nondichao Bachalou provided rich information about the oral traditions surrounding the political aftermath of Télé's disappearance. Their insights have profoundly shaped this chapter in order to convert this incident from a bizarre historical footnote into an exploration of social anxieties and political transformations centered around the life of a single girl.[4] The endurance of the Télé Affair in oral tradition more than eighty years later attests to its importance to colonial Dahomeans, their Beninese descendants, and the royal family.

The Young Life of Télé Acapovi: A "Borrowed" Child in the Lawson Household

The Télé Affair provides an illuminating perspective on the differences between the ideals of child entrustment and the actual girl transfers that occurred in colonial households. The rumors about Télé's disappearance made her case an exceptional one. Due to the lack of eyewitness testimony or physical evidence, the investigation relied mainly on hearsay. The numerous pages of documentation speculating on Télé and her possible fates showed the French administration's concern with the matter. Between 1936 and 1938, the colonial administration compiled extensive secondhand information about Télé's young life, her birth family, and her social mother, Mathilde.

Throughout the two-year investigation into Télé's disappearance, colonial officials discovered that her situation was significantly different from socially accepted forms of entrusting. A fundamental aspect of legitimate arrangements was the maintenance of girls' relationships with their kin. Entrusting implied an ongoing relationship of exchange and affinity between two households.[5] The administration discovered that no such relationship existed between the Lawsons and the Acapovis, Télé's family, either before or during Télé's time in the Lawson household.[6] No one from her natal lineage had maintained contact with her after she arrived in Abomey. The girl's parents did not even know that their daughter lived in Abomey. Télé's alienation from her family hindered any chance of building trust between the two families; therefore, the circumstances of Télé's transfer violated traditional norms regulating entrustment. The investigators discovered that Mathilde Lawson negotiated with an unnamed intermediary about recruiting a girl to perform domestic labor and sell prepared foods in the streets. This impersonal, brokered exchange offered Télé no safeguards against abuse while living in the

Lawson household. Her story is a reminder of the dangers that girls faced when parents neglected their duty to select trustworthy households for their daughters. It also illustrates what might happen when parents fail to maintain contact with their daughters.

When Mathilde needed help with the labor-intensive tasks of running a household and engaging in market trading, she turned to familial connections in the Aného region of French Togoland to find a girl servant.[7] In the late 1920s or early 1930s, an unnamed third party found a young girl in southeastern Togoland to serve in the Lawson household. Télé had been born in Assoukope, a village across the coastal lagoon from Aného, in 1923 or 1924. According to William Lawson, Télé did not live in her father's household for very long.[8] Lawson stated that Télé lived with him and his wife in Abomey since early childhood.[9] Families typically entrusted their daughters to other households only after the girls reached the age of six to eight. Depending on family circumstances, some girls left home as young as three.[10] While her exact age at the time of entrusting is unknown, Télé was likely in the younger age range. In Télé's case, her parents' divorce led to her entering the Lawson household at such a young age. After the divorce, Télé's mother left her marital home in Assoukope and moved to the Gold Coast; Télé remained with her father. Transferring a girl younger than six to another household usually indicated that the girl's mother was unable to care for her, often due to death or divorce. The practice of entrustment was certainly not limited to cases of divorce, but when the mother left a household due to divorce, the father had little choice but to entrust his female children to female kin or another woman. After his divorce and the departure of his wife, Télé's father gave her to an intermediary who then transferred the girl to the Lawsons. According to various depositions, Télé had lived with the Lawsons in Abomey for seven to ten years before her disappearance in 1936. This means that she had been transferred sometime between the years 1927 and 1930 when she was between four and seven.

In the early 1930s, the Great Depression began to impact African families, forcing them to find unconventional ways to provide for their children.[11] This might explain why Télé's transfer to the Lawsons did not follow social conventions of entrustment. The onset of the Great Depression and new colonial taxation demands in 1929–1930 left West African households in dire financial straits as they tried to pay their taxes.[12] The depression, however, caused currency to almost disappear from Dahomey during much of the

1930s.[13] In this unprecedented environment of economic hardship, Dahomeans manipulated child entrustment into a new form of child transfer. In a 1938 report, Denise Savineau, with the Colonial Education Service, suggested an alternative phrase to the commonly used *un enfant confié* (an entrusted child) that more accurately described Télé's and others' situation: *un enfant prêté* (a borrowed child). Savineau described borrowed children as those "who come from surrounding villages; where the chiefs bother the people for taxes." Savineau observed that since the colonial government forced impoverished families to pay taxes for "even the little ones," parents were forced to "move their children away, and the people of the city take them voluntarily because in Porto-Novo one does not pay for them."[14] Urban centers along the coast such as Ouidah, Porto-Novo, and Cotonou—classified as *communes-mixtes*, or territories comprising both indigenous and European people—were tax havens for juvenile dependents. Part of the reason for this loophole was to ensure that the growing European businesses in these colonial economic centers had a sufficient supply of child labor. As Savineau observes, this resulted in an influx of juvenile laborers from more rural areas. In her field notes from Dahomey, Savineau states: "Borrowed children [are] a widespread phenomenon of free domestic staff found again and again throughout southern Dahomey."[15] Her choice of terminology emphasized that no long-term emotional ties existed or developed among guardians, parents, and child. Borrowing, as opposed to entrusting, focused on the eventual termination rather than the evolution of the relationship between two households. As Télé's story shows, the borrowing of children spread beyond the *communes-mixtes* to Abomey when households were wealthy enough to pay taxes on juvenile dependents.

Dahomeans never used the term *borrowed child* when referring to entrusting arrangements in tribunals, nor did Beninese when asked about fostering relationships during the colonial era.[16] Borrowing seems to represent a temporary change in the practice of entrusting that allowed households to manage the economic hardship of colonial taxation during the depression decade. Borrowing was a more impersonal arrangement than entrusting, and it occurred in the context of a widespread economic crisis rather than as a voluntary, intentional transfer. Télé was just one among a growing number of vulnerable children whose terms of transfer diverged from accepted social norms. The circumstances of Télé's transfer showed that previous forms of accountability based on constructed bonds of kinship had deteriorated in the

1930s. Old value systems succumbed to economic hardships and allowed for the emergence of new types of child transfer, such as borrowed children. The practice of borrowed children, as described by Savineau and experienced by Télé, resulted in new forms of girl vulnerability because of its focus on short-term needs rather than long-term relationships.[17]

April 11, 1936: The Day Télé Disappeared

Télé's experience in her mistress's household and the streets of Abomey resembled that of entrusted girls. A typical day in the Lawson household began with rising at five in the morning, fetching water, and bathing. This was followed by chores such as sweeping or laundry. Then Télé would grind beans or yams to make the base of *boulettes*, fried dough balls, which Dahomeans ate as a midday snack or a light meal when away from home. After grinding the legumes, Télé added chopped onions, spices, and a little butter or an egg to create dough. She rolled the dough into bite-sized balls and fried them. Perhaps before rolling and frying the balls, she prepared a spicy pepper sauce into which the boulettes could be dipped. Once cooked, the balls were stacked in a pyramid on a platter. Télé left the house with the platter balanced on her head and sold the boulettes in the street as an itinerant hawker. She returned to the Lawson household each day only after she sold all of her goods.

On April 11, 1936, Télé walked the streets of Abomey selling boulettes. Nothing seemed amiss as she performed her daily routine of hawking food. Many Abomeyans recalled seeing Télé before she disappeared. Victorin Feliho, a merchant and friend of William Lawson, saw Télé hawking in front of his house at around eleven that morning. Nakloko, an Abomeyan woman, also recalled seeing her in the afternoon between four and four thirty near the hospital.[18] Ayoko, the last person who saw Télé that day, walked with her at dusk from the city center toward the Lawson household. Ayoko reached her house first and left Télé.[19] Ayoko claimed that when the two parted, Télé began to follow a man carrying a lantern. She disappeared between seven and eight that night, only about one and a half miles from the Lawsons' home.[20] What happened after she left Ayoko has remained a subject of debate since April 1936.

Early in the investigation, Henri Martinet, lieutenant governor of Dahomey, refused to open a judicial inquiry because he was not convinced by William Lawson's testimony that a crime had been committed.[21] Various officials believed that Télé had simply left the Lawson household of her own accord to rejoin one of her parents.[22] In late 1936, investigators Sardier and Colombani of the Political Affairs Bureau each separately dismissed this theory after locating Télé's parents in December. Upon learning of their daughter's disappearance, both parents actively participated in the search for their daughter in Togoland. The parents' involvement and concern forced administrators to dismiss the theory that she had rejoined either of them.

The fact that Télé had not contacted her family over the years cast further doubt on the district attorney's hypothesis. Lieutenant Governor Martinet observed: "The judicial inquiry actually in course brought out that the true [biological] parents of Télé did not know where their daughter was, she [Télé] had not directly been entrusted to Lawson by them. They were astonished to learn that their child was in Abomey with persons unknown to them."[23] Under these circumstances, Télé could not have predicted whether her parents would have supported her running away from the Lawson household. Because she was so young when she was transferred and a long time had passed since she had last spoken to her parents, returning to her father's home would have been a risky option. Télé likely did not know where her mother lived on the Gold Coast. West African girls such as Télé understood that if they ran away from their mistresses and returned to their natal homes, their parents had few options other than to return them to the households from which they had fled or to place them with another household where their conditions might be worse.[24]

After confirming that Télé had not returned to either of her parents, French administrators continued to insist that she had run away, ignoring other criminal possibilities. The investigators' focus shifted from Télé's parents to the Lawsons. They tried to find out what possible motives other than homesickness Télé might have had for running away. French authorities' suspicions of the Lawsons increased as more information revealed that they had misled authorities in their initial depositions. Mathilde variously claimed Télé as her niece, cousin, or some distant relative. Mathilde called Télé her *petite niece*, or little niece, a phrase that even today colloquially signifies household subservience rather than a biological relationship.[25] It is not clear whether she purposefully misled authorities because of fear of prosecution or if she used this accepted term in a casual manner. When the commandant interviewed Mathilde again in June 1937, she clarified that Télé was her younger cousin rather than her niece.[26] Télé's father refuted these claims, saying that he did not know the Lawsons. On July 29, 1937, the lieutenant governor definitively stated that Télé was in no way related to either William or Mathilde Lawson. This early investigation revealed French misgivings about colonial girl entrustment. French administrators assumed that a natural preference existed for a household based on biological connectedness and organized around a nuclear family.

The issue of Télé's relationship with the Lawsons was significant for the French investigators' treatment of the case. Because Télé was not related to the Lawson family, the colonial administration found it easy to believe that her mistress had mistreated her. According to this logic, Télé therefore felt no loyalty or affection for Mathilde Lawson; the woman was just her harsh mistress. Ayoko confirmed the administration's suspicions that Mathilde Lawson was abusive, stating that she punished Télé severely for slight infractions. According to Ayoko, Télé feared returning to the Lawsons' house on April 11, 1936, because she had lost forty centimes, a relatively small amount of money considering that one hundred centimes equaled one franc. She believed that her mistress would beat her.[27] From the French administrators' point of view, Télé's escape from such a situation was both expected and perhaps justified.

By the 1930s, transferred girls had long been an integral part of African colonial households. Women's financial success depended on attracting girls into relationships of dependence in their households. Jean Bartel, district commandant of Abomey in 1938, repeatedly argued that Télé's disappearance was nothing unusual: "The case of Télé Acapovi is frequent. A young girl is entrusted, as a servant, by her family to relatives or to friends. One day she takes flight."[28] French administrators in Dahomey used the phrase *une enfant confiée* (an entrusted child), demonstrating their recognition of the legitimacy and ubiquity of this customary arrangement. They did not, however, grasp that Télé's and other girls' transfers were not actually entrustment, at least not according to its accepted, traditional definition. Bartel ignored the fact that Mathilde was neither a relative nor a friend of Télé's parents. The authorities' failure to make this important distinction between entrustment and alternative arrangements revealed their simplistic view of child transfers.

The comments made by Télé's parents and colonial administrators revealed overlapping but distinct anxieties about the changes to the practice of girl dependence. On the one hand, French administrators in Dahomey tried to stabilize the African family and support patriarchal authority. On the other hand, Télé's parents were concerned about the violation of customary child transfer norms that alienated them from their daughter.

The Search for Télé: Rumors and Anxieties

The disappearance of a young street hawker would have been unremarkable except for its associated rumors. Initially, the colonial administration in Abomey handled the case like any other disappearance. The district commandant sent an inquiry to the canton chiefs for information, but there were no details regarding Télé's location. Administrators spent years searching for her, continually revising their theories about her whereabouts. In the first year, their suspicions were centered on Télé's parents and the Lawsons. The scandal surrounding Télé's disappearance gained momentum in the absence of any definitive evidence supporting either scenario.

In April 1929, the colonial administration named Justin Aho the district chief of Oumbégamé, a region in the district of Abomey.[29] Upon his nomination, Aho faced a crisis of legitimacy. The official recognition and support of colonial authorities did not supplant older conceptions of legitimacy in the eyes of his subjects. Aho relied on the outward signs of precolonial kingship to ostentatiously display his claim to an inherited royal authority. In 1930 when Frederic Gadmer visited Abomey and photographed the girl near the ruins of Gezo's palace, he also took a portrait of Aho.[30] In it, Aho is adorned with the accoutrements and insignia of Dahomean kings of generations past. This image bears a striking resemblance to those of his ancestor king Béhanzin, the last independent king of Dahomey famed for his anti-colonial resistance. Both Béhanzin and Aho wear sandals, a symbol of kingship and part of a sumptuary regime that allowed only the king and foreigners to don shoes.[31] Aho wielded a *makpo* or *récade*, a figural or ceremonial weapon used to authenticate a messenger and his message, which rested against his shoulder.[32] Many Abomeyans seeing this image or witnessing Aho attired in such a manner still remembered Béhanzin. These elders attached significance to these clearly displayed symbols of precolonial authority. Beyond insignia, Aho further demonstrated his power through including his wives in this portrait. Aho, like his eighteenth-century predecessors Agaja or Tegbessu pictured in chapter 1, surrounded himself with his wives who communicated their subservient status through their positioning, actions, and the items that they held. One wife shielded Aho from the sun with a parasol, another symbol of royal status. Another wife knelt before Aho holding a bowl-like object, probably a royal spittoon that had been a constant accessory for past Dahomean kings.[33] Aho consciously chose to include these precolonial symbols of royalty and stature in his portrait. Through this visual composition, Aho emphasized that his legitimacy came not from the French but from his royal ancestors.

Abomeyans alleged that Aho had sacrificed Télé to strengthen his authority among other members of the royal family, to silence the belief that he was a usurper, and to rebuild the institutional strength of the royal family through a supernatural ritual. Historically, Dahomean monarchs derived a significant portion of their power from executing vodun rituals. In Dahomey and other West African precolonial kingdoms, ritual human sacrifice was practiced as part of a wider belief system that involved intimate links between this world and the realm of dead ancestors. These links created a mutual dependence between the two worlds.[34] The Dahomean king's prerogative to share human blood with his ancestors via ritual sacrifice was one manifestation of his authority.[35] According to historian Robin Law, human sacrifice in the precolonial Kingdom of Dahomey "was not a remediable excess, but a central and indispensable part of its ideological superstructure."[36] For centuries before the colonial era, Abomeyans linked political power and military success to royals' adherence to rituals. The royal family's decline in the early years of colonial rule was blamed on their lack of dedication to rituals. During the first decades of the twentieth century, the colonial government tried to dismantle the authority of the royal family.[37] The political decline of the royal family, significant social upheaval, and widespread economic hardship in the wake of colonization coincided with the abandonment of the practice of human sacrifice. For many Dahomeans, human sacrifice represented Abomey's ongoing freedom from European domination.[38] Human sacrifice, or at least the belief in its existence, served Aho's personal political agenda and, if actually performed, fulfilled ritual purposes of the cult of the ancestors. For centuries, the Abomeyan royal lineage had relied on an adherence to vodun ceremonial rituals to legitimate its authority. French colonial rule outlawed the practice of human sacrifice and deprived the monarchy of this source of legitimacy.[39]

Did Aho try to revive this "macabre ceremony" to strengthen his authority and rebuild the stature of the royal family?[40] After a year of dismissing this possibility, colonial authorities searched Aho's compound.[41] They discovered no evidence of human sacrifice, only the carcass of a cow.[42] Aho assured the administration that "hateful and jealous adversaries" had spread the rumor about human sacrifice to support their accusations of his corrupt practices and abuse of power.[43] French authorities declared that no sacrifice had been performed, yet they acknowledged that the rumor alone augmented Aho's prestige and authority in the region.[44] Aho's ever-increasing power and wealth during the 1930s proved to Abomeyans that he must have appeased the ancestors in some way.

French administrators in Abomey dismissed the timing of Télé's disappearance and the vodun ceremonies at the end of the dry season as "troubling" but coincidental and unrelated.[45] They agreed with Aho that Télé had simply run away. To convincingly establish the royal interpretation of Télé as a mistreated servant who had run away, the official investigation needed to answer two questions: Why did she do so? Where did she go? French colonial officials at all levels—from local authorities to the governor-general in Dakar and the minister of colonies in Paris—considered possible answers to these questions. Their speculation revealed French colonial anxieties about girl transfers. Girls unhappy with the entrustment arrangements made by their families used the only strategy available to them: running away. During the colonial period, women and girls throughout Africa ran away from undesirable and dangerous situations.[46] Throughout the investigation, French officials in Abomey believed that Télé was just another of these runaway girls. Lieutenant Governor Martinet admitted, "These sorts of runaways are not uncommon along the coastal littoral."[47] By "these sorts," Martinet referenced a phenomenon that Commandant Bartel explained in greater detail: "One day she takes flight, goes 'to cling to a man' [sic] who, when she is of age, and if she is not yet reclaimed before [that time], he marries her [without paying the dowry].... It is the case of thousands of girls of Dahomey."[48] This assessment shows that concerns among authorities about girlhood focused on the erosion of patriarchal authority and precocious sexuality. The questioning of William Lawson further revealed this French agenda. In Lawson's first interview in November 1936, officials asked "if she [Télé] had followed a boy." Lawson insisted that Télé was too young to have run away with a lover. Christian Merlo, a French administrator tasked with investigating Télé's disappearance, revisited this line of questioning when he asked Lawson: "Do you think that Télé was still a virgin?"[49]

By late 1936, the French administration's hypothesis that Télé had simply run away to either reunite with her parents or live with a lover was not convincing. French officials could no longer ignore the rumors that Télé had been ritually sacrificed due to events in the neighboring French mandate of Togoland. In July 1936, the French imperial tribunal in Togoland tried a vodun priest named Aglao along with fourteen adherents of his vodun cult house as codefendants; each was charged with various levels of involvement in a series of ritualistic crimes, including the sacrifice of a missing girl.[50] The tribunal investigated the mysterious deaths of twelve women, all of whom had died shortly after they entered the vodun cult house, as well as the disappearance of two girls. During a search of the cult house complex, French authorities discovered five intact human skeletons, a skeleton with no head, and various other human bones.[51] On July 24, 1936, the criminal tribunal of Aného convicted Aglao and his codefendants.[52] After all appeals were exhausted, the French imperial administration executed Aglao, Gouna, and Lanta in October 1936 for performing human sacrifices.[53] The convictions of fifteen men and the execution of three of them proved that authorities could no longer dismiss human sacrifice as exclusively a precolonial practice that French influence had successfully eradicated.

The confirmation of ritual sacrifice being performed in a French-mandated territory one hundred miles to the southwest of Abomey lent credence to the allegations against Aho. Finally, in November 1936, the month following the execution of Aglao and his two codefendants and more than six months after Télé's disappearance, the French colonial government in Dahomey took official action in the Télé Affair. After much pressure from the federation-level government in Dakar, Dahomean officials formally opened an overdue official judicial inquiry into Télé's disappearance.[54] At this point, however, the charge to be investigated was kidnapping committed by an unknown perpetrator. Neither Justin Aho's name nor the charge of murder was mentioned in the initial legal dossier despite both being the subject of rumors and newspaper articles. The judicial inquiry, in which Aho was the primary suspect, began in earnest with his formal deposition on April 10, 1937, one day before the one-year anniversary of Télé's disappearance.

Solving the Télé Affair became even more important when, on April 13, 1937, a four-year-old girl named Sena disappeared from a field near Parahoué, in the Athiémé district of Dahomey. Allegedly, Jerôme Badou had followed Aho's example and murdered Sena in a human sacrifice ritual. Badou, like

Justin Aho, was the great grandson of King Gezo. His connection to the royal family and his ability to speak fluent French made him an attractive collaborator for the French administration to appoint to indirectly rule for them. In 1935 after the dismissal of a popular local chief, the French administration appointed Badou to govern the "difficult" district of Lonkly, a region in the southwestern corner of the colony far removed from Abomey. The French administration failed to grasp that the people of this region near Athiémé would not accept an Abomeyan prince as a legitimate authority over them; rather Badou and his ancestors were seen as foreign conquerors. Initially, Badou struggled to govern this unruly region. Local rumor maintained that Badou was emboldened by the fact that Aho had not been charged with Télé's murder. Dahomeans asserted that by performing a ritual sacrifice, Badou hoped to increase his prestige as Aho had done. While Badou had been baptized as a Catholic during his youth, he never entirely abandoned vodun. By the 1930s, he reportedly resumed practicing this indigenous faith and rejected Catholicism.[55]

Sena's and Télé's disappearances were newsworthy because both of the alleged perpetrators belonged to Abomey's royal lineage and both had parlayed this connection into attaining chiefly offices within the colonial bureaucracy. Although the disappearances were similar, administrators investigated Aho more rigorously than Badou. Colonial authorities, both French and indigenous, focused their energies on Télé's disappearance for more than two years. The girls' ages played a crucial role in how the cases were handled. Sena's young age allowed no plausible alternatives to either criminal activity or tragedy. From April 1937, Télé's file grew rapidly and contained over one hundred documents by December 1937.[56]

Pressure on Dahomey's lieutenant governor and the commandant of the district of Abomey to resolve the case increased in October 1937 when *Notre voix*, a leftist newspaper sponsored by the French Section of the Workers' International, became interested in the matter. On November 29, 1937, Marcel de Coppet, governor-general of AOF, sent copies of the article from *Notre voix* titled: "In Dahomey—The Resumption of Human Sacrifice?" to the minister of colonies, Marius Moutet, and the lieutenant governor of Dahomey, Henri Martinet. The article speculated that two chiefs had abducted the two missing girls and then sacrificed both. The question mark at the end of the article's title alluded to the unverified nature of the rumors concerning the missing girls.[57] The scandalous accusations of human sacrifice occurring in a French imperial possession got the attention of the highest levels of colonial officials in France and throughout West Africa. After all, France had justified its conquest of the precolonial Kingdom of Dahomey forty years earlier when it promised to eradicate human sacrifice and stop the rivers of blood described by many nineteenth-century travelers. The article circulated from Côte d'Ivoire to Senegal and then to France and Dahomey.[58] The newspaper's connection to an international socialist organization raised the stakes for the colonial government to disprove the allegations that France's civilizing mission had failed to end this barbaric practice.[59] The article sounded an international alarm, which threatened France's identity as a civilizing imperial power.[60]

The administration invested copious amounts of time and energy in an effort to discover Télé's fate once it became clear that her disappearance might not be an isolated event. Authorities desperately wanted to substantiate their claim that "the macabre ceremonies [suggested by rumors] are from another age."[61] The administration chose Justin Aho as an indigenous collaborator because he had served in the French army and traveled to France. To admit that a man such as he had committed a ritual murder undermined all French pretensions about the success of the civilizing mission over the last forty years. Commandant Bartel refuted the possibility that such a thing could have happened: "Our population Dahoméene is too advanced, too close to us today and despite legitimate respect the population has for their ancestral religion and its *Kutomé*, for accomplishing these acts so savage and so inhumane."[62] In frustration and desperation, on December 5, 1937, Commandant Bartel issued an ultimatum to Aho: find the girl or go to jail. After futilely protesting that he could not be held responsible for Télé's disappearance, Aho or members of his family presented three girls, each of whom on different occasions they claimed were Télé.[63] One girl, however, lacked Télé's scarification marks. Neither the Lawsons nor Ayoko recognized the second girl presented to them. Miraculously, after the girls were dismissed as impostors, Aho located the "real" Télé on February 4, 1938. He presented her to the authorities, who confirmed her identity with Mathilde Lawson. Télé had been found!

In his report to his superior, Bartel urged the administration in Dakar to close the case and move on from the scandal. Bartel advised: "In closing I hope that the discovery of Télé puts a final period to the 'Affairs of Abomey' and that this district so rich in all sorts of possibilities, will retake its rapid economic expansion of a local political base hindered for the last two years."[64] Abomeyans were more skeptical than Bartel. They claimed that this girl was also an impostor. To save himself and his family, Aho had allegedly purchased a girl and presented her to the French authorities as Télé. In the process of trying to pass off the first three girls as Télé, Aho had become an expert on the confirmation process, and he paid off the appropriate people to ensure that "Télé" was indeed found.[65]

Télé, the genuine one or perhaps an impostor, confirmed official gossip on February 18, 1938, when she admitted that she had run away because she was afraid of Mathilde Lawson's abuse. Télé testified that she went to French Togoland and worked in a household as a domestic servant for the past two years. Abomeyans thought that Télé's return and testimony were suspicious and far too convenient. Her testimony just happened to exonerate all administrators and indigenous chiefs of culpability. To this day, most Abomeyans reject the royal/official version and continue to insist that Aho successfully performed a ritualistic murder to procure supernatural support and strengthen his power.

Conclusion

During the twilight hours after selling food in the market and streets of Abomey, Télé vanished on her way home. The traditional archive preserved the young life of Télé because, like Aholoupé, three decades earlier, the accused perpetrator was a member of the Abomeyan royal family. Popular concerns centered around abusive child transfer arrangements that lacked trust, the sexual and labor exploitation of girls lured away from their households by suitors, and a political economy that still valued girls as resources.

The few known details about Télé's disappearance have been exaggerated by rumors. The "truth" became virtually irrelevant in the flood of hearsay and gossip. The rumors became a popularly accepted reality in Abomey and revealed concerns about girl transfer in the colonial era.[66] The talk surrounding Télé's disappearance reflected Dahomeans' anxieties regarding the shifting norms of girlhood during the 1930s. The hearsay collected during the investigation revealed Dahomeans' unease about the new practice of borrowed girls as a way to deal with the economic hardship of the Great Depression. Commandant Bartel, the French administrator in Abomey who insisted that Télé had run away, was quick to point out that the real scandal in the Télé

Affair was indigenous child transfer norms. His diagnosis of the case may have been convenient for him, but it also reflected Dahomeans' concerns about the evolution of these practices. Dahomeans valued the practice of entrustment, but the concept of borrowing girls corrupted the normative ideals of entrusting.

Borrowed girls were vulnerable to a host of commonplace abuses, such as being mistreated or punished by a harsh mistress. Unlike entrusted girls, borrowed girls did not maintain strong ties to their families and had few avenues through which to protest poor conditions. Télé's alienation from her family prevented her from reporting her mistreatment. In the event that Télé ran away, neither her parents nor guardians knew where to look for her. The long search for Télé was a cautionary tale to parents to keep in touch with their daughters after they moved to another household. The Télé Affair shows that there was a popular fear that borrowed girls were also vulnerable to more sensationalized dangers, such as kidnapping, sex trafficking, and ritual sacrifice.

"Jeune Dahoméenne" by Edmond Fortier © Musée du quai Branly—Jacques Chirac, Dist. RMN-Grand Palais/Art Resource NY.

Conclusion
Obscured Histories of Girlhood

The Bonds of Kinship in Dahomey looks at key points in the life stories of ten dependent West African girls: Àiná, Aholoupé, Houmé, Fovi, Mahoun, Akouéle, Ahoussi, Saba, Ahoudjo, and Télé. These girls were assigned various dependent roles that bonded them to the women who acted as their guardians and mistresses. The portraits presented here offer glimpses into their lives that are necessarily incomplete. This book reveals ephemeral moments of Dahomean girls' life histories recorded in Atlantic and colonial archives. These girls were exceptional because most girls mentioned in the archival record were unnamed, such as the one shown in Edmond Fortier's "Young Dahomean Girl."[1] This anonymous girl and others who appear in recorded images, oral traditions, and written documents contributed to the collective biographies and prosopographically inspired narratives contained in this book. Each chapter focuses on an individual's life or a small group of individuals, but their stories are not exclusively their own—they also draw on the experiences of unnamed girls. The book begins by discussing an anonymous girl and ends by featuring another anonymous girl acknowledging these unnamed individuals' contributions. The case studies presented herein owe a debt to the anonymous girls whose stories and experiences make the lives of Àiná, Aholoupé, Houmé, Fovi, Mahoun, Akouéle, Ahoussi, Saba, Ahoudjo, and Télé more complex and multidimensional.

The young Dahomean in Fortier's picture is looking down with a serious expression. She appears to be in her early teens, and her physical strength is evident in how she balances the trays of goods atop her head.

The viewer might infer that she has carried many such loads and so is unbothered by the weight of the trays. There is an elegance to her ease and nonchalance. How many hours each day did she carry goods on her head to be able to do so without strain or hesitancy? What is the significance of the beaded necklace and bracelets she is wearing? Why did she choose to adorn her body with jewelry on a workday in the market? The answers to these questions may seem insignificant, but to a historian of girlhood, these details provide a starting point for the historical narrative, focusing on the real-life experiences of Dahomean girls rather than cultural ideals or adult expectations. Every part of each available fragment of information is valuable, no matter how incomplete it might be. This girl hawker who encountered Fortier in the streets of colonial Dahomey selected that necklace and those bracelets without knowing she would be photographed that day. What did these pieces mean to her? Did she wear them every day? Who gave them to her? Did she make them herself? Images like this one introduced the material contexts in which Dahomean girls lived, emphasized their individuality, and created space to reflect on girls' interior lives. Each chapter has focused on a particular girl and the world she inhabited. The reader enters these worlds through the images of girls that open the chapters.

The Bonds of Kinship in Dahomey centers around the inadequate documentation of girlhood. Very limited documentation exists of girls as historical subjects, even if the primary source data is empirically rich.[2] This book has shown just how rich fragmentary evidence can become through probing the tension between the knowable and the imaginable. Admittedly, this book outlines a history that is at times suggestive rather than definitive.[3] Although the archive preserved no complete biographies, *The Bonds of Kinship in Dahomey* relied on the available traditions, documents, and images to narrate a history of the experiences of girlhood in the early modern and modern eras of what is today the southern portion of the Republic of Benin.[4] By focusing on the lived experiences of individual girls, this book demonstrates how some girls easily adjusted to these shifting contexts and successfully forged paths for themselves that allowed them to achieve social mobility; liberate themselves from undesirable or abusive circumstances; and build extrafamilial networks that supported them in times of physical, emotional, psychological, and economic distress. These achievements did not ease the pain caused by a long separation from family; harsh physical and mental discipline and abuse;

the trauma of sexual assault; or, for enslaved girls, the horrors of capture, sale, and alienation.

These individual portraits of girls' lives show that over the course of the three centuries discussed, there was a steady need for girls' labor. Households sought and incorporated girls in specific relationships of obligation at particular times because of developments in both the local and global political economies. *The Bonds of Kinship in Dahomey* argues that throughout the eighteenth, nineteenth, and twentieth centuries, girlhood and the traditional institutions of girl transfers that defined it evolved along with the major political and economic transformations that reverberated throughout the Bight of Benin.[5] The pivotal transformations of Dahomean history are examined, including the eighteenth-century expansion of the Kingdom of Dahomey, the kingdom's extensive participation in the transatlantic slave trade, the abolition of said trade, the evolution of African slavery and other forms of coerced dependence during the era of legitimate trade in palm products, the imposition and consolidation of French colonial rule, the effects of colonial laws on household dependency, the shift from the French imperial policy of assimilation to association, and the coping strategies of West Africans to extractive colonial taxation during the Great Depression. This book shows how the Dahomean monarchy, the global economy, and colonial courts reshaped girlhood norms in this region of West Africa.

Economic fluctuations in the Atlantic world resulted in continual renegotiations about the dependent status of girls and their obligations to parents, guardians, mistresses, and masters. Girls' labor became a contested subject whereby numerous social and political forces struggled to control this increasingly valuable resource.[6] The transnational economic changes of the eighteenth through twentieth centuries seemed to have increased girls' vulnerability to enslavement, labor exploitation, and sexual abuse in ways that alarmed Dahomean society. This unease is disproportionately represented in the archives. Undoubtedly, many harmonious arrangements of entrusting existed promoting the value of the practice into the twenty-first century. The long-standing ideals that validated fostering attested to the fact that these must have existed extensively in Dahomean society.

This book looks at how important girl transfers were to both the political economy and women's economic independence. These two forms of power competed with each other over resources, and their rivalry intensified after the mid-nineteenth-century transition to the legitimate trade in palm products. Even though women's status in Dahomey, and throughout Africa, declined in the nineteenth century, Dahomean women such as Agbessipé found innovative ways to benefit from the practice of girl transfer. Others, such as Fohoumbo and Natala, successfully defended their access to the social capital and labor value they received from girl transfer arrangements.

There was a drastic divide between Dahomean free girlhood and captive girlhood. Free girls whose kin voluntarily transferred daughters and maintained ties with them offered some degree of protection. Enslaved girls had to build a support network from scratch and even then often remained at the mercy of their mistresses or masters. For Dahomeans, voluntary forms of girl transfer, such as entrusting, were distinguished from enslavement by the fact that kinship ties remained intact. Parents' love for their children did not stop them from putting them to work or transferring them to attain societal worth.[7] Although an entrusted girl, a pawn, and a slave could find themselves in very similar situations, the distinctions in status were meaningful to Dahomeans. A uniting factor among all forms of dependency discussed in this book—fostered, collected, pawned, enslaved, runaway, and borrowed girls—was the social and economic wealth adults received from their right to control these girls' mobility and labor.[8] Enslaved girls had a unique status because their mistress or master controlled their sexuality and reproductive abilities.

As this book demonstrates, the 1930s brought significant attention to the subject of girl transfers. The debates surrounding girlhood norms were not resolved. Forms of girl transfer that stray from the ideals of entrustment continue to be scrutinized in Benin. In the last four decades, the ideals supporting girl transfers have come under increasing attack because of how vulnerable girls are to abuse in foster homes. Najat Maalla M'jid, a United Nations (UN) special rapporteur on children's issues, visited the West African nation of Benin in October and November 2013—the same period during which I was conducting research on similar subjects from a historical perspective. She summarized her observations of children's vulnerability: "It is unacceptable that so many, too many children in Benin are victims of violence, abuse or exploitation on the pretext of traditions, customs or poverty." She admitted that the actual scale of the phenomena remained difficult to determine, but she believed there existed "an alarming number of incidents of violence and economic and/or sexual exploitation suffered in particular by girls." Though she praised Benin for its "relatively complete legal framework regarding child protection," she observed widespread disregard for the laws intended to protect children generally and girls more specifically.[9] Ostensibly, the UN had given the special rapporteur a gender-neutral assignment to monitor all children, but her mandated topics of child sale, child prostitution, and child pornography had deeply gendered histories. Maalla M'jid's report reflected this and focused on girls in Bénin. She described how valuable and traditional practices had been corrupted and how in the contemporary context these changes had created exploitative situations where girls were subjected to abuse. The life stories of the girls and women presented in *The Bonds of Kinship in Dahomey* show that traditions of girl transfer cannot be dismissed as a "pretext." Any discussion of the contemporary problems concerning girl transfer, child labor, child sexual abuse, and guardianship needs to acknowledge this deeper history and respectfully engage with the ideals that continue to valorize girl circulation and social motherhood.

Popular recollections about customary childhood norms ignored the precolonial transformations in girl transfer practices and how experiences of the phenomenon were inherently gendered. Policymakers and anthropologists often reinforced this perception by depicting precolonial times as a hermetically sealed golden age that legitimized the popular point of view.[10] Anthropologist and activist Neil Howard points to this narrative of recent corruption as an impediment to crafting effective policies at the local level.[11] Maalla M'jid's report remains the most recent, comprehensive, detailed report of a UN special rapporteur on issues of child labor and exploitation in Benin. However, as recently as 2021, the US Office to Monitor and Combat Trafficking in Persons (TIP Office) wrote a report that repeated Maalla M'jid's earlier claims. The report pointed out that "trafficking in the country [Benin] is predominantly internal and involves Beninese children" who are exploited as domestic servants, market hawkers, farm and trade "apprentices," and handicraft manufacturers. This 2021 report, like that of Maalla M'jid's eight years earlier, criticized the "traditional practice known as *vidomégòn*" for exploiting girls in the sectors of urban domestic servitude and open-air market hawking.[12]

When I asked my Beninese informants about the traditions mentioned by Maala M'jid and the TIP Office and when they became corrupted, most of them said that the corruption of traditional girlhood norms probably began in the 1990s and definitely no earlier than the postindependence period.[13] Beninese people admitted that modern-day practices of placing girls as domestic servants were often harmful. They contrasted these developments with older, valued practices of entrusting girls to households. Despite widespread criticism of contemporary abusive practices, Beninese people emphasized the benefits of girl entrustment.

The most recent controversy concerns placed children, or vidomégòn. The practice of entrusting children has existed since the Atlantic Era and undergone significant changes over the centuries, but my informants' narrations ignored these earlier developments. They categorically denounced modern "placement" as exploitative but praised historical "entrustment" as virtuous.[14] However, the history of entrustment, and girl transfers more broadly, is more complicated than this contrast suggests.

Beninese collective memory dramatically diverged from the international narrative that Maalla M'jid and the TIP Office reiterated in their reports. To the present day, West African biological parents willingly transfer their daughters at relatively young ages into foster homes. Parents relocate their daughters to other households where these girls live for many years as a crucial component of being "well raised."[15] Beninese people justified the institution of girl entrustment because it developed kinship ties and produced new forms of relatedness that transcended biology.[16] These relationships would ideally offer more resources for girls when they needed them. The shortcoming of collective memory is that Beninese people often thought of child entrustment as a timeless, fixed, and stable tradition that existed before the twentieth century. *The Bonds of Kinship in Dahomey* explores the *longue durée* history of this practice and ones related to it in order to ground the collective memory in historical time and individual experiences.

Girl transfers, in multiple forms, drew from deeply rooted historical norms that valued extending kinship networks by creating social bonds based on the transfer of a girl from one household to another.[17] West Africans have not, until lately and still not universally, emulated the modern Western European tradition of a conjugally based family ideal.[18] The Euro-American belief that children, especially girls, spend their entire childhoods in the homes of their biological parents does not apply to the West African experience. Historically, African familial structures and household organizations differed fundamentally from that of the nuclear family model.[19] One of these differences was the borrowing, loaning, and entrusting of children between households as an important means of constructing kinship networks that extended beyond biological or emotional relationships.[20] Girl transfers, both historically and in the present day, were fundamental to how the royal family and elite traders accumulated their wealth.

The Bonds of Kinship in Dahomey asserts that in Dahomey in the past—and perhaps even in Benin now—girls' labor was an important component to understanding (1) the evolutions of the political economy, (2) women's economic strategies during the precolonial and colonial eras, and (3) relationships of household dependency and the hierarchies among them. The current understanding of Beninese girlhood no longer supports the notion of a dichotomy between tradition and modernity because precolonial girlhood norms and their ideals have endured into the present day.

GLOSSARY OF FOREIGN TERMS

Fon

agojie—battalions of female warriors, often referred to in European sources as "Amazons."
ahosi—literally "wives of the king," but it can include any dependent, follower, or subordinate of the king. The term usually refers to women and girls living in the royal palaces as well as ministers of both sexes.
cankie—a staple foodstuff referred to as "the diet of the masses." A maize-based dough that is rolled into balls and wrapped in plantain leaves, it is sold by hawkers as a street food.
devi—a domestic slave who has lived in a household for a long time and has therefore become a trusted member. The master or mistress gave these individuals additional responsibilities and liberties because of their long-term service and loyalty.
gbablito—a category of enslaved persons in Dahomey that were identified by their occupation as puncheon rollers. This term was created after the expansion of the palm oil export trade in the 1840s.
gbanú—Fon term for "pawning." Pawning was a form of servitude that functioned as a way of ensuring that debts were repaid. In this type of legal dependency, a pawn was held in the lender's household until the borrower repaid the entire loan. In the period between the loan and repayment, the pawn's work benefited the credit-giving household in which she lived.
glési—literally "wives of the cultivated land." The term was first used to refer to enslaved persons working in agriculture. Later, it described their descendants who, though born in Dahomey and thus free, still belonged to a distinct group

of serf-like laborers who were bound to the land worked by their enslaved ancestors. Eventually, the term *glési* became synonymous with "farm laborer."

kannoumon—literally "people of the cord." It is the broadest category of any enslaved person within Dahomean society.

Hwetanu—These annual ceremonies were an essential element of ritual observance, political statecraft, and economic redistribution in the precolonial Kingdom of Dahomey. The ceremonies elevated the monarchy, reaffirmed the royal family's spiritual legitimacy, stimulated the economy, and emphasized the king's absolute power in terms of judicial punishment and military leadership.

nɛsúxwê—the vodun cult dedicated to the royal family's ancestors. The Hwetanu ceremonies were performed to honor these ancestors as well as appease them in the world of the dead.

pagne—a swath of cloth about eight feet long and four feet wide that West Africans wrapped around their chest or waist to clothe themselves.

récade—a carved staff or baton assigned to an elite member of the Kingdom of Dahomey. These staffs were sent with messengers to confirm the authenticity of the communication.

vidaho—the prince who was designated as heir apparent of the Dahomean king.

vidomégòn—literally "placed child." In the late twentieth and early twenty-first centuries, this practice of child transfer has been widely condemned as abusive to children.

vodunsi—literally "wives of the *vodun*." The term referred to any member of a specific cult house who, through their initiation, "married" the vodun to whom the house was dedicated.

yovo—a term used to describe a foreigner or outsider, encompassing a diverse "white" community of Europeans, multiracial Africans, and Africans from Sierra Leone and the Gold Coast who visited or lived in the Kingdom of Dahomey. *Yovo* developed a racial connotation and was often used to refer to the identity of whiteness. Yovos were not exclusively phenotypically "white."

Yorùbá

ifolé—a dependent born in a household to subservient outsiders. These home-born slaves were trusted more than newer arrivals and given more responsibilities and liberties.

iwofa—often translated as "pawning." Pawning was a form of involuntary servitude that functioned as a way of ensuring that debts were repaid. In this type of legal dependency, a pawn was held in the lender's household until the borrower repaid the entire loan. In the period between the loan and repayment, the pawn's work benefited the credit-giving household in which she lived.

French

chambre d'homolgation—"court of validation" that functioned as a review board at the apex of the indigenous court structure in French West Africa. It was composed of a group of professionally trained magistrates who reviewed the protocols and judgments of lower-level courts, which were staffed by appointed colonial administrators and indigenous assessors, none of whom had formal legal training.

communes-mixtes—referred to coastal enclaves where both indigenous and European populations lived alongside one another. This designation allowed for special tax districts where children were not taxed. In the 1930s, Ouidah, Cotonou, and Porto-Novo were all given this designation and drew in transferred children as an essential component of their workforce.

une enfant confiée—literally "an entrusted child."

un enfant prêté—literally "a borrowed child."

femme du pays—literally "country wife." The term was often used to describe an African woman who married a European man according to the customs of her culture.

levées—tax obligations owed to the king.

manellos—metal bracelets that served as a form of currency, often made of copper, brass, and iron. During the early modern and modern eras, these were used in African and transatlantic trade.

petite niece—literally "little niece." It was and still is used as a euphemism for a subservient girl incorporated into the household.

procès-verbal—a legal document compiled during the investigation of a crime that recorded the testimony of victim(s), the accused, witnesses, and others.

NOTES

Introduction

1. This image appeared in Alexandre L. d'Albéca, *La France au Dahomey* (Paris: Hachette, 1895), 154. This rendering was based on a photograph taken by d'Albéca, Resident of France's Establishments in the Gulf of Guinée from 1887 to 1888 and the Superior Commandant of Guinée and Resident of Ouidah from 1892 to 1893. This digitized version came from the Schomburg Center for Research in Black Culture, Jean Blackwell Hutson Research and Reference Division, New York Public Library. "Une Marchande de Tissus." New York Public Library Digital Collections, accessed March 18, 2022, https://digitalcollections.nypl.org/items/510d47de-0fbb-a3d9-e040-e00a18064a99. D'Albéca included this image in multiple texts that he published in 1894 and 1895. In 1894, the image appeared as "Une marchande à Cotonou" in a series of articles that appeared in *Le Tour de Monde*. This publication credits Berg as the artist who transformed the photograph into an engraving.

2. Christraud M. Geary, *In and Out of Focus: Images from Central Africa, 1885–1960* (London: Philip Wilson, 2002), 28–29. D'Albéca did this by obscuring the background and context, leaving even the locale vague enough to be identified as Cotonou in some published contexts, including the image in his commentary on Mina women in Grand Popo.

3. Nkiru Uwechia Nzegwu, *Family Matters: Feminist Concepts in African Philosophy of Culture*, SUNY Series, Feminist Philosophy (Albany: State University of New York Press, 2006), 11.

4. Rodet and Razy discuss how child migration takes a variety of forms. They argue that the terminology selected to describe these forms must be mindful of this variety. I agree with the distinctions they make in particular with their

limited usage of *circulation*. Marie Rodet and Elodie Razy, "Introduction: Child Migration in Africa: Key Issues & New Perspectives," in *Children on the Move in Africa: Past & Present Experiences of Migration*, ed. Elodie Razy and Marie Rodet (Suffolk: James Currey, 2016), 1–5.

5. Rhiannon Stephens's approach to motherhood in Uganda has influenced this book's conceptualization of girlhood as a social institution; see Rhiannon Stephens, *A History of African Motherhood: The Case of Uganda, 700–1900* (Cambridge: Cambridge University Press, 2013).

6. Sarah Maza makes a similar and more general point in Sarah Maza, "The Kids Aren't All Right: Historians and the Problem of Childhood," *American Historical Review* 125, no. 4 (October 2020): 1282.

7. This definition of pawnship is drawn from a variety of scholarly perspectives, see Paul E. Lovejoy, "Pawnship, Debt, and 'Freedom' in Atlantic Africa during the Era of the Slave Trade: A Reassessment," *The Journal of African History* 55, no. 1 (March 2014): 55–78; Toyin Falola and Paul Lovejoy, eds., *Pawnship, Slavery, and Colonialism in Africa* (Trenton: Africa World Press, 2003); Paul E. Lovejoy and David Richardson, "The Business of Slaving: Pawnship in Western Africa, c. 1600–1810," *Journal of African History* 42, no. 1 (2001): 67–89; Toyin Falola, ed., *Pawnship in Africa : Debt Bondage in Historical Perspective* (Boulder: Westview Press, 1994); Beverly Grier, "Pawns, Porters, and Petty Traders: Women in the Transition to Cash Crop Agriculture in Colonial Ghana," *Signs* 17, no. 2 (Winter 1992): 304–28.

8. These age estimates are based primarily on colonial era records.

9. Igor Kopytoff and Suzanne Miers, "Introduction: African 'Slavery' as an Institution of Marginality," in *Slavery in Africa: Historical and Anthropological Perspectives*, ed. Suzanne Miers and Igor Kopytoff (Madison: University of Wisconsin Press, 1977), 7.

10. This periodization encapsulates the effects of Atlanticization on the history of Dahomean girlhood. Ndubueze L. Mbah, historian of Atlantic West Africa, defines Atlanticization as a series of successive political economies whereby Africans and their "local traditions, gender ideologies, sociopolitical systems, commercial networks, and knowledge systems" engaged with Atlantic ones. Africans then selectively reconciled these Atlantic influences with their existing norms. In Dahomey, Atlanticization began in the 1720s when the kingdom expanded its territory to the Atlantic littoral, and it—arguably—ended with the protracted colonial efforts at slave emancipation in Africa from the turn of the twentieth century through the 1930s. In the 1940s, the Atlantic Era was eclipsed by a new supranational postwar world order framed by Cold War and decolonial politics.

11. For more on issues regarding the defining of African childhood by a rigid chronological age, see Saheed Aderinto, "Introduction: Colonialism and the

Invention of Modern Nigerian Childhood," in *Children and Childhood in Colonial Nigerian Histories* (New York: Palgrave Macmillan, 2015), 4–6. Also, this may reflect a colonial or French conception that was heavily debated at the time. In 1939, the Mandel Decree established fourteen as the minimum age of marriage for girls in French West Africa. The language used in documentation seems to be referring to social age, which was often indicated through attire or the labor tasks assigned to certain age groups. To further explore the issues of designating child versus adult status in African history, see Elodie Razy and Marie Rodet, eds., *Children on the Move in Africa: Past and Present Experiences of Migration* (Suffolk: James Currey, 2016), 11–14.

12. For similar observations on other regions of Africa, see Corrie Decker, "A Feminist Methodology of Age-Grading and History in Africa," *American Historical Review* 125, no. 2 (April 2020): 420–21. This age designation seems to have been the product of a colonial idea in global circulation. For example, the Indian Penal Code, introduced in 1862 to the subcontinent and subsequently applied to British colonies in East Africa, established the age of fourteen as the threshold for consent. See ibid., 418.

13. Nineteenth-century European missionaries, traders, and administrators observed that girls' statuses and roles within the household changed when they were around seven years of age. Edouard Foà, *Le Dahomey: Histoire, Géographie, Moeurs, Coutumes, Commerce, Industrie, Expeditions Françaises (1891–1894)* (Paris: A. Hennuyer, 1895), 192–94. Africanist scholars studying other African countries or groups also use fourteen as a benchmark to distinguish between childhood or girlhood and adolescence or young adulthood. For example, see Beverly Grier, "Child Labor and Africanist Scholarship: A Critical Overview," *African Studies Review* 47, no. 2 (September 1, 2004): 4.

14. Decker makes this general point about maturation in Africa as an earned status; see Decker, "Feminist," 420.

15. Dr. Euloge Akodjetin interview, January 28, 2014. Sonia Mahame interview, January 21, 2014. Guirlene March interview, January 20, 2014. Erdmute Alber, "The Transfer of Belonging: Theories on Child Fostering in West Africa Reviewed," in *Child Fostering in West Africa: New Perspectives on Theory and Practice* (Leiden: Brill, 2013), 96.

16. Since the sixteenth century, Gbe-speaking ethnic groups, including the subgroups of the Aja, Ewe, Fon, Gen/Mina, and Phla-Phera, had been one of the dominant cultural forces along the Bight of Benin. See Meera Venkatachalam, *Slavery, Memory, and Religion in Southeastern Ghana, c. 1850–Present* (New York: Cambridge University Press, 2015), 25–26. James H. Sweet, *Domingos Álvares, African Healing, and the Intellectual History of the Atlantic World* (Chapel Hill: University of North Carolina Press, 2011), 14. For a general discussion of the designation *Gbe group*, see Robin Law, *The Slave Coast of West*

Africa, 1550–1750: The Impact of the Atlantic Slave Trade on an African Society (Oxford: Oxford University Press, 1991), 21–23; Edna G. Bay, *Wives of the Leopard: Gender, Politics, and Culture in the Kingdom of Dahomey* (Charlottesville: University of Virginia Press, 1998), 41–42.

17. For Northern Benin, see Erdmute Alber, *Transfers of Belonging: Child Fostering in West Africa in the 20th Century* (Boston: Brill, 2018). Erdmute Alber, "No School without Foster Families in Northern Benin: A Social Historical Approach," in *Parenting after the Century of the Child* (Burlington, VT: Ashgate, 2010), 57–78; Alber, *Transfers of Belonging*; Alber, "Denying Biological Parenthood: Fosterage in Northern Benin," *Ethnos* 68, no. 4 (December 2003): 487–506. For Ghana, see Esther Goody, *Parenthood and Social Reproduction: Fostering and Occupational Roles in West Africa* (Cambridge: Cambridge University Press, 1982); Cati Coe, "Disputes over Transfers of Belonging in the Gold Coast in the 1870s: Fosterage or Debt Pawning?," in *Child Fostering in West Africa: New Perspectives on Theory and Practice* (Leiden: Brill, 2013), 201–20; Coe, *The Scattered Family: Parenting, African Migrants, and Global Inequality* (Chicago: University of Chicago Press, 2013); Coe, "How Debt Became Care: Child Pawning and Its Transformations in Akuapem, the Gold Coast, 1874–1929," *Africa* 82, no. 2 (May 2012): 287–311; Coe, "Domestic Violence and Child Circulation in the Southeastern Gold Coast, 1905–28," in *Domestic Violence and the Law in Colonial and Postcolonial Africa*, New African Histories (Athens: Ohio University Press, 2010), 54–73. For Togo, see Suzanne Lallemand, *Adoption et Mariage: Les Kotokoli du centre du Togo*, Anthropologie—Connaissance des hommes (Paris: Éditions l'Harmattan, 1994).

18. Anthropological literature commonly describes what I am calling idiomatic kinship as "fictive" kinship, but I agree with Rhiannon Stephens's objections to using this terminology. I have preferred to use *idiomatic kinship* when referring to social bonds created among unrelated individuals that are as strong as any biological or affinal ones. In Dahomey, there is a rich history of such idiomatic bonds being important, including those ritualized with the ceremony of a blood pact. For more on this phenomenon, see Paul Hazoumé, *Le pacte de sang au Dahomey*. Travaux et mémoires de l'Institut d'ethnologie; 25 (Paris: Institut d'ethnologie, 1937). For a more detailed discussion and longer list of reasons, see Alber, *Transfers of Belonging*, 41–42. Alber, "Transfer of Belonging," 86. Some of Alber's points are not relevant for this time period, for example, attending school; other factors are simply not addressed in the sources, such as elder care.

19. Suzanne Lallemand, *La circulation des enfants en société traditionnelle: prêt, don, échange* (Paris: Editions L'Harmattan, 1993), 34.

20. Melville J. Herskovits, *Dahomey: An Ancient West African Kingdom*, vol. 1 (New York: J. J. Augustin, 1938), 275–76. For a more in-depth discussion of views of juvenile sexuality in the colony of Dahomey, see Jessica Reuther,

"Irresponsible Boys, Promiscuous Girls: Maturity, Gender, and Rape Myths in the Criminal Tribunals of Colonial Dahomey, 1924–1940," *La Revue d'histoire de l'enfance "irrégulière"* 20 (November 2018), https://journals.openedition.org/rhei/4209?lang=en.

21. For more on the sexual dimensions of slavery, see the entire collection *Sex, Power, and Slavery*, ed. Gwyn Campbell and Elizabeth Elbourne (Athens: Ohio University Press, 2014), 61–82, but, especially, Martin A. Klein, "Sexuality and Slavery in the Western Sudan."

22. Decker, "Feminist," 419–20.

23. In Dahomey, it was not until the mid-twentieth century that an individual's age or birthdate was considered to be an important identifying feature that needed to be preserved.

24. Rodet and Razy point out that childhood—and girlhood as a gendered subcategory within it—is multifaceted in that it is "a biological, age and social category, as well as a period of the life cycle, which is historically, socially and culturally constructed." See Rodet and Razy, "Introduction," 1. Here I show that the category was consistent; however, the historical, social, and cultural construction of the term varied.

25. Lynn M. Thomas, *Politics of the Womb: Women, Reproduction, and the State in Kenya* (Berkeley: University of California Press, 2003); Janice Patricia Boddy, *Civilizing Women: British Crusades in Colonial Sudan* (Princeton: Princeton University Press, 2007); Abosede A. George, *Making Modern Girls: A History of Girlhood, Labor, and Social Development in Colonial Lagos* (Athens: Ohio University Press, 2014); Saheed Aderinto, *When Sex Threatened the State: Illicit Sexuality, Nationalism, and Politics in Colonial Nigeria, 1900–1958* (Urbana: University of Illinois Press, 2015); Jessica Cammaert, *Undesirable Practices: Women, Children, and the Politics of the Body in Northern Ghana, 1930–1972* (Lincoln: University of Nebraska Press, 2016); Robin Phylisia Chapdelaine, *The Persistence of Slavery: An Economic History of Child Trafficking in Nigeria* (Amherst: University of Massachusetts Press, 2021).

26. Maria Lugones, "The Coloniality of Gender," in *The Palgrave Handbook of Gender and Development* (London: Palgrave Macmillan, 2016), 1–17.

27. Mona Etienne, "Maternité sociale, rapports d'adoption et pouvoir des femmes chez les Baoulé (Côte d'Ivoire)," *L'Homme* 19, nos. 3/4 (1979): 63–107; Caroline H. Bledsoe, *Women and Marriage in Kpelle Society* (Stanford: Stanford University Press, 1980); Goody, *Parenthood and Social Reproduction*; Lallemand, *La circulation des enfants*; Lallemand, *Adoption et mariage*.

28. Goody, *Parenthood and Social Reproduction*, 7–19. For Alber's commentary on Goody's contribution to the field, see Alber, "Transfer of Belonging," 80–89.

29. Lallemand, *La circulation des enfants*. Alber, "Transfer of Belonging," 89–90.

30. Alber, *Transfers of Belonging*, 35, 46.

31. Janet Carsten, "Introduction: Cultures of Relatedness," in *Cultures of Relatedness: New Approaches to the Study of Kinship*, ed. Janet Carsten (Cambridge: Cambridge University Press, 2000), 1–36. Tatjana Thelen and Erdmute Alber, "Reconnecting State and Kinship: Temporalities, Scales, Classifications," in *Reconnecting State and Kinship*, ed. Tatjana Thelen and Erdmute Alber (Philadelphia: University of Pennsylvania Press, 2018), 11–12.

32. Claude Meillassoux forcefully argues that the institutions of slavery and kinship "are strictly antinomic." Orlando Patterson's concept of social death similarly strips slaves of kinship through their natal alienation.

33. Anthony Reid, "'Closed' and 'Open' Slave Systems in Pre-Colonial Southeast Asia," in *Critical Readings on Global Slavery*, Critical Readings (Leiden: Brill, 2018), 1462.

34. Dahomeans attributed meaning to enslavement, both transatlantic and intra-African, as a fateful hardship through which some individuals emerged stronger and with unique attributes. Edna G. Bay, "Protection, Political Exile, and the Atlantic Slave Trade: History and Collective Memory in Dahomey," *Slavery & Abolition* 22, no. 1 (2001): 52, 56–58.

35. Kopytoff and Miers, "Introduction," 14.

36. Miller discusses enslaved persons in general seeking to construct belonging as a coping mechanism for their alienation; see Joseph C. Miller, "A Historical Appreciation of the Biographical Turn," in *Biography and the Black Atlantic*, ed. Lisa A. Lindsay and John Wood Sweet, The Early Modern Americas (Philadelphia: University of Pennsylvania Press, 2014), 33–35.

37. In the context of French Sudan (modern-day Mali), Emily Burrill makes a similar point that "slavery and kinship were bonds that tied." She points out that the two statuses, especially for women, were not necessarily antithetical to each other. Emily S. Burrill, *States of Marriage: Gender, Justice, and Rights in Colonial Mali* (Athens: Ohio University Press, 2015), 57.

38. Marshall Sahlins, "What Kinship Is (Part One)," *Journal of the Royal Anthropological Institute* 17, no. 1 (March 2011): 5–11. Sahlins makes this point about global kinship practices generally, not specifically, regarding the Gbe.

39. Thelen and Alber, "Reconnecting," 11–12. This point of the processual understanding of kinship is at the heart of the field of "new kinship studies." For more on this field, see Carsten, "Introduction." For ethnographic insights into the preeminence and importance of kinship not based on biology or consanguinity in Dahomey, see Hazoumé, *Le pacte de sang*.

40. Bay, *Wives*, 144.

41. Grier, "Child Labor and Africanist Scholarship," 7–8; Claire C. Robertson and Martin A. Klein, eds., *Women and Slavery in Africa* (Portsmouth, NH: Heinemann, 1997); Claire C. Robertson and Marsha Robinson, "Re-Modeling

Slavery As If Women Mattered," in *Women and Slavery: The Modern Atlantic*, vol. 2 (Athens: Ohio University Press, 2007), 253–83.

42. Fretwell, "'Domesticating the Unfamiliar': Afropolitan Dress in the West African Kingdom of Dahomey," *Radical History Review*, no. 144 (October 2022): 19–20.

43. Nupur Chaudhuri, Sherry J. Katz, and Mary Elizabeth Perry, "Introduction," in *Contesting Archives: Finding Women in the Sources*, ed. Nupur Chaudhuri, Sherry J. Katz, and Mary Elizabeth Perry (Urbana: University of Illinois Press, 2010), xiv–xv.

44. Luc Garcia, *Le royaume du Dahomé face à la pénétration coloniale: affrontements et incompréhension (1875–1894)* (Paris: Editions Karthala, 1988), 7.

45. Aderinto, "Introduction," 3.

46. This is not to say that European men did not interact with Dahomean women. Their cited primary informants were male. Marisa Fuentes makes a similar observation about slaveholders' power in determining the narratives preserved about the enslaved; see Marisa J. Fuentes, *Dispossessed Lives: Enslaved Women, Violence, and the Archive* (Philadelphia: University of Pennsylvania Press, 2016), 4–5.

47. Geary, *In and Out*, 16–17. Geary does not discuss this particular image but makes this more general point.

48. Cécile Fromont, *Images on a Mission in Early Modern Kongo and Angola* (University Park: Pennsylvania State University Press, 2022), 10.

49. Colleen E. Kriger, *Cloth in West African History* (Lanham, MD: AltaMira, 2006), 2.

50. Kristin Kastner, "Fashioning Dakar's Urban Society: Sartorial Code-Mixing in Senegal," *Sociologus* 69, no. 2 (2019): 167. Geary discusses how Africans recognized the importance of this sartorial language when they were the subjects of photographs, but it extended beyond this momentary display as well. Geary, *In and Out*, 85–86.

51. The fabric seller's position makes it difficult to determine if her legs are covered by loose trousers or a pagne. See d'Albéca, *La France au Dahomey*, 159.

52. Jean Allman, "Fashioning Africa: Power and the Politics of Dress," in *Fashioning Africa: Power and the Politics of Dress*, ed. Jean Allman (Bloomington: Indiana University Press, 2004), 1–2.

53. Kelly Mohs Gage makes a similar argument about the many purposes of cloth turbans worn by African women in Rio de Janeiro, Brazil. Her works repeatedly note that "Mina" women wore these intricate turbans. Kelly Mohs Gage, "Forced Crossing: The Dress of African Slave Women in Rio de Janeiro, Brazil, 1861," *Dress: The Journal of the Costume Society of America* 39, no. 2 (October 1, 2013): 111–33.

54. Kelly Mohs Gage, "Forced Crossing: The Dress of African Slave Women in Rio de Janeiro, Brazil, 1861," *Dress: The Journal of the Costume Society of America* 39, no. 2 (October 1, 2013): 123–24.

55. Patricia Hayes and Gary Minkley, "Introduction: Africa and the Ambivalence of Seeing," in *Ambivalent: Photography and Visibility in African History*, ed. Patricia Hayes and Gary Minkley, New African Histories (Athens: Ohio University Press, 2019), 3.

56. Patricia Hayes and Gary Minkley, *Ambivalent: Photography and Visibility in African History* (Athens: Ohio University Press, 2019), 2; Elizabeth Edwards, *Raw Histories: Photographs, Anthropology and Museums*, Materializing Culture (Oxford: Berg, 2001), 4.

57. Shawn Michelle Smith, "Introduction: First Photographs," in *At the Edge of Sight: Photography and the Unseen* (Raleigh, NC: Duke University Press, 2013), 4–7.

58. Patricia Hayes, "Empty Photographs: Ethnography and the Lacunae of African History," in *Ambivalent: Photography and Visibility in African History* (Athens: Ohio University Press, 2019), 61–62; Michel-Rolph Trouillot, *Silencing the Past: Power and Production of History* (Boston: Beacon, 1995), 26–27.

59. Bay, "Protection, Political Exile, and the Atlantic Slave Trade," 45. Marisa Fuentes's methodology of stretching fragments about the lives of enslaved women has influenced my own regarding entrusted girls. For a brief explanation of Fuentes's methodology, see Fuentes, *Dispossessed Lives*, 7–8.

60. Lisa A. Lindsay and John Wood Sweet, "Introduction: Biography and the Black Atlantic," in *Biography and the Black Atlantic*, ed. Lisa A. Lindsay and John Wood Sweet (Philadelphia: University of Pennsylvania Press, 2014), 15.

61. A similar point is made about the life stories of slaves in the Atlantic world and subaltern people more broadly. See ibid., 3–4.

62. Holding precolonial or early colonial African history to the same quantitative thresholds as research in other areas during different periods would bolster the Hegelian myth that Africa does not have history. Despite my exhaustive research of published travelogues, archives in four countries, and digitized archives, the information compiled for chapters 3 and 4 examines a few instances in the documentary record where female householders and runaway girls are mentioned. Andrej Svorenčik, "The Missing Link: Prosopography in the History of Economics," *History of Political Economy* 50, no. 3 (September 2018): 605–13.

63. Given unlimited time and funding, I would have liked to conduct further oral research on the individuals featured in chapters 3 and 4. I did triangulate the data as much as possible. When I conducted oral interviews in 2013–2014, I had not yet discovered the individuals on whom these chapters focus or decided to pursue a prosopographical approach.

1. The Value of Girls to the Royal Household of Dahomey, 1720s–1870s

1. Robin Law, "An Alternative Text of King Agaja of Dahomey's Letter to King George I of England, 1726," *History in Africa* 29 (2002): 264–68.

2. Scholars agree that Agaja's reign ended in 1740. The date of his accession to the throne, though, is debated with some sources giving 1708, 1716, or even 1718 as the beginning of his reign. Akinjogbin cites Dalzel as the earliest source that gave a specific date, and he designated 1708 as the beginning of Agaja's reign. I am not weighing in on the controversy. I. A. Akinjogbin, *Dahomey and Its Neighbours, 1708–1818* (Cambridge: Cambridge University Press, 1967), 39. "The King of Dahomy's Levée" by Francis Chesham, from Archibald Dalzel, *The History of Dahomy an Inland Kingdom of Africa; Compiled from Authentic Memoirs; with an Introduction and Notes* (London: T. Spilsbury and Son, 1793), Plate 1 on unnumbered page facing viii. For an alternative analysis of this image, see Roberto Zaugg, "The King's Chinese Spittoon: Global Commodities, Court Culture and Vodun in the Kingdoms of Hueda and Dahomey (Seventeenth to Nineteenth Centuries)," *Annales: Histoire, Sciences Sociales* 73, no. 1 (2018): 142–45.

3. I. A. Akinjogbin, "Archibald Dalzel: Slave Trader and Historian of Dahomey," *Journal of African History* 7, no. 1 (January 1, 1966): 70.

4. Jane I. Guyer and Samuel M. Eno Belinga, "Wealth in People as Wealth in Knowledge: Accumulation and Composition in Equatorial Africa," *The Journal of African History* 36, no. 1 (January 1, 1995): 92.

5. Jane I. Guyer, "Wealth in People and Self-Realization in Equatorial Africa," *Man*, New Series, 28, no. 2 (June 1993): 246.

6. Chesham's depiction included both Dalzel's and Snelgrave's influences; however, he chose to omit certain elements, such as the armed ahosi who acted as the king's bodyguard, even though Dalzel described these women as part of the monarch's ever-present entourage. Other than this notable omission, Chesham was faithful to Dalzel's detailed description of the ahosi.

7. Dalzel, *History of Dahomy*, xvii.

8. Ibid., 33–35. The man kissing the ground appeared much closer than twenty feet, and the seated European visitors even closer. Chesham foreshortened this distance for the scene's composition.

9. Bay, *Wives*, 11.

10. For a discussion of the long-standing and enduring association of tobacco smoking and the spittoon with the royalty of the region, see Zaugg, "The King's Chinese Spittoon."

11. Leslie Peirce makes a similar observation about proximity to the ruler in the Ottoman court: Leslie P. Peirce, *The Imperial Harem: Women and Sovereignty in the Ottoman Empire* (Oxford: Oxford University Press, 1993), 11.

12. Bay, *Wives*; Edna G. Bay, "Belief, Legitimacy and the Kpojito: An Institutional History of the 'Queen Mother' in Precolonial Dahomey," *Journal of African History* 36, no. 1 (January 1995): 1–27; Edna Bay, "Servitude and Worldly Success in the Palace of Dahomey," in *Women and Slavery in Africa*, ed. Claire C. Robertson and Martin A. Klein (Portsmouth, NH: Heinemann, 1983), 340–67; Suzanne Preston Blier, "The Path of the Leopard: Motherhood and Majesty in Early Danhomè," *Journal of African History* 36, no. 3 (1995): 391–417.

13. Law, "Alternative," 266.

14. The figure of two thousand ahosi would quadruple in the nineteenth century with a projected eight thousand ahosi housed within palace walls. The European visitors who cited these numbers for the palace failed to state if these figures included only adult women or if girls, slaves, or the female warriors known as *agojie*—who were also technically ahosi—were included as well. William Smith, *A New Voyage to Guinea* (London: Frank Cass, 1967), 183.

15. Ibid., 200–201. Barbot, *Barbot on Guinea*, vol. 2, Second Series no. 176 (Hakluyt Society, n.d.), 638.

16. Bay, *Wives*, 113–14.

17. Law, "Alternative," 266.

18. Not all ahosi entered the palace as girls. For example, the kpojito Hwanjile was an adult woman who had already given birth to two children and trained as a vodun priestess before she entered the palace. Bay, *Wives*, 91.

19. Robert Norris, *Memoirs of the Reign of Bossa Ahádee, King of Dahomy, an Inland Country of Guiney, to Which Are Added the Author's Journey to Abomey, the Capital, and a Short Account of the African Slave Trade*, 1st ed., new impression (London: Frank Cass, 1966). Norris wrote and published his memoirs explicitly as a defense of the slave trade in reaction to the rising abolitionist sentiment in Great Britain. Norris's shortcomings are well documented; see Robin Law, "The Slave-Trader as Historian: Robert Norris and the History of Dahomey," *History in Africa* 16 (1989): 223–24.

20. Édouard Dunglas published his history in two parts in different volumes of the *Études Dahoméennes*. Édouard Dunglas, "Contribution à l'histoire du Moyen-Dahomey: Royaumes d'Abomey, de Kétou et de Ouidah," *Études Dahoméennes* 19, no. 1 (1957): 17–185. and Édouard Dunglas, "Contribution à l'histoire Du Moyen-Dahomey: Royaumes d'Abomey, de Kétou et de Ouidah," *Études Dahoméennes* 20, no. 2 (1957): 3–152.

21. Bay, *Wives*, 35–37.

22. Zaugg similarly employs such an approach: Zaugg, "The King's Chinese Spittoon," 120.

23. A household could give a child to another family during a crisis and use the transfer to manage that emergency. Erdmute Alber, *Transfers of Belonging: Child Fostering in West Africa in the 20th Century* (Boston: Brill, 2018), 86.

24. I. A. Akinjogbin, "The Expansion of Oyo and the Rise of Dahomey, 1600–1800," in *History of West Africa*, ed. J. F. A. Ajayi and Michael Crowder, vol. 1 (New York: Columbia University Press, 1972), 313–14. Akinjogbin, *Dahomey*, 11–14.

25. For a discussion of the controversies surrounding the exact date, see Robin Law, *Ouidah: The Social History of a West African Slaving "Port," 1727–1892* (Athens: Ohio University Press, 2004), 20–25.

26. Robin Law, *The Slave Coast of West Africa, 1550–1750: The Impact of the Atlantic Slave Trade on an African Society* (Oxford: Oxford University Press, 1991), 225–60.

27. This was not unique to West Africa. In the East African Kingdom of Buganda, for example, princes' maternal kin raised children outside the king's palace. Rhiannon Stephens, *A History of African Motherhood: The Case of Uganda, 700–1900* (Cambridge: Cambridge University Press, 2013), 117–18.

28. Delbée, "Journal du voyage du Sieur Delbée, commissaire general de la marine, aux isles, dans la coste de Guynée, pour l'établissement du commerce en ces pays, en l'année 1669," in *Relation de ce qui s'est passé dans les Isles et terre-ferme de l'Amérique, pendant la dernière guerre avec l'Angleterre, et depuis en exécution du traitté de Breda*, by Jean de Clodoré (Paris: Chez Gervais Clozier, 1671), 443. Jean Baptiste Labat, *Voyage Du Chevalier Des Marchais En Guinée, Isles Voisines, et à Cayenne, Fait En 1725, 1726 & 1727* (Amsterdam: Aux dépens de la Compagnie, 1731), 260.

29. John K. Thornton, *A Cultural History of the Atlantic World, 1250–1820* (Cambridge: Cambridge University Press, 2012), 60, 212–13.

30. Tezifon is believed to have been born around 1600. This is based on Delbée's estimate that Tezifon was approximately seventy years old in 1670. Delbée, "Journal du voyage," 422.

31. Ray A. Kea, "From Catholicism to Moravian Pietism: The World of Marotta/Magdalena, a Woman of Popo and St. Thomas," in *The Creation of the British Atlantic World* (Baltimore: Johns Hopkins University Press, 2005), 118–19.

32. Akinjogbin, *Dahomey*, 28.

33. Other Africans during the early modern era did embrace Catholicism and converted to the global religion, such as Nzinga Mbemba, also known as Afonso I of the Kingdom of Kongo, and Dona Beatriz Kimpa Vita and her followers, due to their contact with Portugal and European missionaries. Cécile Fromont, *The Art of Conversion: Christian Visual Culture in the Kingdom of Kongo*, Omohundro Institute of Early American History and Culture (Chapel Hill: University of North Carolina Press, 2014); John K. Thornton, *The Kongolese Saint Anthony: Dona Beatriz Kimpa Vita and the Antonian Movement, 1684–1706* (Cambridge: Cambridge University Press, 1998).

34. Pernille Ipsen, *Daughters of the Trade: Atlantic Slavers and Interracial Marriage on the Gold Coast* (Philadelphia: University of Pennsylvania Press, 2014), 30–35.

35. Akinjogbin, *Dahomey*, 35–43.

36. Labat, *Voyage Du Chevalier*, 42–43.

37. Akinjogbin, *Dahomey*, 18.

38. Labat, *Voyage Du Chevalier*, 42.

39. Law notes that succession in the Kingdom of Hueda throughout this period was highly contested and never "wholly regular"; see Law, *Slave Coast*, 76–77. Sandra T. Barnes, "Gender and the Politics of Support and Protection in Precolonial West Africa," *Annals of the New York Academy of Sciences* 810, no. 1 (1997): 1–18.

40. This was common in the region throughout the precolonial era and continued to be practiced in the Kingdoms of Dahomey and Hogbonou (Porto-Novo) through the nineteenth century. See Bay, *Wives*, 88.

41. Ibid., 144.

42. William Bosman, *A New and Accurate Description of the Coast of Guinea: Divided into the Gold, the Slave, and the Ivory Coasts*, 4th English ed. (London: Frank Cass, 1967), 345.

43. Ibid., 345.

44. Martin Klein, "Sex, Power, and Family Life in the Harem: A Comparative Study," in *Women and Slavery: Africa, the Indian Ocean World, and the Medieval North Atlantic*, ed. Gwyn Campbell, Suzanne Miers, and Joseph C. Miller, vol. 1 (Athens: Ohio University Press, 2007), 70–71.

45. Each king maintained multiple palaces. The numbers varied. Bulfinch Lambe claimed that Agaja owned eleven palaces. See Smith, *New Voyage to Guinea*, 179.

46. Law, *Slave Coast*, 261; Blier, "Path of the Leopard," 391; Akinjogbin, *Dahomey*, 13.

47. Akinjogbin, *Dahomey*, 59.

48. Bosman, *New and Accurate Description*, 339; William Snelgrave, *A New Account of Some Parts of Guinea and the Slave-Trade* (London: James, John, and Paul Knapton, 1734), 65. Barbot, *Barbot on Guinea*, 638–41.

49. For more information on the sugar revolution, see B. W. Higman, "The Sugar Revolution," *Economic History Review* 53, no. 2 (2000): 213–36.

50. Bay, *Wives*, 41.

51. Bulfinch Lambe's letter is reproduced in full with an introduction and annotations. See Robin Law, "Further Light on Bulfinch Lambe and the 'Emperor of Pawpaw:' King Agaja of Dahomey's Letter to King George I of England, 1726," *History in Africa* 17 (1990): 217. Law also published an alternative translation; see Law, "Alternative."

52. Smith, *New Voyage to Guinea*, 200–1. Bosman, *New and Accurate Description*, 345. Reynaud Desmarchais claimed that the king of Hueda sold his wives specifically to Europeans. Labat, *Voyage Du Chevalier*, 82. J. A. Skertchly, *Dahomey as It Is: Being a Narrative of Eight Months' Residence in That Country...* (London: Chapman and Hall, 1874), 490–95.

53. These were the three primary grains of the era that women ground into flour. See Patrick Manning, *Slavery, Colonialism, and Economic Growth in Dahomey, 1640–1960* (Cambridge: Cambridge University Press, 1982), 72.

54. We know very little about the division of labor inside the palace because of restrictions placed on who could enter it. J. Monroe and Anneke Janzen, "The Dahomean Feast: Royal Women, Private Politics, and Culinary Practices in Atlantic West Africa," *African Archaeological Review* 31, no. 2 (June 2014): 308–9.

55. John Duncan, *Travels in Western Africa in 1845 & 1846: A Journey from Whydah, through the Kingdom of Dahomey, to Adofoodia, in the Interior*, vol. 1 (London: Richard Bentley, 1847), 257.

56. Hwetanu, or Huetanù, literally means the "yearly head business." Hwetanu was celebrated in order for the royal living to appease and propitiate the dead ancestors in Kutomé, "the land of the dead" or "the shadow world." In English, Hwetanu is often referred to as "Customs," and the French called it *Coutumes*, both cognates of the Fon term *Kutomé* in their respective languages. See Robin Law, "'My Head Belongs to the King': On the Political and Ritual Significance of Decapitation in Precolonial Dahomey," *Journal of African History* 30, no. 3 (January 1, 1989): 403. Note that Hwetanu, or Customs, took place annually, but on the death of a king, a more elaborate celebration called Grand Customs was held to complete the coronation of a successor. For a discussion of the distinction between the annual Customs and Grand Customs, see Catherine Coquery-Vidrovitch, "La Fête Des Coutumes Au Dahomey: Historique Et Essai D'interprétation," *Annales: Histoire, Sciences Sociales* 19, no. 4 (1964): 703.

57. Eleanor Aho Agoli-Agbo interview, February 19, 2014. Robin Law, "Human Sacrifice in Precolonial West Africa," *African Affairs* 84, no. 334 (January 1985): 75.

58. For more information on feasting at these annual rituals, see Monroe and Janzen, "Dahomean Feast." For a list of all eyewitness European accounts of Kutomé, see Coquery-Vidrovitch, "La Fête," 715–16.

59. Coquery-Vidrovitch, "La Fête," 696.

60. This is the task that the ahosi in the right-hand edge of Chesham's image were performing. Duncan, *Travels*, 1:257; Archibald R. Ridgway, "Journal of a Visit to Dahomey; or, the Snake Country," *New Monthly Magazine* 81, no. 3 (1847): 305.

61. Heidi Nast, *Concubines and Power Five Hundred Years in a Northern Nigerian Palace* (Minneapolis: University of Minnesota Press, 2005), 17.

62. Akinjogbin, *Dahomey*, 107–11. Law, *Slave Coast*, 325–26.

63. Law, "Slave-Trader as Historian," 225–26.

64. Robin Law, "Ideologies of Royal Power: The Dissolution and Reconstruction of Political Authority on the 'Slave Coast,' 1680–1750," *Africa: Journal of the International African Institute* 57, no. 3 (1987): 322–23.

65. Bay, *Wives*, 70.

66. Lorelle D. Semley, *Mother Is Gold, Father Is Glass: Gender and Colonialism in a Yoruba Town* (Bloomington: Indiana University Press, 2011), 43.

67. Dahomey was not unique in this regard among West African states. As Heidi Nast has shown, Kano similarly recognized children's value to the political economy; see Nast, *Concubines*, 41.

68. Norris was undeniably a racist, which affected his observations and interpretations of events. This portrayal supported Norris's proslavery propaganda. Norris, along with Snelgrave and Dalzel, developed the narrative that justified the transatlantic slave trade as a better, more humane alternative to living in the despotic kingdom. Bay, *Wives*, 29–30. Law, *Slave Coast*, 1–2. Tegbesu infamously engaged in a reign of terror whereby no official was safe from arbitrary execution or forced exile. Akinjogbin, *Dahomey*, 120–21.

69. Law, "Slave-Trader as Historian," 219.

70. Bay, *Wives*, 124. Law, "My Head Belongs to the King."

71. For a more in-depth discussion of the complexities of this expression and its political and ritual ramifications, see Law, "My Head Belongs to the King."

72. Norris, *Memoirs of the Reign*, 88.

73. Ibid., 88–89.

74. Bay observes that in the precolonial period, ownership of this type of wealth was viewed as wrong or despotic, but it becomes laudatory after the colonial conquest. Bay, *Wives*, 31–32.

75. Édouard Dunglas, "Contribution à l'histoire Du Moyen-Dahomey: Royaumes d'Abomey, de Kétou et de Ouidah," *Études Dahoméennes* 20, no. 2 (1957): 3–4. Dunglas admits that this "curious" tradition is not unanimously accepted. Some scholars, such as Akinjogbin, dismiss this detail of royal tradition as "curious" and a case of misattribution; others, such as Bay, give it more credence. Akinjogbin, *Dahomey*, 62; Bay, *Wives*, 160.

76. It is possible that this actually refers to the children of his six designated wives who could produce heirs. Three to four, however, does seem unusually low. Even Behanzin was reputed to have sixty children despite the challenges he faced; see Auguste Le Hérissé, *L'ancien Royaume Du Dahomey, Moeurs, Religion, Histoire*, 1911, 35.

77. Dunglas, "Moyen Dahomey," 3–4.

78. For more on the office of vidaho, see Maurice A. Glélé, *Le Danxomẹ: du pouvoir Aja à la nation Fon* (Paris: Nubia, 1974), 85–106.

79. Akinjogbin collapsed the alleged two distinct vidahos of Tegbesu into one person: Junipera/Gnansonou (reign name Kpengla). Akinjogbin, *Dahomey*, 117.

80. Dunglas, "Moyen Dahomey," 180.

81. Norris makes this statement twice word for word. Norris, *Memoirs of the Reign*, 89, 158.

82. Ibid., 4. There exists no data from the eighteenth century to speculate on a normal age for child transfers at the time. Later examples of child circulation do support the norm of children leaving their natal homes as young as three. This is based on ages given in twentieth-century documents in Series 1M of the Archives Nationales du Bénin. Oral tradition later asserted that girls left their natal homes between seven and nine years old as the estimated norm.

83. Norris, *Memoirs of the Reign*, 88–89.

84. Snelgrave, *New Account*, 78. Note that Snelgrave has irregular pagination, and there are two pages numbered 78.

85. Ibid., 31–35.

86. Ibid., 90–92. The date of the establishment of Dahomey's tributary status is disputed. Akinjogbin citing Brathwaite dates it to 1730. Some scholars, such as Asiwaju, state that Dahomey's tributary status commenced in 1748. A. I. Asiwaju, "Dahomey, Yorubaland, Borgu and Benin in the Nineteenth Century," in *General History of Africa*, vol. 6: Africa in the Nineteenth Century until the 1880s (Berkeley: University of California Press, 1989), 704.

87. The dates of when Dahomey initiated and terminated its payments to Oyo are disputed. Asiwaju, "Dahomey," 704, 709–10.

88. Bay, *Wives*, 137.

89. All three died under mysterious circumstances. Kpengla died of "smallpox," a term that could signify any misfortune and might have referred to the loss of his legitimacy rather than an actual illness. Elisée A. Soumonni, "Disease, Religion and Medicine: Smallpox in Nineteenth-Century Benin," *História, Ciências, Saúde—Manguinhos* 19 (December 2012): 35–45. Agonglo was either assassinated by an armed palace woman or poisoned by a coalition that included Prince Dogan and a royal woman. An outline of the controversy is presented in Ana Lucia Araujo, "Dahomey, Portugal and Bahia: King Adandozan and the Atlantic Slave Trade," *Slavery & Abolition* 33, no. 1 (March 2012): 5.

90. Akinjogbin, *Dahomey*, 195.

91. France left its fort vacant in 1797 due to the cataclysmic effects of the French and Haitian Revolutions. Great Britain followed suit in 1812 for different reasons. By this point, Great Britain attempted to reformulate its international agenda based around an abolitionist agenda. Brazilians continued to occupy Portugal's fort and engaged in continuing slave trading.

92. Akinjogbin, *Dahomey*, 187–88.

93. It is unclear whether Labarthe observed this collection himself or if he relied on any of the memoirs of the French naval officers who visited the region in 1784–1790. For a full list of the memoirs he might have consulted, see viii–ix in the "Avertissement" written in the front matter of Labarthe. He does not cite Norris. Pierre Labarthe, *Voyage à La Côte de Guinée, Ou Descriptions Des Côtes d'Afrique Depuis Le Cap Tagrin Jusqu'au ca de Lopez-Gonzalves* (Paris: Chez DeBray, 1803), 117. There were culturally constructed limits on the king's viable options for Dahomean subjects. Only convicted criminals could be sold into the transatlantic trade, but it is well documented that the king used spurious criminal convictions as a tool to dispose of political rivals and ideological challengers. For an example of the sale of ideological threat, see James H. Sweet, *Domingos Álvares, African Healing, and the Intellectual History of the Atlantic World* (Chapel Hill: University of North Carolina Press, 2011).

94. Labarthe, *Voyage*, 120.

95. Antoine Edme Pruneau de Pommegorge, *Description de la nigritie* (Amsterdam: Chez Maradan, 1789), 165–66. Stanley B. Alpern, *Abson and Company: Slave Traders in Eighteenth-Century West Africa* (London: Hurst, 2019), 97.

96. Dalzel, *History of Dahomy*, 47.

97. Duncan, *Travels*, 1:231. Duncan estimates eight thousand. Ridgway, "Journal," 304. Just a few years earlier, Ridgway estimated four thousand to five thousand female guards. Fraser estimated five thousand in 1851–1852. In 1862, Enschott gave the highest estimate at ten thousand. For a table of these figures indicating the source of the estimate, see endnote 20 in Hélène d'Almeida-Topor, *Les amazones: Une armée de femmes dans l'Afrique précoloniale* (Paris: Rochevignes, 1984), 174.

98. Auguste Bouët, "Le Royaume de Dahomey: Relation Du Voyage de M. Le Lieutenant de Vaisseau Auguste Bouët, Envoyé En Mission Près Du Roi Du Dahomey, En Mai 1851," *L'Illustration, Journel Universel*, July 17, 1852, 42, July 24, 1852, and July 31, 1852.

99. Frederick Edwyn Forbes, *Dahomey and the Dahomans: Being the Journals of Two Missions of the King of Dahomey . . . in the Years 1849 and 1850*, vol. 2 (London: Longman, 1851), 115.

100. Bouët, "Le Royaume."

101. Skertchly, *Dahomey*, 454–55.

102. Ibid.

103. Bouët, "Le Royaume," 60. Repin reiterates Bouet's point that the agojie recruits are selected from elite families. Pierre-Clément Repin, "Voyage au Dahomey," *Le Tour du monde: nouveau journal des voyages* 7, first semester (1863): 92.

104. Forbes, *Dahomey*, 2:118.

105. A. Vallon, "Le Royaume de Dahomey: Côtes occidentales d'Afrique," *Revue Maritime et Coloniale* 2 (August 1861): 347.

106. Forbes, *Dahomey*, 2:113.

107. A. Vallon, "Le Royaume de Dahomey: Voyage à Abomey," *Revue Maritime et Coloniale* 3 (October 1861): 349.

108. Vallon, "Côtes," 351. Elisée Soumonni, "Disease, Religion and Medicine: Smallpox in Nineteenth-Century Benin," *História, Ciências, Saúde—Manguinhos* 19, no. suppl. 1 (December 2012): 39–40. Glèlè's agojie troops, like that of his father Gezo, suffered serious losses during a subsequent attack on Abeokuta in 1864. Borghero describes the attack based on informants' recollections and the preserved battleground strewn with bones two months after the March 1864 attack. Francesco Borghero, *Journal du premier missionnaire du Dahomey, 1860–1864*, ed. Renzo Mandirola (Monee, IL: SMA, 2018), 301–3.

109. d'Almeida-Topor, *Les amazones*, 39.

110. Richard Francis Burton, *A Mission to Gelele, King of Dahome: With Notices of the So Called*, vol. 2 (London: Tinsley Brothers, 1864), 45.

111. P. Chautard, *Le Dahomey* (Lyon: Librairie Emmanuel Vitte, 1890), 9–10.

112. Vallon, "Côtes," 345–46; Skertchly, *Dahomey*, 457.

113. Richard Francis Burton, *A Mission to Gelele, King of Dahome: With Notices of the So Called*, vol. 1 (London: Tinsley Brothers, 1864), 169. There did not seem to be a set number of recruits each year. The palace's fluctuating needs determined both the frequency and number of girls conscripted.

114. Repin, "Le Tour du monde," 92–93.

115. Ibid., 92. By the nineteenth century, there were few elephants remaining in the kingdom, and the king's prohibition of its importation indicated that it was a prestige commodity.

116. Burton distinguishes young girls as those with "nude bosom." Burton, *Mission to Gelele*, 2:11. Robin Law, ed., *Dahomey and the Ending of the Trans-Atlantic Slave Trade: The Journals and Correspondence of Vice-Consul Louis Fraser, 1851–1852*, Fontes Historiae Africanae 10 (Oxford: Oxford University Press, 2012), 56.

117. Burton, *Mission to Gelele*, 2:164.

118. Ibid., 2:260.

119. Skertchly, *Dahomey*, 448. Burton, *Mission to Gelele*, 2:52.

120. Ibid., 2:259.

121. Ibid., 2:165 & 259. Freed immigrant communities also produced agricultural products. Later visitors confirm the continuation of this practice of reserving agricultural labor for slaves. Alexandre L. d'Albéca, *La France au Dahomey* (Paris: Hachette, 1895), 121. Sweeping was also an occupation reserved for the enslaved; Skertchly, *Dahomey*, 401. Agojie did act as porters to carry palm oil to the coast.

122. Law, *Beecroft's Journal*, 143.

123. Burton, *Mission to Gelele*, 1:226.

124. Burton, *Mission to Gelele*, 2:260–61.

125. The king staffed multiple palaces in this region. Skertchly, *Dahomey*, 110, 457.

126. Law, *Dahomey and the Ending*, 56.

127. Burton, *Mission to Gelele*, 1:127.

128. Ibid., 159–60. Law, *Dahomey and the Ending*, 54, 198. In 1871, Skertchly said this was no longer an agojie monopoly. Skertchly, *Dahomey*, 25, 85, & 271.

129. Peter Morton-Williams, "A Yoruba Woman Remembers Servitude in a Palace of Dahomey, in the Reigns of Kings Glele and Behanzin," *Africa: Journal of the International African Institute* 63, no. 1 (1993): 111.

130. Skertchly, *Dahomey*, 293. The Yemadje family of male tailors took up the appliqué arts during the reign of King Agonglo (1789–1797). There is no clear division between the Yemadje's appliqué work and the agojie's work. Blier says that the Yemadje family "are credited with adding motifs in cloth to royal parasols, hammocks, and cushions" as well as sewing the *tokpon* tent. Suzanne Preston Blier, *The Royal Arts of Africa: The Majesty of Form* (New York: Harry N. Abrams, 1998), 119–20.

131. Skertchly, *Dahomey*, 178–299. Skertchly devotes four chapters of his text to describing the So-sin ceremonies in detail. For more on the differences of So-sin and Attoh, see Edna Bay, "On the Trail of the Bush King: A Dahomean Lesson in the Use of Evidence," *History in Africa* 6 (1979): 1–15.

132. While no other European visitors credited agojie with producing royal appliqué arts and scholars today attribute the craft to the Yemadje artisan workshop, Skertchly, due to the length of his sojourn and Glèlè's reputed fondness for him, was given greater access to the operations of the royal palace than other visitors. Skertchly, *Dahomey*, 189. Skertchly was remembered fondly in oral histories, unlike other visitors, such as Richard Burton. Glèlè's affection for Skertchly led to make him a prince. Bay, *Wives*, 31.

133. Bay, *Wives*, 145–46.

134. Ibid., 118.

135. A similar observation about the Ottoman harem and its relationship to other Ottoman households was made by Leslie Peirce; see Leslie P. Peirce, *The Imperial Harem: Women and Sovereignty in the Ottoman Empire* (Oxford: Oxford University Press, 1993), 6–7.

136. Bay, *Wives*, 145–46.

137. Patrick Manning, *Slavery and African Life* (Cambridge: Cambridge University Press, 1990), 67–68; Bay, *Wives*, 146.

2. Dashing and Entrusting Girls

1. The term *dash* likely came from the Portuguese *dação* or *das me*. It has also been suggested that the word has common origins in Portuguese and Fanti.

See footnote 47 in Christina Brauner, "Connecting Things: Trading Companies and Diplomatic Gift-Giving on the Gold and Slave Coasts in the Seventeenth and Eighteenth Centuries," *Journal of Early Modern History* 20 (2016): 421. Enrique Martino, "Dash-Peonage: The Contradictions of Debt Bondage in the Colonial Plantations of Fernando Pó," *Africa* 87, no. 1 (February 2017): 54.

2. For more information on gift giving and Atlantic trade, see Ana Lucia Araujo, *The Gift: How Objects of Prestige Shaped the Atlantic Slave Trade and Colonialism* (Cambridge: Cambridge University Press, 2024).

3. For a discussion on power imbalances in gift exchanges along the Slave Coast during the seventeenth and eighteenth centuries, see Brauner, "Connecting Things." The king often gave favored subjects one or two captive females at Hwetanu to make the bestowing a conspicuous act of royal largesse. Blanchely, "Au Dahomey: Relation Du Deuxième Voyage Fait En 1850, Dans Le Royaume Du Dahomey, Par M. Blanchely Aîné, En Compagnie de M. Esprit Cases, Nouvel Agent de La Factorerie Française Régis Aîné, de Whydah," *Les Missions Catholiques* 23 (January–December 1891): 576.

4. While all European-authored documents give her name as Sarah Bonetta Forbes, she signed her marriage certificate with Àìná, a Yorùbá name, before her Anglicized name. Isis Davis-Marks, "The Little-Known Story of Queen Victoria's Black Goddaughter," *Smithsonian Magazine*, October 8, 2020, https://www.smithsonianmag.com/smart-news/english-heritage-presents-portrait-queen-victorias-black-goddaughter-180976008/. For more on Yorùbá naming practices, see Samuel Johnson, *The History of the Yorubas from the Earliest Times to the Beginning of the British Protectorate*, repr. (London: Forgotten Books, 2012), 79; Abosede A. George, *Making Modern Girls: A History of Girlhood, Labor, and Social Development in Colonial Lagos* (Athens: Ohio University Press, 2014), 1–2. Johnson states that girls are named on the seventh day. George says the naming ceremony takes place on the eighth day, which, according to Johnson, is reserved for twins of both sexes.

5. This information is derived from an online search for the meaning of the name. https://www.Yorùbáname.com/entries/A%CC%80i%CC%80na%CD%81.

6. J. A. Skertchly, *Dahomey as It Is: Being a Narrative of Eight Months' Residence in That Country* . . . (London: Chapman and Hall, 1874), 156.

7. Robin Law, *Consul John Beecroft's Journal of His Mission to Dahomey, 1850*, Fontes Historiae Africanae 17 (Oxford: Oxford University Press, 2019), 195. Forbes omitted this detail in his published account. Robin Law has included "Lieutenant Forbes' Journal" in the appendices of Consul Beecroft's journal.

8. For a discussion of the significance of human gift-giving interpreted through a gendered lens, see Gayle S. Rubin, "The Traffic in Women: Notes on

the 'Political Economy' of Sex," in *Deviations: A Gayle Rubin Reader* (Durham, NC: Duke University Press, 2011), 42–47.

9. The British Slave Trade Act of 1807 did not have a profound or immediate effect on the export trade from Dahomey. All Portuguese trade at Ouidah stopped briefly in 1807–1810. Then, in an about-face, the 1810 Anglo-Portuguese Treaty allowed slave trading at Ouidah to continue, but at neighboring ports, such as Porto-Novo, Badagry, Little Popo, and Lagos, the British squadron suppressed trade by seizing ships. Portuguese ships trading at Ouidah were unmolested. The Equipment Act of 1839 exerted much more influence on the trade in human cargo; however, trade continued sporadically throughout the 1850s. For a discussion of the effects of the Equipment Act of 1839 on the western Slave Coast, see Silke Strickrodt, *Afro-European Trade in the Atlantic World: The Western Slave Coast, c. 1550–c. 1885*, Western Africa Series (Suffolk, UK: James Currey, 2015), 197–210.

10. I. A. Akinjogbin, *Dahomey and Its Neighbours, 1708–1818* (Cambridge: Cambridge University Press, 1967), 190–95.

11. Akinwumi Ogundiran, *The Yorùbá: A New History* (Bloomington: Indiana University Press, 2020), 357–58; Paul E. Lovejoy, *Transformations in Slavery: A History of Slavery in Africa*, 2nd ed. (Cambridge: Cambridge University Press, 2000), 145.

12. Lovejoy, *Transformations in Slavery*, 141.

13. Richard L. Roberts, "The End of Slavery, 'Crises' over Trafficking, and the Colonial State in the French Soudan," in *Trafficking in Slavery's Wake: Law and the Experience of Women and Children in Africa*, ed. Benjamin N. Lawrance and Richard L. Roberts (Athens: Ohio University Press, 2012), 65. Lovejoy, *Transformations in Slavery*, 160–84.

14. The Saro diaspora from Sierra Leone spread throughout the Atlantic littoral of West Africa. Sierra Leoneans quickly found the absolutism of the Dahomean monarchy and the hostility of the Afro-Brazilian community of Ouidah to be incommodious to their nascent community. The Mahi captive diaspora had less of an impact on Dahomean society and culture, according to the scant existing documentation.

15. Edna G. Bay, *Wives of the Leopard: Gender, Politics, and Culture in the Kingdom of Dahomey* (Charlottesville: University of Virginia Press, 1998), 188.

16. For an overview of slavery in Dahomey in the nineteenth century, see Lovejoy, *Transformations in Slavery*, 176–82.

17. For more information on the lack of evidence and absence of Europeans, see Robin Law, *Ouidah: The Social History of a West African Slaving "Port," 1727–1892* (Athens: Ohio University Press, 2004), 7. The lack of European documentation of life in the Kingdom of Dahomey was further affected by the fact that after

a successful coup in 1818, King Gezo expunged his brother Adandozan from the oral history and changed the history of the kingdom during the years of Adandozan's reign from 1797 to 1818. For more on the coup and the rewriting of history to erase Adandozan, see Akinjogbin, *Dahomey*, 199–201; Elisée Soumonni, "The Compatibility of the Slave and Palm Oil Trades in Dahomey, 1818–1858," in *From Slave Trade to "Legitimate" Commerce: The Commercial Transition in Nineteenth-Century West Africa*, ed. Robin Law (Cambridge: Cambridge University Press, 1995), 79–81; Bay, *Wives*, 171–76; J. Cameron Monroe, *The Precolonial State in West Africa: Building Power in Dahomey* (New York: Cambridge University Press, 2014), 87–89.

18. Oral tradition insists that this was common, but there are no records that shed further light on this phenomenon.

19. Rosalind Shaw, *Memories of the Slave Trade: Ritual and the Historical Imagination in Sierra Leone* (Chicago: University of Chicago Press, 2002), 20–21.

20. Since at least the 1770s and perhaps earlier, the Òyó Empire protected the Kingdom of Hogbonou. This allegiance prevented Dahomean expansion east of the Weme River, a jointly beneficial arrangement for Hogbonou and Òyó. Robin Law, *The Ọyọ Empire, c. 1600–c. 1836 a West African Imperialism in the Era of the Atlantic Slave Trade* (Oxford: Clarendon, 1977), 175–76. Law gives the later date of the 1770s, whereas Akinjogbin asserts that Òyó involvement in the area of Hogbonou began as early as the 1730s. Akinjogbin, *Dahomey*, 91–92.

21. Law, *The Ọyọ Empire*, 268–73.

22. Bay, *Wives*, 230.

23. Unfortunately, there are no estimates of the number of Yorùbá migrants. Bay simply describes the volume as "massive." Ibid., 188.

24. Lovejoy, *Transformations in Slavery*, 177.

25. Frederick Edwyn Forbes, *Dahomey and the Dahomans: Being the Journals of Two Missions of the King of Dahomey . . . in the Years 1849 and 1850*, vol. 1 (London: Longman, 1851), 14.

26. Bay, *Wives*, 94–95, 110–18.

27. Archibald Dalzel, *The History of Dahomy an Inland Kingdom of Africa; Compiled from Authentic Memoirs; with an Introduction and Notes* (London: T. Spilsbury and Son, 1793), 112.

28. Jean Daniel, *Le palmier à huile au Dahomey*, Revue Coloniale (Paris: Librarie Maritime et Coloniale, 1902), 18.

29. European sources variously call this village Leflefun, as Burton called it, or Lefu Lefu, as Forbes called it. Richard Francis Burton, *A Mission to Gelele, King of Dahome: With Notices of the So Called*, vol. 1 (London: Tinsley Brothers, 1864), 190–91. Forbes, *Dahomey*, 1:31, 68. Leflefun was just one of these villages of resettled enslaved communities. After the French conquest, Le Hérissé recorded

the names of six others. Auguste Le Hérissé, *L'ancien Royaume Du Dahomey, Moeurs, Religion, Histoire*, 1911, 52. See also Bay, *Wives*, 188–189.

30. Law, *Ouidah*, 209, 224–25.

31. Burton, *Mission*, 1:187. Auguste Bouët, "Le Royaume de Dahomey: Relation Du Voyage de M. Le Lieutenant de Vaisseau Auguste Bouët, Envoyé En Mission Près Du Roi Du Dahomey, En Mai 1851," *L'Illustration, Journel Universel*, July 17, 1852, 42.

32. Boniface I. Obichere, "Women and Slavery in the Kingdom of Dahomey," *Revue Française d'histoire d'outre mer* 65, no. 1 (1978): 7.

33. Ibid., 7.

34. Other ethnic groups were victims of Dahomean predations, but the continuous integration of large numbers of Yorùbá throughout much of the nineteenth century set them apart from the other communities. Another distinguishing factor was that notable elite Yorùbá could provide support to ambitious and fortunate members of this community. Alexandre L. d' Albéca, *La France au Dahomey* (Paris: Hachette, 1895), 193.

35. Many scholars who relied on members of the royal family as informants claim that glési were not slaves. After a careful review of the earliest primary sources that mention glési, I disagree because their servile status was inherited, and they had no freedom of movement. Glési was the only category of enslaved people that resembled certain elements of chattel slavery and diverged from the tradition of social mobility in an "open" slave society. During the 1970s, the Glèlè branch of the royal family denied that glési were ever enslaved, but primary sources lead me to believe that, during the nineteenth century, glési were enslaved individuals or marginal individuals descended from enslaved persons. For a list of Fon terms for various enslaved individuals, see Obichere, "Women and Slavery in the Kingdom of Dahomey," 7. Note that Obichere does not include glési in his list, as his citations indicate that he agrees with Maurice Ahanhanzo Glélé; see Maurice A. Glélé, *Le Danxomę: du pouvoir Aja à la nation Fon* (Paris: Nubia, 1974), 156–57.

36. There were many words to describe slaves in Fon, but the term *glési* was first recorded by Auguste Le Hérissé during the early twentieth century, indicating a relatively recent provenance of this status. Le Hérissé, *L'ancien Royaume*, 57. Bay, *Wives*, 191.

37. d'Albéca, *La France au Dahomey*, 121. Glélé, *Le Danxomę*, 156–57.

38. Brauner, "Connecting Things," 422.

39. Burton, *Mission*, 1:217.

40. Marcel Mauss, *The Gift: Expanded Edition*, trans. Jane I. Guyer (Chicago: Hau Books, 2016), 57–58.

41. Robin Law, ed., *Dahomey and the Ending of the Trans-Atlantic Slave Trade: The Journals and Correspondence of Vice-Consul Louis Fraser, 1851–1852*, Fontes Historiae Africanae 10 (Oxford: Oxford University Press, 2012), 68.

42. Burton, *Mission*, 1:57.

43. Burton, *Mission*, 2:244. In his letter, Commander Wilmot confirmed that he identified captives' origins in this manner.

44. For analyses of Yorùbá scarification and its significance, see Lisa A. Lindsay, "Remembering His Country Marks: A Nigerian American Family and Its 'African' Ancestor," in *Biography and the Black Atlantic* (Philadelphia: University of Pennsylvania Press, 2014), 192–208. Olatunji Ojo, "Beyond Diversity: Women, Scarification and Yoruba Identity," *History in Africa* 35 (2008): 347–74.

45. Skertchly, *Dahomey*, 488; Pierre Bouche, *Sept Ans En Afrique Occidentale: La Côte Des Esclaves et Le Dahomey* (Paris: Librarie Plon, 1885), 26–28.

46. For example, in the 1820s, Yorùbá speakers in Sierra Leone were given the ethnic identity of "Aku," an onomatopoeic term derived from the common Yorùbá greeting of *e ku*. Bouche, *Sept Ans*, 77; Robin Law, "Ethnicity and the Slave Trade: 'Lucumi' and 'Nago' as Ethnonyms in West Africa," *History in Africa* 24 (1997): 206. Patrick Manning, *Slavery, Colonialism, and Economic Growth in Dahomey, 1640–1960* (Cambridge: Cambridge University Press, 1982), 48.

47. The literature on the British involvement in the abolition of the slave trade is voluminous. Some scholarly works that discuss the efforts to abolish slavery in precolonial Africa include Suzanne Miers, "Slavery and the Slave Trade as International Issues 1890–1939," in *Slavery and Colonial Rule in Africa*, Slave and Post-Slave Societies and Cultures 8 (Routledge: Frank Cass, 1999), 16–37; Kevin Grant, *A Civilised Savagery: Britain and the New Slaveries in Africa, 1884–1926* (New York: Routledge, 2005); Sandra E. Greene, "Modern 'Trokosi' and the 1807 Abolition in Ghana: Connecting Past and Present," *William and Mary Quarterly* 66, no. 4 (2009): 959–74.

48. Rhiannon Stephens, *A History of African Motherhood: The Case of Uganda, 700–1900* (Cambridge: Cambridge University Press, 2013), 25–26.

49. Law points out in the introduction that one of the unique elements of Fraser's journal was his acknowledgment of African interpreters. Law, *Dahomey and the Ending*, 16, 33.

50. Madiki was also sometimes referred to as Mark. After the British abandonment of the William's Fort in Ouidah in 1810, the king of Dahomey continued to appoint an English governor to the fort.

51. Interpreters were known for taken liberties with translations in order to keep all parties involved happy. Bouche, *Sept Ans*, 68–69.

52. Before his participation in Fraser's mission, Lemon served Freeman in 1843, Forbes in 1849, and Forbes and Beecroft in 1850. Robin Law, "The English Interpreters in Dahomey, 1843–1852," *Journal of Imperial and Commonwealth History* 44, no. 5 (2016): 731–33.

53. The transatlantic slave exports continued until 1863. Law, *Dahomey and the Ending*, 2.

54. Burton, *Mission to Gelele*, 2:133.

55. Ibid., 2:251.

56. For a brief biography of Freeman, see Boston University, ed., "Freeman, Thomas Birch (1809–1890): British Methodist Missionary to West Africa," in *The History of Missiology* (Boston: School of Theology, Boston University, n.d.), accessed October 3, 2020. https://www.bu.edu/missiology/missionary-biography/e-f/freeman-thomas-birch-1809-1890/#:~:text=Freeman%20was%20born%20in%20Twyford,because%20of%20his%20Methodist%20activism.

57. Burton, *Mission*, 1:80.

58. Ibid., 1:81; Burton, *Mission*, 2:194.

59. Skertchly, *Dahomey*, 305. Skertchly would leave these four girls and four male Mahi captives dashed to him in their natal region as he traveled. Glèlè subsequently gave Skertchly three more slave girls and three more slave boys; see ibid., 433.

60. The idiom of *entrustment* can be found, for example, in Benin, Côte d'Ivoire, and Kenya. Mathias Deshusses, "Du confiage à l'esclavage 'Petites bonnes' ivoiriennes en France (The 'Misfortunes' of Fosterage in France: The Case of 'Little Maids' from the Ivory Coast)," *Cahiers d'Études Africaines* 45, nos. 179/180 (January 1, 2005): 731–50; Parker MacDonald Shipton, *The Nature of Entrustment: Intimacy, Exchange, and the Sacred in Africa*, Yale Agrarian Studies (New Haven, CT: Yale University Press, 2007).

61. Shipton, *Nature of Entrustment*, 81–91.

62. Thomas B. Freeman, *Journal of Various Visits to the Kingdoms of Ashanti, Aku and Dahomi, in Western Africa*, 2nd ed. (London: John Mason, 1844), 273. This seems to be the final occurrence when gifted girls are described as slaves.

63. This definition comes from https://www.wordreference.com/definition/presents.

64. Freeman, *Journal of Various Visits*, 273. Ridgway, who accompanied Freeman, only mentions the gifts of slave girls, not the children entrusted for education. Archibald R. Ridgway, "Journal of a Visit to Dahomey; or, the Snake Country," *New Monthly Magazine* 81, no. 3 (1847): 410–11.

65. This definition comes from https://www.wordreference.com/definition/placing.

66. Unfortunately, no European recorded the Fon terms used at this time for these different statuses. Historians could speculate that an entrusted child was vidomégòn because of the co-occurrence of "placed in the care of" in the European accounts. Contemporary Beninese do not recall a Fon term equivalent to *entrusted child*. The closest term they acknowledge is *vidomégòn*, but they deny that precolonial practices resembled the contemporary one. This term is highly politicized in the contemporary moment and condemned as exploitative.

Beninese do not equate historical forms of child circulation with vidomégòn. When speaking historically, Beninese insisted on using the French phrase *enfant confié(e)*. Hospice Hounyoton, a Beninese social scientist, defines *vidomégòn* "as a social, ancestral and cultural practice consisting for a parent, a clan, a tribe or a family in *entrusting or placing* a child under the custody of a person other than his own parents. It is a kind of externalization of the child's education." For a more detailed, albeit historically vague, discussion of the origin of the term *vidomégòn*, see Hospice Hounyoton, "Child Slaves: The Case of Vidomegon Children in Benin," in *Child Exploitation in the Global South*, ed. J. Ballet and A. Bhukuth (London: Palgrave Macmillan, 2019), 173–201.

67. They came from Gezo's household, but it is unclear if they were biologically related to him. These also could have been *sou dofi*, or captive children, raised in the palace and fully socialized into Fon society. Freeman, *Journal of Various Visits*, 273. For more information about the category of *sou dofi*, see Hélène d'Almeida-Topor, *Les amazones: Une armée de femmes dans l'Afrique précoloniale* (Paris: Rochevignes, 1984), 51.

68. Law, *Beecroft's Journal*, 151.

69. Pierre-Clément Repin, "Voyage au Dahomey," *Le Tour du monde: nouveau journal des voyages* 7, first semester (1863): 66.

70. A. Vallon, "Le Royaume de Dahomey: Voyage à Abomey," *Revue Maritime et Coloniale* 3, no. October (1861): 353.

71. Ibid., 356. For a less detailed account of the same events, see Repin, "Le Tour du monde," 95. Repin does not use the term *entrusted*.

72. Law, *Beecroft's Journal*, 125–26. Forbes disagrees with this event in his published journals. Forbes, *Dahomey*, 1:155. The Catholic mission and school was founded by the Société des Missions africaines de Lyon in Ouidah in 1861. See Manning, *Slavery, Colonialism, and Economic Growth*, 55.

73. The Catholic and Wesleyan missions' clearest influence was on boyhood. Girls remained relatively marginal to the missionaries' activities except for being baptized by Catholic priests. Dahomean girls' educational opportunities at the Christian missions in Ouidah were much more limited and indirect. Francesco Borghero, *Journal du premier missionnaire du Dahomey, 1860–1864*, ed. Renzo Mandirola (Monee, IL: SMA, 2018), 254–56.

74. Ibid., 92, 133.

75. Edna Bay supports this assertion, saying that "Gezo welcomed, indeed courted, contacts with Europeans." Bay, *Wives*, 183. There had been less interruption with the Brazilian and Portuguese communities in Ouidah.

76. Bay uses the phrase *precious commodity* to describe women. Ibid., 148.

77. Lisa A. Lindsay and John Wood Sweet, "Introduction: Biography and the Black Atlantic," in *Biography and the Black Atlantic*, ed. Lisa A. Lindsay and John Wood Sweet (Philadelphia: University of Pennsylvania Press, 2014), 11.

3. Agbessipé and Her Mother

1. Yorùbá culture commonly named people in this manner, so this might be a preferred form of address rather than an attempt at anonymity. Peter Morton-Williams, "A Yoruba Woman Remembers Servitude in a Palace of Dahomey, in the Reigns of Kings Glele and Behanzin," *Africa: Journal of the International African Institute* 63, no. 1 (1993): 103. The daughter is referred to as Agbessipé, the name of the female-headed lineage that she founded. She may have had other names, but Reynier did not record her personal names. The female head of this lineage in 1917 (when Reynier completed his survey) is listed as Agbessi-Danga. Presumably, the woman leading the house took the name Agbessi or some form of it in a positional succession like the kpojito did. For more information on positional succession, see Edna G. Bay, *Wives of the Leopard: Gender, Politics, and Culture in the Kingdom of Dahomey* (Charlottesville: University of Virginia Press, 1998), 38–39.

2. This dating assumes that Agbessipé was indeed the *femme du pays* mentioned in Frederick Edwyn Forbes, *Dahomey and the Dahomans: Being the Journals of Two Missions of the King of Dahomey . . . in the Years 1849 and 1850*, vol. 1, 2 vols. (London: Longman, 1851). The fragmentary evidence concerning this will be weighed in the following sections.

3. Auguste Le Hérissé, *L'ancien Royaume Du Dahomey, Moeurs, Religion, Histoire*, 1911, 227–28.

4. Robin Law, *Ouidah: The Social History of a West African Slaving "Port," 1727–1892* (Athens: Ohio University Press, 2004), 76–78.

5. As Reid points out, these concepts were developed by James Watson much earlier. Anthony Reid, "'Closed' and 'Open' Slave Systems in Pre-Colonial Southeast Asia," in *Critical Readings on Global Slavery*, Critical Readings (Leiden: Brill, 2018), 1462. This "openness" did not preclude prejudice against those people with recent family histories of enslavement. Descendants of enslaved persons sometimes found the obstacles to social mobility to be insurmountable. As Lempereur states, descendants were "strongly marked" by their ancestors' status while enslaved. Enslaved persons who held "elite," skilled professions, such as Afa diviners, had greater resources than did agricultural laborers. Samuel Lempereur, "A Path from Slavery to Freedom: The Case of the Ologuoudou Family in Southern Benin," *African Economic History* 48, no. 1 (2020): 22–24. Certain groups, though, such as the Afro-Brazilian community, resisted this norm and more vigilantly policed and reinforced status differences across generations.

6. Emmanuel Akyeampong, "History, Memory, Slave-Trade and Slavery in Anlo (Ghana)," *Slavery and Abolition* 22, no. 3 (December 2001): 1.

7. Lempereur, "A Path from Slavery to Freedom," 28.

8. Walter C. Rucker, *Gold Coast Diasporas: Identity, Culture, and Power* (Bloomington: Indiana University Press, 2015), 15.

9. Heidi Nast, *Concubines and Power Five Hundred Years in a Northern Nigerian Palace* (Minneapolis : University of Minnesota Press, 2005), 7–8.

10. Bay, *Wives*, 81–84, 94, 186–92.

11. Reynier, "Ouidah: Organisation Du Commandement [1917]," *Mémoire Du Bénin* 2 (1993): 30.

12. For more on these women, see Jessica Reuther, "Merchant Queens and the Politics of Housebreaking in Ouidah" *Africa Today* (forthcoming).

13. A prosoprographically inspired approach is explained in the introduction of this book. As defined by Andrej Svorečník, prosopography "identifies and draws relationships between various people within a specific, well defined historical or social context by collecting and analyzing relevant biographical data." Prosopography is the study of shared biographical details of individuals in aggregate. It was developed for situations where there is insufficient primary source evidence to write an individual life history or collective biography.

14. Ada Ferrer, "Slavery, Freedom, and the Work of Speculation," *Small Axe* 23, no. 1 (March 2019): 220–28.

15. It is also possible that the woman described in Forbes's account did not belong to a lineage that survived until 1917. Alternatively, she might have been part of the Avloko lineage, which had several daughters taken as wives by Europeans.

16. It is possible that this country wife was briefly a member of an entrepreneurial elite that was not recorded in the oral traditions of Ouidah half a century later.

17. Future historians could engage in collecting oral histories about Agbessipé or other women mentioned in Reynier's census. Unfortunately, the COVID-19 pandemic prevented me from following up on this individual.

18. Bay, *Wives*, 199. While this statement is true for women of the Mina ethnic group as well, this chapter focuses on a Yorùbá woman because of the available documentation. Mina women were also active and successful traders who developed networks stretching from Grand-Popo and Agoué to Ouidah. Ouidah was not, properly speaking, an Atlantic port because it was located approximately two and a half miles inland, north of the lagoon that separated it from the seaside. Law, *Ouidah*, 18.

19. For more on religious innovation, see Law, *Ouidah*, 88–92. Suzanne Preston Blier, *African Vodun: Art, Psychology, and Power* (Chicago: University of Chicago Press, 1995).

20. The French term *mise en gage* encompasses a variety of West African forms of dependence that differed depending on the society in which the pawn exchange occurred. Here I define the term broadly with regard to how it was

defined in the French colonial tribunals. In each indigenous language, there is a term (or terms) that connotes distinctly different arrangements governed by accepted social norms. *Mise en gage* is an umbrella term. In Fon, the term for *pawn* was *gbánu*, and in Yorùbá, iwofa. Dr. Felix Iroko emphasized that Nago (Yorùbá) forms of child circulation, including pawning, were not identical to Fon ones in Dahomey. See Dr. Felix Iroko interview, February 2, 2014 . The cases from Dahomey show that Dahomeans did not agree with the French definition of pawning as illicit or applicable to the particular child transfer arrangements. Melville Herskovits describes a hierarchy of pawns within the households. I am skeptical of the clear-cut "rules" he outlines and believe that the choice of whom to pawn involved a more complex rationale, one that factored in economic, social, and emotional logic depending on the situation. See Melville J. Herskovits, *Dahomey: An Ancient West African Kingdom*, vol. 1 (New York: J. J. Augustin, 1938), 82–83. Many other scholars have defined pawning. For the Yorùbá definition of iwofa, see Samuel Johnson, *The History of the Yorubas from the Earliest Times to the Beginning of the British Protectorate*, repr. (London: Forgotten Books, 2012), 126–30; Olatunji Ojo, "'Èmú' (Àmúyá): The Yorùbá Institution of Panyarring or Seizure for Debt," *African Economic History*, no. 35 (2007): 34. See especially the works cited in footnote 13 of Ojo. For iwofa, see also Elisha P. Renne, "Childhood Memories and Contemporary Parenting in Ekiti, Nigeria," *Africa (Edinburgh University Press)* 75, no. 1 (March 2005): 63–82.

21. As Lovejoy points out, in practice, pawnship could overlap or evolve into a situation of slavery, particularly when the pawn was not redeemed in a prompt manner. Paul E. Lovejoy, "Pawnship, Debt, and 'Freedom' in Atlantic Africa during the Era of the Slave Trade: A Reassessment," *Journal of African History* 55, no. 1 (March 2014): 55–78.

22. Ibid.

23. Ndubueze L. Mbah, *Emergent Masculinities: Gendered Power and Social Change in the Biafran Atlantic Age* (Athens: Ohio University Press, 2019), 95.

24. Bay, *Wives*, 169. Robin Law, "Ouidah as a Multiethnic Community," in *The Black Urban Atlantic in the Age of the Slave Trade*, ed. Jorge Cañizares-Esguerra, Matt D. Childs, and James Sidbury (Philadelphia: University of Pennsylvania Press, 2013), 42–44. David Eltis and David Richardson, "West Africa and the Transatlantic Slave Trade: New Evidence of Long-Run Trends," *Slavery & Abolition* 18, no. 1 (April 1997): 19.

25. These forts were sometimes called trading factories since they were not fortified. This date does not mark the beginning of European involvement. The Portuguese had explored and traded at Ouidah since the 1580s. Law, *Ouidah*, 29–34. All of the forts predated the Dahomean conquest of the Kingdom of Hueda.

26. Ibid., 9–12.

27. Eltis and Richardson, "West Africa and the Transatlantic Slave Trade," 17, 22; Law, *Ouidah*, 2.

28. Rebecca Shumway, "Castle Slaves of the Eighteenth-Century Gold Coast (Ghana)," *Slavery & Abolition* 35, no. 1 (2014): 84.

29. Law, *Ouidah*, 31–33.

30. Ibid., 155.

31. Richard Francis Burton, *A Mission to Gelele, King of Dahome: With Notices of the So Called*, vol. 1 (London: Tinsley Brothers, 1864), 35, 63.

32. Delbée, "Journal du voyage du Sieur Delbée, commissaire general de la marine, aux isles, dans la coste de Guynée, pour l'établissement du commerce en ces pays, en l'année 1669," in *Relation de ce qui s'est passé dans les Isles et terre-ferme de l'Amérique, pendant la dernière guerre avec l'Angleterre, et depuis en exécution du traitté de Breda*, by Jean de Clodoré (Paris: Chez Gervais Clozier, 1671), 384–86. William Smith, *A New Voyage to Guinea* (London: Frank Cass, 1967), 166–67. Before developing trading forts and relationships with Kru canoe men on the Gold Coast, Europeans' lack of knowledge of navigating the surf prevented them from landing along the Slave Coast. Law, *Ouidah*, 29.

33. Shumway, "Castle Slaves," 84. In other areas of Africa, this category of slaves associated with the European slave-trading companies of various nations were called castle slaves, company's slaves, committee's slaves, and service slaves, all of whom facilitated the transshipment of slaves and, later, "legitimate" agricultural products. I have chosen the term *fort slaves* because it is most commonly used in the historical documents related to Ouidah.

34. Ibid., 84.

35. Law, *Ouidah*, 39, 76. Bernard Schnapper, *La Politique et Le Commerce Français Dans Le Golfe de Guinée de 1838 à 1871* (Paris: Mouton, 1961), 163.

36. Pernille Ipsen, *Daughters of the Trade: Atlantic Slavers and Interracial Marriage on the Gold Coast* (Philadelphia: University of Pennsylvania Press, 2014), 8.

37. Reynier, "Ouidah," 39–40.

38. The oral tradition, as recorded by Reynier, does not include any exact dates connected with Agbessipé. Reynier, "Ouidah," 39.

39. These numbers are presented in table 3.1 in Law, *Ouidah*, 74. For the 1803 number, he cites John M'Leod, *A Voyage to Africa with Some Account of the Manners and Customs of the Dahomian People* (London: John Murray, 1820), 13, and the British Parliamentary Papers for the 1841 figure.

40. Law, *Ouidah*, 161–62.

41. Reynier, "Ouidah," 39.

42. Ipsen, *Daughters*, 20.

43. For more on *signares* on Gorée Island and Senegambia, see Jessica Marie Johnson, *Wicked Flesh: Black Women, Intimacy, and Freedom in the Atlantic World* (Philadelphia: University of Pennsylvania Press, 2020), 16–77; Hilary Jones,

The Métis of Senegal: Urban Life and Politics in French West Africa (Bloomington: Indiana University Press, 2013); Hilary Jones, "From Mariage à La Mode to Weddings at Town Hall: Marriage, Colonialism, and Mixed-Race Society in Nineteenth-Century Senegal," *International Journal of African Historical Studies* 38, no. 1 (2005): 27–48; George Brooks, *Eurafricans in Western Africa: Commerce, Social Status, Gender, and Religious Observance from the Sixteenth to the Eighteenth Century* (Athens: Ohio University Press, 2003); George E. Brooks, "The Signares of Saint-Louis and Gorée: Women Entrepreneurs in Eighteenth-Century Senegal," in *Women in Africa: Studies in Social and Economic Change*, ed. Nancy J. Hafkin and Edna G. Bay (Stanford: Stanford University Press, 1976), 19–44. For the Gold Coast, see Ipsen, *Daughters*.

44. Law, *Ouidah*, 163–65.

45. For a better-documented and more detailed account of a similar *cassare* union in the Gold Coast, see the biography of Wulff Joseph Wulff and his wife, Sara Malm Wulff: "Chapter 5: Familiar Circles" in Ipsen, *Daughters*, 140–74.

46. Reynier, "Ouidah," 39.

47. Patrick Manning, *Slavery, Colonialism, and Economic Growth in Dahomey, 1640–1960* (Cambridge: Cambridge University Press, 1982), 54.

48. Rucker, *Gold Coast Diasporas*, 21.

49. For more information on pawning in the Gold Coast, see Randy J. Sparks, "Gold Coast Merchant Families, Pawning, and the Eighteenth-Century British Slave Trade," *William and Mary Quarterly* 70, no. 2 (April 2013): 317–40; Cati Coe, "Disputes over Transfers of Belonging in the Gold Coast in the 1870s: Fosterage or Debt Pawning?," in *Child Fostering in West Africa: New Perspectives on Theory and Practice* (Leiden: Brill, 2013), 201–20; Coe, "How Debt Became Care: Child Pawning and Its Transformations in Akuapem, the Gold Coast, 1874–1929," *Africa* 82, no. 2 (May 2012): 287–311; Ipsen, *Daughters*, 133–37. For more information on pawning in Yorùbáland, see Judith Byfield, "Pawns and Politics: The Pawnship Debate in Western Nigeria," in *Pawnship, Slavery, and Colonialism in Africa*, ed. Paul E. Lovejoy and Toyin Falola (Trenton: Africa World Press, 2003), 357–85.

50. While the Yorùbá term *iwofa* is often translated as "pawn," this English equivalent is imperfect. See Johnson, *History of the Yorùbás*, 126–27.

51. Lovejoy, "Pawnship, Debt, and 'Freedom,'" 59; Paul E. Lovejoy and David Richardson, "The Business of Slaving: Pawnship in Western Africa, c. 1600–1810," *Journal of African History* 42, no. 1 (2001): 67–89; Sparks, "Gold Coast Merchant Families"; Toyin Falola, ed., *Pawnship in Africa: Debt Bondage in Historical Perspective* (Boulder, CO: Westview Press, 1994).

52. Ipsen, *Daughters*, 133.

53. Law states that Agaja only suppressed panyarring. I argue that he suppressed pawning for the same reasons. Robin Law, "Finance and Credit in

Precolonial Dahomey," in *Credit, Currencies, and Culture: African Financial Institutions in Historical Perspective*, ed. Endre Stiansen and Jane I. Guyer (Uppsala: Nordiska Afrikainstitutet, 1999), 31–32. Law admits that pawning in precolonial Dahomey has "little contemporary evidence that bears directly upon the subject." He found four "reasonably clear allusions to it," though he admits they are ambiguous. I would like to point out that only one of these possible instances of pawning in Dahomey predates the mid-nineteenth century. Robin Law, "On Pawning and Enslavement for Debt in the Precolonial Slave Coast," in *Pawnship, Slavery, and Colonialism in Africa* (Trenton, NJ: African World, 2003), 55–69. In both of Law's chapters cited here, his evidence is from either the 1720s when Dahomey was struggling to establish control or the mid-nineteenth century or later. The one exception is the manuscript by de Chenevert and Bullet, "Réflexions sur Juda par les Sieurs de Chenevert et abbé Bullet" (June 1, 1776), MS 111, Archives Nationale d'Outre Mer. This is an instance of a request of self-pawning of three adults. The incident also seemed to shock the Frenchmen. De Chenevert and Bullet reject the request because "so-called free men were slaves of the king"; de Chenevert and Bullet, 59. Lovejoy's more recent article supports my claim that pawning, at least in multiracial African commercial exchanges, was suppressed in the Kingdom of Dahomey until the mid-nineteenth century. Lovejoy, "Pawnship, Debt, and 'Freedom.'"

54. Forbes, *Dahomey*, 1:146.

55. Lovejoy, "Pawnship, Debt, and 'Freedom,'" 78.

56. For more on Gezo's usurpation, see Maurice A. Glélé, *Le Danxomę: du pouvoir Aja à la nation Fon* (Paris: Nubia, 1974), 115–26.

57. Law, *Ouidah*, 116, 178. Law, "Finance and Credit," 25.

58. Law, "Finance and Credit," 37.

59. Ibid.; Law, "On Pawning."

60. Endre Stiansen and Jane I. Guyer, "Introduction," in *Credit, Currencies and Culture: African Financial Institutions in Historical Perspective*, ed. Endre Stiansen and Jane I. Guyer (Uppsala: Nordiska Afrikainstitutet, 1999), 14–15, http://nai.diva-portal.org/smash/record.jsf?pid=diva2%3A272162&dswid=5719.

61. Forbes, *Dahomey*, 1:149–50.

62. See "Chapter 5: The Evolution of 'Nharship' in Senegambia" in Brooks, *Eurafricans in Western Africa*, 122–60. Jones, *Métis of Senegal*. Ipsen, *Daughters*. Vanessa S. Oliveira, "Spouses & Commercial Partners: Immigrant Men & Locally Born Women in Luanda, 1831–1859," in *African Women in the Atlantic World: Property, Vulnerability, & Mobility, 1660–1880*, ed. Mariana P. Candido and Adam Jones (Suffolk: James Currey, 2019), 217–32.

63. Forbes, *Dahomey and the Dahomans*, 1:149–50.

64. Johnson, *History of the Yorùbás*, 129.

65. See chapter 2 of this book for more detail on articulations of entrusting in the early to mid-nineteenth century.

66. Forbes, *Dahomey*, 1:139–40.

67. Le Hérissé, *L'ancien Royaume*, 203–26; "Chapter XVI: Marriage" in Herskovits, *Dahomey*, 1:300–33.

68. Martin Lynn says that the exporting of palm oil from West Africa started at least as early as 1588. Martin Lynn, *Commerce and Economic Change in West Africa: The Palm Oil Trade in the Nineteenth Century*, African Studies Series 93 (Cambridge: Cambridge University Press, 1997), 12.

69. Ibid., 21.

70. Pierre Bouche, *Sept Ans En Afrique Occidentale: La Côte Des Esclaves et Le Dahomey* (Paris: Librarie Plon, 1885), 61; Louis Brunet and Louis Giethlen, *Dahomey et Dépendances*, Exposition Universelle de 1900—Les Colonies Françaises (Paris: Augustin Challamel, 1900), 283. While none of the sources on Dahomey from the nineteenth century give a measurable quantity for "enormous," Dona J. E. Maier cited a German official, Preuss, who estimated that African households in palm-producing areas in southeastern Ghana and southern Togo consumed a minimum of ten grams of palm oil per person per day. Donna J. E. Maier, "Precolonial Palm Oil Production and Gender Division of Labor in Nineteenth-Century Gold Coast and Togoland," *African Economic History* 37 (2009): 5.

71. Bay, *Wives*, 193–96; Robin Law, "'Legitimate' Trade and Gender Relations in Yorubaland and Dahomey," in *From Slave Trade to "Legitimate" Commerce: The Commercial Transition in Nineteenth-Century West Africa*, ed. Robin Law, African Studies Series 86 (Cambridge: Cambridge University Press, 1995), 196; Lynn, *Commerce and Economic Change*, 52. For a description of men's skilled labor in harvesting the palm fruit, see Edouard Foà, *Le Dahomey: Histoire, Géographie, Moeurs, Coutumes, Commerce, Industrie, Expeditions Françaises (1891–1894)* (Paris: A. Hennuyer, 1895), 138.

72. E. Chaudoin, *Trois mois de captivité au Dahomey* (Paris: Hachette, 1891), 65.

73. Foà, *Le Dahomey*, 139.

74. Chaudoin, *Trois mois*, 65. Foà, *Le Dahomey*, 139.

75. John Duncan, *Travels in Western Africa in 1845 & 1846: A Journey from Whydah, through the Kingdom of Dahomey, to Adofoodia, in the Interior*, vol. 1 (London: Richard Bentley, 1847), 196. Three to six liters of oil alone weighed between six and twelve pounds, not including the weight of the vessel.

76. Forbes, *Dahomey*, 1:114. Chaudoin also confirms male and female traders both selling palm oil and kernels. Chaudoin, *Trois mois*, 54–55.

77. Forbes, *Dahomey*, 1:114–15.

78. There might have been systemic issues concerning the availability of slaves at this time that hindered her ability to acquire enslaved laborers. The primary way of obtaining slaves in Dahomey in the nineteenth century remained the yearly raids by the king's armies. In the early years of developing palm

plantations in the Abomey plateau, slaves may have been difficult to acquire if one did not have political connections. Established Dahomean slave traders and ministers would have had connections that Agbessipé did not. Perhaps she lacked the means to purchase slaves until after these merchants and officials had gathered the workers they needed for their own plantations.

79. Law, *Ouidah*, 72–74. For the population statistics of Ouidah, see Hélène d'Almeida-Topor, *Histoire Économique du Dahomey (Bénin) (1890–1920)*, vol. 1, Collection racines du présent (Paris: L'Harmattan, 1995), 22.

80. Law, *Ouidah*, 76–77. M. Béraud, "Note Sur Le Dahomé," *Bulletin de La Société de Géographie*, 5th Series, 12 (1866): 380. Forbes estimates that slaves composed nine-tenths of the city's population in 1850. Forbes, *Dahomey*, 1:14.

81. Padraic X. Scanlan, *Freedom's Debtors: British Antislavery in Sierra Leone in the Age of Revolution* (New Haven, CT: Yale University Press, 2017), 13–15.

82. Oliveira, "Spouses & Commercial Partners," 228. Rucker, *Gold Coast Diasporas*, 15.

83. Mbah, *Emergent*, 125.

84. Reynier, "Ouidah," 39–40. He does not clarify whether this figure included juvenile dependents or if these were in addition to this figure.

85. In Dahomey, the king owned all land in the kingdom, but he granted usufruct rights to individuals. Law, *Ouidah*, 85. Agbessipé could not have actually owned the land of the plantation that she operated. At some point, Agbessipé's descendants gained access to a plot of land and planted a palm orchard in Ouakpé, located three miles from the center of Ouidah.

86. Law, *Ouidah*, 262.

87. Law, "Finance and Credit," 32.

88. Law, *Ouidah*, 248–49.

89. Law, 121–22. Bay, *Wives*, 235–36. While Dahomean kings had always exercised their prerogative to confiscate private goods upon the death of lineage heads or on a criminal conviction, Gezo suspended the arbitrary seizures of property during his reign. He had, after all, relied on his alliance with the merchant community in Ouidah and his friendship with slave merchant Francisco Félix da Souza to execute a successful coup against his brother Adandozan.

90. Glèlè invoked the traditional prerogative of the king seizing property and infamously "plundered" Ouidah many times in the 1860s. Law, *Ouidah*, 248–49.

91. Bay, *Wives*, 188.

92. Asiwaju, "Dahomey, Yorùbáland, Borgu and Benin in the Nineteenth Century," 718–19.

93. Kristin Mann, "Shifting Paradigms in the Study of the African Diaspora and of Atlantic History and Culture," in *Rethinking the African Diaspora: The Making of a Black Atlantic World in the Bight of Benin and Brazil* (London: Frank Cass, 2001), 5. Sweet makes a similar point about African diasporas in the

Portuguese world; see James H. Sweet, *Recreating Africa: Culture, Kinship, and Religion in the African-Portuguese World, 1441–1770* (Chapel Hill: University of North Carolina Press, 2003), 1–2.

94. Catherine Coquery-Vidrovitch, "De La Traite Des Esclave à l'exportation de l'huile de Palme et Des Palmistes Au Dahomey: XIXe Siècle," in *The Development of Indigenous Trade and Markets in West Africa*, ed. Claude Meillassoux (Oxford: Oxford University Press, 1971), 108, 116–17.

95. Law, *Ouidah*, 121. Bay, *Wives*, 234–36.

96. Adam Jones and Mariana P. Candido, *African Women in the Atlantic World: Property, Vulnerability & Mobility, 1660–1880* (Suffolk: James Currey, 2019), 6.

97. Reynier, "Ouidah," 39–40.

98. Mbah, *Emergent*, 114.

99. Bay, *Wives*, 239.

100. Jean-Marie Bayol, "Le Lieutenant Gouverneur Bayol à Colonies, Paris," January 1, 1890, DAHO I 1b, Archives Nationale d'Outre Mer.

4. A Runaway Girl amid the Turmoil of Conquest

1. The entry says 1894–1909, but its first publication was in 1900 in Louis Brunet and Louis Giethlen, *Dahomey et Dépendances*, Exposition Universelle de 1900—Les Colonies Françaises (Paris: Augustin Challamel, 1900).

2. Samuel Crowther, *Vocabulary of the Yoruba Language* (London: Seeleys, 1852), 131, https://archive.org/details/vocabularyofyoruoocrow.

3. As an industry, kernel export developed to compensate for the decline in global palm oil prices from the 1870s to 1890s. A. G. Hopkins, *An Economic History of West Africa* (New York: Columbia University Press, 1976), 139.

4. The story of Aholoupé has been preserved and is easily found in digitized form through the Archives de la traite. This digitized archive contains a carefully curated set of two hundred and fifty documents concerning slavery and the slave trade during the late nineteenth and early twentieth centuries. See https://dan.ilemi.net/Archives-de-la-traite.html. The project was financed by the Norwegian Agency for Development Cooperation (Norad) and executed by the United Nations Educational, Scientific and Cultural Organization (UNESCO) and the International Council on Archives (ICA). The Introduction section describes further details about the curation process and the individuals involved. See https://dan.ilemi.net/spip.php?article11.

5. For a contemporaneous example at the end of the nineteenth century, see Trevor R. Getz and Liz Clarke, *Abina and the Important Men: A Graphic History*, 2nd ed. (New York: Oxford University Press, 2016); Trevor R. Getz and Lindsay Ehrisman, "The Marriages of Abina Mansah: Escaping the Boundaries of 'Slavery' as a Category in Historical Analysis," *Journal of West African History* 1,

no. 1 (Spring 2015): 93–118. Richard Roberts has shown that during the first two decades of the twentieth century, enslaved women fled households in modern-day Mali in large numbers. Richard Roberts, *Litigants and Households: African Disputes and Colonial Courts in the French Soudan, 1895–1912*, Social History of Africa (Portsmouth, NH: Heinemann, 2005). Emily Burrill has built on Roberts's work on colonial French Sudan (modern-day Mali). For runaway wives, see especially chapter 3 in Emily S. Burrill, *States of Marriage: Gender, Justice, and Rights in Colonial Mali* (Athens: Ohio University Press, 2015). Brett Shadle has similarly documented an interwar crisis of "girl cases" in Gusiiland in Kenya. Brett Lindsay Shadle, *"Girl Cases": Marriage and Colonialism in Gusiiland, Kenya, 1890–1970* (Portsmouth, NH: Heinemann, 2006).

6. Jean Allman and Victoria Tashjian, *"I Will Not Eat Stone": A Women's History of Colonial Asante* (Portsmouth: Heinemann, 2000), 148; Shadle, *Girl Cases*, xxvii.

7. As early as 1864, Richard Burton reported that Glèlè had a film over his corneas that made his eyes appear cloudy. He predicted that it would lead to complete blindness. Richard Francis Burton, *A Mission to Gelele, King of Dahome: With Notices of the So Called*, vol. 1 (London: Tinsley Brothers, 1864), 234. Edna G. Bay, *Wives of the Leopard: Gender, Politics, and Culture in the Kingdom of Dahomey* (Charlottesville: University of Virginia Press, 1998), 276–77.

8. The nature of the girl's relationship with Kossouhow is never defined. She was either a member of his lineage or a child born in his household to enslaved parents. Aholoupé is mentioned in the correspondence concerning Minister Kodokoué's imprisonment and appeal for release. This documentation contains very limited information about her life, focusing more on the legitimacy of Kodokoué's claims that she was not his slave and he did not sell her. "Affaire Des Ministres Dahoméens Internés à Porto Novo," February 1897, ap 1897 3 0–2, Archives de la traite, http://www.dan.ilemi.net/Archives-de-la-traite.html. Banamè is in the Zou department of modern-day Benin and under the jurisdiction of Zagnanado commune.

9. Bay, *Wives*, 225, 259–65, 276–77. The struggle for succession became more destabilized in 1876 when Glèlè's vidaho, or heir apparent, died under mysterious circumstances.

10. The documents do not state where he lived, but ministers usually resided in the political capital of Abomey. Some ministers such as the *yovogan*, the "chief of the foreigners" tasked with being the king's representative to Atlantic traders, lived in Ouidah. Ministers could also have multiple residences. Kodokoué likely had a residence in Abomey and its hinterland where he controlled a palm plantation.

11. "Affaire Des Ministres."

12. E. Chaudoin, *Trois mois de captivité au Dahomey* (Paris: Hachette, 1891), 330. Training across a wide variety of societies in West Africa began at around six

to eight years of age. Christine Whyte, "Mothering Solidarity: Infant-Feeding, Vulnerability and Poverty in West Africa since the Seventeenth Century," *Past and Present*, 246, no. suppl. 15 (2020): 64.

13. Women estimated that *ablo* (a mixture of ground maize, water, and a leavening agent), another food consumed on a regular basis, required nine hours of preparation, not including the grinding of the maize.

14. J. A. Skertchly, *Dahomey as It Is: Being a Narrative of Eight Months' Residence in That Country* ... (London: Chapman and Hall, 1874), 490. These maize-based products included *akassa* (an emulsified cornmeal and water mixture that results in a white, gelatinous, translucent porridge), cankie (a mixture of ground maize and water that is rolled into balls and wrapped in plantain leaves), *ablo* (a mixture of ground maize, water, and a leavening agent boiled in a dish), and *dakoh* (a mixture of ground maize and palm oil baked in an open pot).

15. The methods used to grind and cook these staple foods remained largely untouched by technological innovations. It can be assumed that women and girls worked together in the grinding process.

16. Skertchly, *Dahomey*, 490–92. John Duncan, *Travels in Western Africa in 1845 & 1846: A Journey from Whydah, through the Kingdom of Dahomey, to Adofoodia, in the Interior*, vol. 1 (London: Richard Bentley, 1847), 101. John Adams, *Remarks on the Country Extending from Cape Palmas to the River Congo* (London: Frank Cass, [1823] 1966), 90–91; Frederick Edwyn Forbes, *Dahomey and the Dahomans: Being the Journals of Two Missions of the King of Dahomey . . . in the Years 1849 and 1850*, vol. 1 (London: Longman, 1851), 29.

17. Skertchly, *Dahomey*, 56–57.

18. Burton, *Mission*, 1:127. It is difficult to determine the exact weight of the loads women and girls carried on their heads. Forbes states that women carried loads of twenty thousand cowrie shells and 2.5 gallons of rum in kegs, the latter of which would weigh approximately 19.75 pounds. Forbes, *Dahomey*, 1851, 1:51–52.

19. For this statement to have become a proverb by the 1850s, hawking had to be commonplace in the region at least a generation or two earlier or in the late eighteenth century or early nineteenth at the latest. Forbes, *Dahomey*, 100.

20. Luc Garcia, *Le royaume du Dahomé face à la pénétration coloniale: affrontements et incompréhension (1875–1894)* (Paris: Editions Karthala, 1988), 206–10.

21. "Affaire Des Ministres."

22. Ibid.

23. Kelly M. Duke Bryant, "Runaways, Dutiful Daughters, and Brides: Family Strategies of Formerly Enslaved Girls in Senegal, 1895–1911," *Women, Gender, and Families of Color* 7, no. 1 (Spring 2019): 44–46.

24. Preteen girls fled marriages that they perceived to be undesirable for any reason. Shadle, *Girl Cases*; Rodet, "Continuum of Gendered Violence."

25. Michel D. K. Videgla, *Un état ouest-africain: le royaume Goun de Hogbonou (Porto-Novo) des origines à 1908* (PhD diss., University of Paris 1-Panthéon-Sorbonne 1999, 2002), 487–90.

26. In the nineteenth century, Hogbonou struggled to maintain its autonomy under threat from both the Kingdom of Dahomey and the British Empire. In February 1861, Hogbonou's independence faced significant danger when the British navy bombarded Porto-Novo. This altered King Sodji's (r. 1848–1864) views of his kingdom's relationships with European powers. He considered France to be an attractive ally to challenge both British and Dahomean aggression. Colin W. Newbury, *The Western Slave Coast and Its Rulers: European Trade and Administration among the Yoruba and Adja-Speaking Peoples of South-Western Nigeria, Southern Dahomey, and Togo* (Oxford: Clarendon, 1961), 64–68. Elisée A. Soumonni, "Porto-Novo, Between the French and the British, 1861–1884," *Journal of the Historical Society of Nigeria* 12, nos. 3/4 (December 1984): 53–54.

27. After the British annexation of Lagos in August 1861, the French felt increased pressure to expand their claims to territories along the Slave Coast and counter British attempts to dominate the region. Brunet and Giethlen, *Dahomey et Dépendances*, 70–73. Newbury, *Western Slave Coast*, 99.

28. After 1881, these predatory attacks increased in frequency and extent. Alexandre L. d'Albéca, *La France au Dahomey* (Paris: Hachette, 1895), 18–19; P. Chautard, *Le Dahomey* (Lyon: Librairie Emmanuel Vitte, 1890), 23. For a discussion of why the early protectorate lapsed, see Newbury, *Western Slave Coast*, 71–76, 103, 107. Silke Strickrodt, *Afro-European Trade in the Atlantic World: The Western Slave Coast, c. 1550–c. 1885*, Western Africa Series (Suffolk: James Currey, 2015), 225–27. The British also increased pressure on Toffa to renew the protectorate when its forces again blockaded Porto-Novo and the surrounding coast in 1876.

29. J. F. Ade Ajayi and Robert Smith, *Yoruba Warfare in the Nineteenth Century* (Cambridge: Cambridge University Press, 1964); A. I. Asiwaju, "Dahomey, Yorubaland, Borgu and Benin in the Nineteenth Century," in *General History of Africa*, vol. 6: Africa in the Nineteenth Century until the 1880s: 699–723 (Berkeley: University of California Press, 1989); I.A. Akinjogbin, ed., *War and Peace in Yorùbáland, 1793–1893* (Ibadan: Heinemann Educational Books, 1998). Aribidesi Usman and Toyin Falola, *The Yoruba: From Prehistory to the Present* (Cambridge: Cambridge University Press, 2019), 177–201.

30. For monthly on-the-ground reports concerning the French conquest of the region, see ANOM DAHO I. "Depêche télégraphique Colonel à Marine," October 6, 1892, DAHO I 8, Archives Nationale d'Outre Mer.

31. A. Hagen, "La Colonie de Porto-Novo et Le Roi Toffa," *Revue d'ethnographie* 6 (March–April 1887): 84.

32. Patrick Manning, *Slavery, Colonialism, and Economic Growth in Dahomey, 1640–1960* (Cambridge: Cambridge University Press, 1982), 61.

33. "État statistique de la population pendant l'année 1890," January 1, 1892. Hélène d'Almeida-Topor, *Histoire Économique du Dahomey (Bénin) (1890–1920)*, vol. 1, Collection racines du présent (Paris: L'Harmattan, 1995), 22.

34. Brunet and Giethlen, *Dahomey et Dépendances*, 46–48.

35. By the midcentury, the enslaved population reached numbers as high as nine-tenths to two-thirds of the Kingdom of Dahomey. Robin Law, *Ouidah: The Social History of a West African Slaving "Port," 1727–1892* (Athens: Ohio University Press, 2004), 77. Béraud claims two-thirds were enslaved; see M. Béraud, "Note Sur Le Dahomé," *Bulletin de La Société de Géographie*, 5th Series, 12 (1866): 380. These high estimates of the proportion of the enslaved population seem to have reflected the unique composition of Ouidah. Patrick Manning has suggested that a more accurate estimate of the preconquest population in the 1890s would be one-fourth to one-third currently or formerly enslaved, with higher concentrations and proportions of slaves in and around Ouidah and Abomey. Manning, *Slavery, Colonialism, and Economic Growth*, 192. Early colonial administrators estimated that slaves made up one-sixth to one-fifth of the population in the former Fon Kingdom.

36. I have not found any European estimates regarding how much of the total population was enslaved in the Kingdom of Hogbonou at any given time. European sources often referred to the Kingdom of Hogbonou by the Portuguese designation of its capital, Porto-Novo. It is not always clear when the reference is to the kingdom or to the city. In this context, Lieutenant Gellé's use of *Port-Novo* does seem to refer to the kingdom. Lieutenant de vaisseau Gellé, "Notice Sur Porto-Novo (Côte Occidentale d'afrique)," *Revue Maritime et Coloniale*, March 1864, 426.

37. Padraic X. Scanlan, *Freedom's Debtors: British Antislavery in Sierra Leone in the Age of Revolution* (New Haven, CT: Yale University Press, 2017), 13–15.

38. Jules de Cuverville, "N. 471 Situation Politique Au Dahomey: Le Contre-Amerial de Cuverville, Commandant En Chef La Division Navale de l'Atlantique Nord à Monsieur Le Ministre de La Marine—Paris," November 5, 1890, DAHO I 3, Archives Nationale d'Outre Mer.

39. For a discussion of this vulnerability in East Africa, see Elisabeth McMahon, "Trafficking and Reenslavement: The Social Vulnerability of Women and Children in Nineteenth-Century East Africa," in *Trafficking in Slavery's Wake: Law and the Experience of Women and Children in Africa*, New African Histories (Athens: Ohio University Press, 2012), 29–44.

40. The palm oil and kernel industry grew dramatically during the 1860s–1880s. J. (Abbé) Laffitte, *Le Pays Des Nègres* (Tours: Alfred Mame et fils, 1876), 102. J. (Abbé) Laffitte, *Le Dahomé: souvenirs de voyage et de mission* (Tours: Alfred Mame et fils, 1873), ix, http://gallica.bnf.fr/ark:/12148/bpt6k6209298w.

41. "Recettes douanières au 31 Décembre de chacune des années 1893, 1894, 1895, 1896, 1897, 1898, 1899, 1900, 1901, & 1902, effectuées par les bureaux de

Porto Novo, Cotonou, Ouidah, Grand Popo, Agoué, & Athiémé," 1902, 1E 8–6, Archives Nationales du Bénin.

42. Bay, *Wives*, 224.

43. Sierra Leoneans developed a monopoly as middlemen in the export trade and bought "almost all" the palm oil sold in the city. Gellé, "Notice Sur Porto-Novo," 421, 429. Law, *Ouidah*, 227. This contrasted with the community Sierra Leoneans found earlier in the nineteenth century in Ouidah where the Sierra Leoneans experienced marginalization and eventual mass emigration no later than the 1850s. Sierra Leoneans remained an active part of the commercial community in Porto-Novo.

44. Europeans did not observe a pronounced gender imbalance in Hogbonou as they had in the Kingdom of Dahomey. There was probably a slight gender imbalance as was common throughout Atlantic Africa.

45. Pierre Bouche, *Sept Ans En Afrique Occidentale: La Côte Des Esclaves et Le Dahomey* (Paris: Librarie Plon, 1885), 54.

46. Hagen, "La Colonie de Porto-Novo et Le Roi Toffa," 106.

47. Adams, *Remarks on the Country*, 87–88.

48. Gellé, "Notice Sur Porto-Novo," 425–27.

49. Hagen, "La Colonie de Porto-Novo et Le Roi Toffa," 106. E. Chappet, *Études Sur Les Côtes Occidentales de l'Afrique: La Côte Des Esclaves* (Lyon: Imprimerie Générale de Lyon, 1881), 10.

50. France exiled Béhanzin first to Martinique and later to Algeria, where he died in 1906. Joseph Adrien Djivo, *Le refus de la colonisation dans l'ancien royaume de Danxome, 1875–1894*, vol. 1: Gbehanzin et Ago-li-Agbo, 2 vols., Langues et cultures du Bénin (Paris: L'Harmattan, 2013).

51. "N. 65 Resident de France à Sagon—Objet: Au Sujet Du Trafic Des Esclaves Dans Le Royaume d'Abomey," June 18, 1895, cd 1895 2, Archives de la traite.

52. "Déposition du chef de Sagon Bocossa," June 15, 1895, 1E2/1 1895 2, Archives de la traite, http://www.dan.ilemi.net/IMG/jpg/1e2_1_1895_2.jpg.

53. "Rapport de M. Le Résident de Sagon," June 4, 1895, 1E2/1 1895 1, Archives de la traite, http://www.dan.ilemi.net/IMG/jpg/1e2_1_1895_1.jpg.

54. "Interrogatoire de Mébôlo," 1894, 1e2/1 1894 1, Archives de la traite, http://www.dan.ilemi.net/IMG/jpg/1e2_1_1894_1.jpg.

55. Résident of Allada, "N. 90," July 22, 1895, 1e2/1 1895 6, Archives de la traite, https://www.dan.ilemi.net/IMG/jpg/1e2_1_1895_6.jpg.

56. Bouche, *Sept Ans*, 156. I have feminized this because, especially in Dahomey, the slave population was overwhelmingly female. For a discussion of this view, see Boniface I. Obichere, "Women and Slavery in the Kingdom of Dahomey," *Revue Française d'histoire d'outre mer* 65, no. 1 (1978): 520.

57. Not every enslaved person did so immediately or ever. Peter Morton-Williams, "A Yoruba Woman Remembers Servitude in a Palace of Dahomey,

in the Reigns of Kings Glele and Behanzin," *Africa: Journal of the International African Institute* 63, no. 1 (1993): 105.

58. This was concentrated in 1896 and 1897. "Affaires Politiques 1896," July 9, 1896, ap1896 3, Archives de la traite, http://www.dan.ilemi.net/Archives-de-la-traite.html.

59. Igor Kopytoff and Suzanne Miers, "Introduction: African 'Slavery' as an Institution of Marginality," in *Slavery in Africa: Historical and Anthropological Perspectives*, ed. Suzanne Miers and Igor Kopytoff (Madison: University of Wisconsin Press, 1977), 29–32.

60. Law, *Ouidah*, 15–16.

61. "Affaire Des Ministres."

62. The digitized collection Archives de la traite of the Archives Nationales du Bénin is replete with correspondence concerning these reclamations and inquiries. See the documents related to the period 1894 to c. 1900, http://www.dan.ilemi.net/Archives-de-la-traite.html.

63. Marie Rodet, "Continuum of Gendered Violence: The Colonial Invention of Female Desertion as a Customary Criminal Offense, French Soudan, 1900–1949," in *Domestic Violence and the Law in Colonial and Postcolonial Africa*, New African Histories (Athens: Ohio University Press, 2010), 74–93.

5. Entrusted or Enslaved?

1. Tribunal du cercle de Porto-Novo, "Jugement n. 5 du 25 Janvier 1909 Affaire Bouou Nonekoue Senou Ouessou Sokola-Caragahoumyo-Hounton-Simenou et Sounen," January 25, 1909, 1M106, Archives Nationales du Bénin.

2. Richard Roberts, *Litigants and Households: African Disputes and Colonial Courts in the French Soudan, 1895–1912* (Portsmouth, NH: Heinemann, 2005), 67–70.

3. Emily S. Burrill, *States of Marriage: Gender, Justice, and Rights in Colonial Mali* (Athens: Ohio University Press, 2015), 57.

4. Trevor R. Getz and Lindsay Ehrisman, "The Marriages of Abina Mansah: Escaping the Boundaries of 'Slavery' as a Category in Historical Analysis," *Journal of West African History* 1, no. 1 (Spring 2015): 96.

5. Ibid., 94.

6. The crime in French was *traite*. Since the 1980s, with Robertson and Klein's now-classic volume *Women and Slavery in Africa*, Africanist scholars have developed a rich literature on gender and slavery. As Martin Klein observes, scholarship on slavery has, until recently, neglected age. For a discussion of why this is so, see Martin Klein, "Children and Slavery in the Western Sudan," in *Child Slaves in the Modern World*, ed. Gwyn Campbell, Suzanne Miers, and Joseph C. Miller (Athens: Ohio University Press, 2011), 124–39. Children have become a subject of increasing interest in edited volumes; see Benjamin N.

Lawrance and Richard L. Roberts, eds., *Trafficking in Slavery's Wake: Law and the Experience of Women and Children in Africa*, New African Histories (Athens: Ohio University Press, 2012). Gwyn Campbell, Suzanne Miers, and Joseph Calder Miller, eds., *Children in Slavery through the Ages* (Athens: Ohio University Press, 2009). Gwyn Campbell, Suzanne Miers, and Joseph C. Miller, *Child Slaves in the Modern World* (Athens: Ohio University Press, 2011). See also Olatunji Ojo, "Child Slaves in Precolonial Nigeria, c. 1725–1860," *Slavery and Abolition* 33, no. 3 (September 2012): 417–34.

7. For more on the thirteen different forms of Fon marriage, see Auguste Le Hérissé, *L'ancien Royaume Du Dahomey, Moeurs, Religion, Histoire*, 1911, 203–26. Melville J. Herskovits, *Dahomey: An Ancient West African Kingdom*, vol. 1 (New York: J. J. Augustin, 1938), 300–333.

8. Marie Rodet, "'Under the Guise of Guardianship and Marriage:' Mobilizing Juvenile and Female Labor in the Aftermath of Slavery in Kayes, French Soudan, 1900–1939," in *Trafficking in Slavery's Wake: Law and the Experience of Women and Children in Africa*, ed. Benjamin N. Lawrance and Richard L. Roberts (Athens: Ohio University Press, 2012), 86.

9. This definition is based on a translation of the term *mise en gage* in Olivier Pétré-Grenouilleau, *Dictionnaire des esclavages*, À présent (Paris: Larousse, 2010), 249–50. The edited volume *Pawnship in Africa* provides an overview of the diversity of pawnship practices across Africa; see Toyin Falola, ed., *Pawnship in Africa: Debt Bondage in Historical Perspective* (Boulder, CO: Westview Press, 1994).

10. Robin Phylisia Chapdelaine, *The Persistence of Slavery: An Economic History of Child Trafficking in Nigeria* (Amherst: University of Massachusetts Press, 2021), 4.

11. Ibid., 77.

12. Edna G. Bay, *Wives of the Leopard: Gender, Politics, and Culture in the Kingdom of Dahomey* (Charlottesville: University of Virginia Press, 1998), 185–186, 190, 207, & 231.

13. Elisabeth McMahon, "Trafficking and Reenslavement: The Social Vulnerability of Women and Children in Nineteenth-Century East Africa," in *Trafficking in Slavery's Wake: Law and the Experience of Women and Children in Africa* (Athens: Ohio University Press, 2012), 29.

14. Tribunal du cercle de Porto-Novo, "Jugement n. 5 du 25 Janvier 1909."

15. This was a continent-wide phenomenon. For more on nineteenth-century kidnapping, see Chapdelaine, *Persistence*, 31–32, 67–69; Elisabeth McMahon, "Trafficking." For an explanation as to why children were a targeted population to kidnap and enslave during the colonial era, see Klein, "Children and Slavery in the Western Sudan."

16. At this time, thirteen or fourteen was an acceptable marriageable age, as there was no minimum age mandated by colonial law. In 1920, Governor-General

Charles Brunet issued a memorandum after a controversial case in Dahomey was overturned on appeal. Marcel de Coppet issued a second memorandum on the subject of precocious marriage in 1937. In 1939, the Mandel Decree was enacted, which formalized these vague condemnations of young marriage by establishing the minimum age of marriage for girls at fourteen and boys at sixteen. This was further revised in 1951 by the Jacquinot Decree. For further discussion on the minimum age of marriage and marriage suspected of concealing slavery in AOF, see Aminata Kane, "Violences sur les femmes, violences des femmes en Afrique Occidentale Francaise (1895–1960): Histoire des femmes d'apres les registres judiciaires" (PhD diss., University of Provence-Aix-Marseille 1, 2008), 69–88.

17. Ernest Noirot, a colonial administrator in AOF, called them "wives of circumstance." Emily S. Burrill, "'Wives of Circumstance': Gender and Slave Emancipation in Late Nineteenth-Century Senegal," *Slavery and Abolition* 29, no. 1 (March 2008): 49–63.

18. It is impossible to tell what form of marriage Bouou might have claimed to have performed because his ethnic identity was not recorded. At this time, the French tribunal often simply documented people as Muslim or non-Muslim. The Fon, according to Herskovits, had thirteen recognized distinct forms of marriage in 1931. Herskovits, *Dahomey*, vol. 1, 302. Houmé's life story as recorded in the colonial tribunal resembled that of Abina Mansah in the Gold Coast; see Trevor R. Getz and Liz Clarke, *Abina and the Important Men: A Graphic History*, 2nd ed. (New York: Oxford University Press, 2016).

19. Roberts, *Litigants and Households*; see "Chapter 2: Contesting Slavery and Marriage in Early Colonial Sikasso," in Burrill, *States of Marriage*, 53–78. This was a transimperial phenomenon that occurred in British colonies as well. For an in-depth analysis of one such case in the British colony of the Gold Coast, see Getz and Clarke, *Abina and the Important Men*.

20. Burrill, *States of Marriage*, 70.

21. Roberts, *Litigants and Households*, 130–32.

22. Marie Rodet has shown that women in the French Sudan used this strategy. Marie Rodet, "'I Ask for Divorce Because My Husband Does Not Let Me Go Back to My Country of Origin with My Brother:' Gender, Family, and the End of Slavery in the Region of Kayes, French Sudan, 1890–1920," in *Sex, Power, and Slavery*, ed. Gwyn Campbell and Elizabeth Elbourne (Athens: Ohio University Press, 2014), 197.

23. Sessou's brother also received the same sentence. Tribunal du cercle de Porto-Novo, "Jugement n. 5 du 25 Janvier 1909."

24. "Rapport sur le jugement rendu le 21 Mai 1909 par le Tribunal de Cercle de Porto Novo dans l'affaire des Nés ALI, GODONOU et YÉOUÉOU, inculpés de trafic de personne et de complicite de trafic," June 8, 1909, 1M106, Archives Nationales du Bénin.

25. For a more theoretical discussion of these aspects of the enslaved person's experience, see Igor Kopytoff and Suzanne Miers, "Introduction: African 'Slavery' as an Institution of Marginality," in *Slavery in Africa: Historical and Anthropological Perspectives*, ed. Suzanne Miers and Igor Kopytoff (Madison: University of Wisconsin Press, 1977), 18–19.

26. A. LeBrun and Aristide Briand, "Décret Portant Réorganisation de La Justice Indigène En Afrique Occidentale Française," *Journal officiel de la République française* 44, no. 227 (August 22, 1912): 7586–89.

27. He traveled throughout AOF for the next eight months and returned to Dakar in June 1914.

28. E. Beurdeley, *La Justice Indigène En Afrique Occidentale Française: Mission d'études 1913–1914*, 1916, http://gallica.bnf.fr/ark:/12148/bpt6k147625h.

29. Ibid., 10.

30. Ginio discusses the rationale for supervising indigenous assessors in these matters. For more discussion of the perceived "limited" capacities of African assessors, see Ruth Ginio, "Negotiating Legal Authority in French West Africa: The Colonial Administration and African Assessors, 1903–1918," in *Intermediaries, Interpreters, and Clerks: African Employees in the Making of Colonial Africa*, ed. Benjamin N. Lawrance, Emily Lynn Osborn, and Richard L. Roberts (Madison: University of Wisconsin Press, 2006), 121–23.

31. The difference in Carde's tone was likely due to the contrasting audiences of each assessment. Beurdeley wrote his assessment for metropolitan policymakers not involved in the day-to-day task of on-the-ground imperial governance. Carde, however, addressed his frank assessment to the administrative hierarchy below him. It served to remind French administrators in West Africa of their responsibilities as colonial legal officers to use the legal system as a tool to promote civilization and transform the consciousness of West Africans. Jules Carde, "Circulaire sur la réorganisation de la Justice indigène," *Journal officiel de l'Afrique occidentale française* 20, no. 1026 (May 24, 1924): 365.

32. The chambre d'homologation handled appeals and reviewed lower-level court decisions and procedures.

33. Alice Conklin, *A Mission to Civilize: The Republican Idea of Empire in France and West Africa, 1895–1930* (Stanford, CA: Stanford University Press, 2001), 91–93.

34. Carde, "Circulaire Carde."

35. Gouverneur général Brévié, "151 A.P. Arrêté promulguant en Afrique occidentale française le décret du 3 décembre 1931, réorganisant la Justice inidgène en Afrique occidentale française," *Journal officiel de l'Afrique occidentale française* (February 6, 1932), 125–34. The 1931 decree marked the beginning of an uphill battle to grant "real" power to France's chiefly intermediaries in West Africa. Henceforth, the personnel of the criminal courts would comprise

five members: the tribunal's president, two French assessors, and two indigenous assessors, the last of which were overwhelmingly chiefs.

36. These statistics were compiled by Bénédicte Brunet-LaRuche based on a sampling of the registers remaining in ANB. Brunet-LaRuche's scholarship is one of the only quantitative analyses of the legal records in colonial Dahomey. Her sample is based on data from over 3,200 register entries. Her sample for the 1930s included one trafficking case out of 738 cases of crimes committed against persons. Bénédicte Brunet-La Ruche, "'Crime et châtiment' aux colonies: poursuivre, juger, sanctionner au Dahomey de 1894 à 1945" (University of Toulouse le Mirail—Toulouse 2, 2013), 428, https://tel.archives-ouvertes.fr/tel-00979289. I find this statistic somewhat problematic, but it represents an overall decline and virtual disappearance of the issues.

37. Richard Roberts makes this argument for French Sudan (modern-day Mali). Roberts, *Litigants and Households*. For a contrasting example in British colonial Asante (modern-day Ghana), see Jean Allman and Victoria Tashjian, *"I Will Not Eat Stone": A Women's History of Colonial Asante* (Portsmouth, NH: Heinemann, 2000).

38. For more on these decrees by the League of Nations, see Chapdelaine, *Persistence*, 83–84. Suzanne Miers, "Slavery and the Slave Trade as International Issues 1890–1939," in *Slavery and Colonial Rule in Africa*, Slave and Post-Slave Societies and Cultures 8 (Routledge: Frank Cass, 1999), 16–37. For international debates about whether to include pawning as a form of slavery, see the Committee of Experts on Slavery files (6B). On pawning, see carton R4156 in the League of Nations archives. Marie Rodet also makes a similar observation, see Rodet, "Under the Guise of Guardianship and Marriage," 91.

39. Cercle de Ouidah, "Procès-verbal d'interrogatoire de Fohoumbo: Affaire Kadja Boco—Rapt d'enfant," August 29, 1932, 1M118, Archives Nationales du Bénin.

40. Marcadé interviewed Fohoumbo, Kadja, and Fovi with the assistance of an interpreter, Benoît Joseph Codjia. All three testimonies stated that Fovi resided with and worked for Fohoumbo from 1926 until 1932.

41. Cercle de Ouidah, "Procès-verbal d'interrogatoire de Fohoumbo." For a succinct analysis of the changing views of the international community and British colonial officials on child pawning in Africa, see "Chapter 3: International Debate on the Welfare of Children, 1920s," in Chapdelaine, *Persistence*, 79–106. For a comparative context about debates surrounding pawning in late-colonial Ghana, see "Chapter 4: Child Slavery, Pawning, and Trafficking in Late-Colonial Bawku, 1941–48," in Jessica Cammaert, *Undesirable Practices: Women, Children, and the Politics of the Body in Northern Ghana, 1930–1972* (Lincoln: University of Nebraska Press, 2016), 117–62.

42. There is extensive and expanding literature on discussions about slavery in the twentieth century and the League of Nations' role in these discussions.

For further information, see Miers, "Slavery," 16–37. Kevin Grant, *A Civilised Savagery: Britain and the New Slaveries in Africa, 1884–1926* (New York: Routledge, 2005). While conducting field research in Dahomey in 1931, American anthropologist Melville Herskovits confirmed that Dahomeans were aware that France condemned pawning as illegal. Herskovits observed: "It is said that the custom of giving persons in pawn exists at the present time, though it is difficult, in view of the attitude of the French government toward anything that *approaches* slavery in any way, to obtain information concerning the extent to which pawning is now practiced." Herskovits, *Dahomey*, 1:82–85.

43. Cercle de Ouidah, "Procès-verbal d'interrogatoire de Fohoumbo."

44. It is unclear whether some or all of this money was a finder's fee for himself or if this money would have gone to the girl's family.

45. Cercle de Ouidah, "Procès-verbal d'interrogatoire de Fohoumbo"; Benoît Joseph Codjia, "Procès-verbal d'interrogatoire de Kadja Boco: Affaire Kadja Boco—Rapt d'enfant," July 30, 1932, 1M118, Archives Nationales du Bénin.

46. Nicolas Argenti gives examples from the contemporary period of how commercial networks facilitated fostering arrangements in Cameroon. Nicolas Argenti, "Things That Don't Come by the Road: Folktales, Fosterage, and Memories of Slavery in the Cameroon Grassfields," *Comparative Studies in Society and History* 52, no. 2 (2010): 247–49.

47. Charles Marcadé, *Procès-verbal d'audition de témoins: Fovi concernant l'Affaire Kadja Boco—Rapt d'enfant* (Commandant le cercle d'Ouidah, 1932).

48. Ibid.

49. This should not be confused with "public motherhood" as defined by Lorelle Semley; see Lorelle Semley, "Public Motherhood in West Africa as Theory and Practice," *Gender & History* 24, no. 3 (November 2012): 600–616. Social mothers did not have the same political power that public mothers did. West Africans have not, until lately and still not universally, emulated the modern, Western European norm of a conjugally based family ideal. Niara Sudarkasa, "Interpreting the African Heritage in Afro-American Family Organization," in *Families in the U.S.: Kinship and Domestic Politics*, ed. Karen V. Hansen and Anita Ilta Garey, Women in the Political Economy (Philadelphia: Temple University Press, 1998), 93–97.

50. Cercle de Ouidah, "Procès-verbal d'interrogatoire de Fohoumbo."

51. Lovejoy argues that not only was pawnship not part of the enslavement practice in Atlantic Africa, but it actually protected pawns from enslavement. Paul E. Lovejoy, "Pawnship, Debt, and 'Freedom' in Atlantic Africa during the Era of the Slave Trade: A Reassessment," *Journal of African History* 55, no. 1 (March 2014): 78. He does, however, distinguish between the pawning of a non-Muslim to a Muslim trader as possibly evolving into enslavement. This, though, would not have been relevant to the Dahomean context because there

was not a Muslim population permanently resident in the precolonial kingdom. Robin Law shows that in the Kingdoms of Allada and Whydah in the eighteenth century, the distinction between pawning and slavery was muddled, and pawnship could often be transformed into slavery. See Robin Law, "On Pawning and Enslavement for Debt in the Precolonial Slave Coast," in *Pawnship, Slavery, and Colonialism in Africa* (Trenton, NJ: African World Press, 2003), 58–62. All evidence points to this not being the case in the Kingdom of Dahomey.

52. Tribunal du 1er degré d'Athiémé, "Extrait du registre des jugements du Tribunal de la Colonie de Dahomey: Jugement N. 201 du 4 Novembre 1935—Affaire Pierre Johnson—Traite," November 4, 1935, 3M185 (184), Archives du Sénégal.

53. Patrick Manning, *Slavery, Colonialism, and Economic Growth in Dahomey, 1640–1960* (Cambridge: Cambridge University Press, 1982), 263–72.

54. Martin Klein and Richard Roberts, "The Resurgence of Pawning in French West Africa during the Depression of the 1930s," in *Pawnship, Slavery, and Colonialism in Africa*, ed. Paul Lovejoy and Toyin Falola (Trenton, NJ: Africa World Press, 2003), 303–6. Chapdelaine, *Persistence*, 152–53.

55. Johnson had not lived there for several years. He was residing in Cotonou at the time of the proceedings. Johnson was prosecuted for traite only after his wife was acquitted.

56. Neither Aledjessi nor Pierre Johnson was charged with additional counts of trafficking for these girls. Seemingly, the administration was content with a conviction for a single count of trafficking. Tribunal du 1er degré d'Athiémé, "Jugement N. 201 du 4 Nov 1935—Johnson."

57. Ibid.

58. Testimonies of D'Anssivi, Agossivi, Lissassi, Tchotchovi, and Hounsi in "Extrait du registre des jugements du Tribunal de la Colonie de Dahomey: Jugement N. 201 du 4 Novembre 1935—Affaire Pierre Johnson—Traite," November 4, 1935, 3M185 (184), Archives du Sénégal.

59. Johnson would eventually be convicted and serve a lengthy prison sentence and punitive exile.

60. Claire Griffiths, "The Savineau Archive," The Savineau Report, 2006, http://www.savineau.hull.ac.uk/.

61. Denise Savineau, "Rapport 6: Le Dahomey," March 9, 1938, 3, Archives Nationales du Senegal, https://www.francophoneafricaarchive.org/wp-content/uploads/2017/07/rapport6.pdf. Savineau's reports from the field are not as polished or structured as her penultimate synthetic report. They are rich in ethnographic notations but are often riddled with grammatical mistakes and incomplete sentences.

62. Ibid., 26.

63. The designation of *communes-mixtes* and the applicable taxation policies for them can be found in the *Journal officiel de la République du Dahomey*.

64. The colonial administration addressed these concerns in the December 12, 1905, decree; Brunet's October 5, 1920, circular, which was reiterated by de Coppet's May 7, 1937, circular and formalized by the Mandel Decree of 1939; and the September 18, 1936, decrees. For detailed discussions of the December 12, 1905, decree abolishing slavery, see Roberts, *Litigants and Households*, and Martin Klein, *Slavery and Colonial Rule in French West Africa* (Cambridge: Cambridge University Press, 1998). For information concerning the circulars and the Mandel Decree, see Kane, "Violences sur les femmes, violences des femmes," 69–80. There is very little literature about the September 18, 1936, decree. Lydon mentions it Ghislaine Lydon, "The Unraveling of a Neglected Source: A Report on Women in Francophone West Africa in the 1930s (La re-decouverte d'une source negligee: un rapport sur la condition des femmes en AOF dans les annees 1930)," *Cahiers d'études africaines* 37, no. 147 (1997): 555–84. Also, Ghislaine Lydon, "Women, Children and the Popular Front's Mission of Inquiry in French West Africa," in *French Colonial Empire and the Popular Front: Hope and Disillusion*, ed. Tony Chafer and Amanda Sackur (London: Macmillan, 1999), 170–87.

65. Berthet, "Référence: Rapport N. 6 présenté par Mme. Savineau, Conseillère technique de l'Enseignement, sur le Dahomey," Letter, June 3, 1938, 8G39 (17), Archives du Sénégal.

66. There exists a vast literature on transformations in slavery. For a foundational and far-reaching text, see Paul Lovejoy, *Transformations in Slavery: A History of Slavery in Africa*, 2nd ed. (Cambridge: Cambridge University Press, 2000). For colonial French West Africa specifically, see Klein, *Slavery*. For a discussion of British colonial courts' criteria, Getz and Ehrisman, "Marriages," 97.

67. Chapdelaine, *Persistence*, 8.

68. Dr. Romauld Michozounnou interview, February 21, 2014.

6. "Why Did You Not Cry Out . . . ?"

1. "Procès-verbal d'audition de témoins—Affaire Stanislas Amoussouvi: Akouélé" (Cercle de Mono, Poste d'Athiémé, June 19, 1929), 1M162, Archives Nationales du Bénin.

2. Ibid.

3. For more information on the quantitative data set that this chapter relies on, see Jessica Reuther, "Street Hawking or Street Walking in Dahomey? Debates about Girls' Sexual Assaults in Colonial Tribunals, 1924–1941," *Journal of African History* 63, no. 3 (November 2022): 371–74.

4. "Procès-verbal d'audition de témoins."

5. For a further explanation of what these roles entailed, see Esther Goody, *Parenthood and Social Reproduction: Fostering and Occupational Roles in West Africa* (Cambridge: Cambridge University Press, 1982), 7–14.

6. In 2013–2014 and 2018, I systematically photographed all legal documents including information related to sexual crimes in Dahomey. These were contained in the 1M and 2M series at the Archives Nationales du Bénin and 3M, 8G, and 5C in the Archives du Sénégal. The 206 cases of *viol* count only those in which rape was the exclusive charge. This figure does not include cases of indecent assault, even though before the 1931 judicial reorganization, indecent assault could be heard in either first- or second-degree criminal tribunals in Dahomey. Many of the cases that were not rape or attempted rape of very young girls or violent rapes of adult women were considered indecent assault, even though today, we would consider many of these rapes or attempted rapes.

7. First, I work on the assumption that *aunt* is often used synonymously with *social mother* or *guardian*. The term can but does not necessarily entail a biological relationship with either of the girl's parents. For a detailed explanation of how this kinship idiom was used, see chapter 7 of this book. See also Melanie Y. Jacquemin, "'Petites nieces' et petites bonnes: le travail des fillettes en milieu urbain de Cote-d'Ivoire," *Journal des africanistes* 70, nos. 1/2 (2001): 105–22. For an analysis of a different subset of cases, see Jessica Reuther, "Irresponsible Boys, Promiscuous Girls: Maturity, Gender, and Rape Myths in the Criminal Tribunals of Colonial Dahomey, 1924–1940," *La Revue d'histoire de l'enfance "irrégulière"* 20 (November 2018), https://journals.openedition.org/rhei/4209?lang=en.

8. This list is compiled from an analysis of all two hundred–plus cases available in the Archives Nationales du Benin.

9. This narrative is primarily based on the procès-verbal given by Akouéle. Some of the details are drawn from the testimonies of Alougba and Ahoussi. "Procès-verbal d'audition de témoins—Affaire Stanislas Amoussouvi : Akouéle" (Cercle de Mono, Poste d'Athiémé, 19 June 1929) ANB 1M162, Archives Nationales du Bénin.

10. Thornberry discusses how older women in South Africa used virginity testing to monitor girls' bodies to ensure their chaste status. Elizabeth Thornberry, "Virginity Testing, History, and the Nostalgia for Custom in Contemporary South Africa," *African Studies Review* 58, no. 3 (December 2015): 134–35.

11. This list of complaints was compiled after an exhaustive review of rape cases contained in series 1M in the ANB.

12. C. B. d'Almeida, "Extrait du registre des jugements du Tribunal du 2e degré de Ouidah: Jugement n. 39 Affaire Adamon—viol," November 21, 1924, ANB 1M154, Archives Nationales du Bénin, 3–4.

13. Ibid.

14. Tribunal du 1e degré de Ouidah, "État des jugements N. 26," December 1931, 1M89, Archives Nationales du Bénin.

15. George, with the help of Wale Makanjuola, surveyed forty-six current and former septuagenarian women traders who recalled that while they were

hawkers in Lagos during the 1940s and 1950s, the chief danger that they faced was being robbed of their goods or money. George acknowledged that the fear of sexual violence may have been downplayed due to these women's reluctance to discuss issues of sexuality or sexual violence with Mr. Makanjuola. Abosede A. George, *Making Modern Girls: A History of Girlhood, Labor, and Social Development in Colonial Lagos* (Athens: Ohio University Press, 2014), 124–27.

16. Tribunal du 2e degré de Ouidah, "État des jugements rendus en matière répressive n. 17 & 18," June 13, 1930, 1M002, Archives Nationales du Bénin.

17. In his testimony, Houmpatin disputed this narrative of events, and the court seemed to believe him. Houmpatin was acquitted of the charges. This chapter, however, privileges the narratives of the girls who testified in the tribunals. The documentation does not invalidate Bodjo's recollection of events.

18. Pieussergues, "Jugement n. 22: Extrait Du Registre Des Jugements Du Tribunal de Cercle d'Allada," May 30, 1918, 1M41, Archives Nationales du Bénin.

19. William L. F. Felstiner, Richard L. Abel, and Austin Sarat, "The Emergence and Transformation of Disputes: Naming, Blaming, Claiming . . .," *Law & Society Review* 15, no. 3/4 (1980–1981): 631–32.

20. For more on this particular reorganization and how it affected the prosecution of rape, see Reuther, "Street Hawking."

21. Ibid.

22. The only time that the 1931 decree mentions age is regarding reaching the age of discernment and when a juvenile should be held accountable for his actions.

23. "Requistions n. 24," July 6, 1932. ANB 1M106, Archives Nationales du Bénin.

24. By the 1930s, Europeans condemned ambulant and itinerant professions as morally dangerous and sought ways to eradicate them. There is comparatively less information on French views concerning children's street trading in West Africa, in part because, unlike British Lagos, no indigenous activist movement existed. "Chapter 4: The Street Hawker, the Street Walker, and the Salvationist Gaze" in George, *Making Modern Girls*, 113–41. George does not use legal records to determine the veracity of this anxiety. Saheed Aderinto, *When Sex Threatened the State: Illicit Sexuality, Nationalism, and Politics in Colonial Nigeria, 1900–1958* (Urbana: University of Illinois Press, 2015), 78–81.

25. The posited blameworthiness of rape victims that plagues prosecutions of the crime of rape in a variety of contexts is one of the reasons rape victims are in a unique position. Rebecca Chennells, "Sentencing: The 'Real Rape' Myth," *Agenda: Empowering Women for Gender Equity* 82, Gender and the Legal System (2009): 32.

26. Tribunal Colonial d'Appel du Dahomey, "Réquisitoire n. 83: Affaire Hounkponou Aglo, Zannou Gankpan, Atchatin, et Avoce Fohoun—viol," August 29, 1939, 1M159, Archives Nationales du Bénin.

27. Tribunal criminel de Ouidah, "Jugement n. 1 du 26 Février 1934: Affaire viol avec violences légères," February 26, 1934, 1M162, Archives Nationales du Bénin.

28. Tribunal criminel de Athieme, "Réquisitoire n. 116: Affaire Agbavo—viol et blessures volontaires," August 12, 1935, 1M82, Archives Nationales du Bénin.

29. Tribunal criminel de Athieme.

30. Throughout the colonial period of 1894–1960, the northern districts were chronically understaffed, and overworked administrators recorded much less documentation concerning the functioning of the courts in these districts. This article analyzes cases from the southern districts of Abomey, Allada, Cotonou, Grand Popo/Mono/Athiémé, Ouidah, Porto-Novo, Savalou, and Zagnanado.

31. For a discussion of these alternative venues, see the section "Dahomeans and Colonial Legal Pluralism" in Reuther, "Street Hawking," 374–76.

32. Thornberry similarly documented the decline in the value and credibility of older women's testimony regarding virginity testing in sex crimes cases in the Eastern Cape. Thornberry, "Virginity Testing, History," 134–38.

7. The Télé Affair (1936–1938)

1. In the course of the investigation, the details of each explanation varied greatly. For a discussion of an official narrative versus popular rumors concerning the death of Émile Mauchamp, a French doctor and colonial officer stationed in Morocco, see Jonathan G. Katz, *Murder in Marrakesh: Émile Mauchamp and the French Colonial Adventure* (Bloomington: Indiana University Press, 2006).

2. William Snelgrave, *A New Account of Some Parts of Guinea and the Slave-Trade* (London: James, John, and Paul Knapton, 1734), 66. Snelgrave's account was based on his travels in West Africa in March–July 1727. He gives a detailed account of human sacrifices in the precolonial kingdom; see ibid., 37–55.

3. Luise White, *Speaking with Vampires: Rumor and History in Colonial Africa* (Berkeley: University of California Press, 2008), 321–22.

4. Dr. Romuald Michozounnou, interview February 21, 2014. Gabin Djimasse, interview, February 18 and 21, 2014. Nondichao Bachalou, interview, February 21, 2014.

5. Parker MacDonald Shipton, *The Nature of Entrustment: Intimacy, Exchange, and the Sacred in Africa*, Yale Agrarian Studies (New Haven, CT: Yale University Press, 2007), 81–91; Nicolas Argenti, "Things That Don't Come by the Road: Folktales, Fosterage, and Memories of Slavery in the Cameroon Grassfields," *Comparative Studies in Society and History* 52, no. 2 (2010): 242–49.

6. Unlike other women, Mathilde was never accused of trafficking the girl, perhaps because no one admitted to a monetary exchange accompanying her transfer.

7. Both she and her husband were originally from Aného. William Lawson moved from Aného to Abomey in 1923. It is unclear when Mathilde joined him. Lawson explained that his status as an outsider in Abomey had created problems when he tried to recruit laborers from the local population.

8. Entrusting was more than simply economic. Shipton, *Nature of Entrustment*, 10–11.

9. No one gave a precise date as to when she was entrusted to the Lawson household. William Lawson, "Monsieur le Procureur de la République," Plainte, November 10, 1936, 5C6, Archives du Sénégal.

10. Leaving home at a very young age in Sierra Leone also reflected some sort of family upheaval. See Christine Whyte, "Mothering Solidarity: Infant-Feeding, Vulnerability and Poverty in West Africa since the Seventeenth Century," *Past and Present*, 246, no. suppl. 15 (2020): 86.

11. Martin Klein and Richard Roberts, "The Resurgence of Pawning in French West Africa during the Depression of the 1930s," in *Pawnship, Slavery, and Colonialism in Africa*, ed. Paul Lovejoy and Toyin Falola (Trenton, NJ: Africa World Press, 2003), 303.

12. For more on French colonial taxation at the time, see Benjamin N. Lawrance, "La Révolte des Femmes: Economic Upheaval and the Gender of Political Authority in Lomé, Togo, 1931–33," *African Studies Review* 46, no. 1 (April 2003): 43–67; Silivi d'Almeida-Ekué, *La révolte des loméennes, 24–25 janvier 1933* (Lomé: Nouvelles éditions africaines du Togo, 1992); Laurent Manière, "Popular Unrest and the Press Campaign against the Capitation Tax in Dahomey, 1929–1935," *Journal of Policy History* 25, no. 3 (July 2013): 385–403. For the effects that this specifically had on children in Nigeria, see chapters 3 and 4 in Robin Phylisia Chapdelaine, *The Persistence of Slavery: An Economic History of Child Trafficking in Nigeria* (Amherst: University of Massachusetts Press, 2021), 107–60.

13. Patrick Manning, *Slavery, Colonialism, and Economic Growth in Dahomey, 1640–1960* (Cambridge: Cambridge University Press, 1982), 255.

14. Savineau's report on Dahomey was just one of eighteen that she wrote on households in AOF. In October 1937, Marcel de Coppet, governor-general of AOF, commissioned Savineau to tour France's colonies and produce reports on women and the family in each. Denise Savineau, "Rapport 6: Le Dahomey," March 9, 1938, 7–8, Archives Nationales du Senegal, https://www.francophoneafricaarchive.org/wp-content/uploads/2017/07/rapport6.pdf.

15. Ibid., 3.

16. In oral interviews, there was great confusion when I asked about "enfant prêté." No Beninese informant seemed to attach significance to this phrase or understand it as something specific.

17. Robin Chapdelaine makes these points about evolutions of pawnship in Nigeria. Chapdelaine, *Persistence*, 33.

18. Amaro Colombani and William Lawson, "Déclaration de Lawson Willem [sic] Mensah, né à Anécho, fils de Mensah Agbahoun et Dedevi Goudoobé," April 10, 1937, 5C6, Archives du Sénégal. Feliho was a known adversary of Justin Aho. He also played a role in encouraging Lawson to report the disappearance.

19. Ayoko stated that Télé had one kilometer to go from Ayoko's house to the Lawsons. See the second inquiry, Le Procureur de la République Roux, "Réquisitoire N. 29 (1937): Rapt de la jeune TELE," April 21, 1937, 5C6, Archives du Sénégal.

20. See the first inquiry, ibid.

21. M. de Coppet, "N. 179 a/s: Activité Fétichiste Dans Le Bas-Dahomey Réapparition Des Cultes Royaux et Sacrifices Humains, Le Gouverneur Général de l'A.O.F. à Monsieur Le Ministre Des Colonies," July 22, 1937, 5C6, Archives du Sénégal.

22. "N. 1158 A.P.A. a/s Disparition fillette TELE," to Monsieur l'administrateur Commandant le Cercle d'Abomey, December 1, 1936, 8G24 (17), Archives du Sénégal.

23. Henri-Étienne Martinet, "N. 1035 A.P.A. Objet: Transmission du Rapport d'enquête de M. l'Inspecteur COLOMBANI," July 29, 1937, 8G24 (17), Archives du Sénégal.

24. Erdmute Alber, *Transfers of Belonging: Child Fostering in West Africa in the 20th Century* (Boston: Brill, 2018), 144–46.

25. Female slavery—and subsequently servitude—was often concealed in court records with kinship terms. Kinship terms implied hierarchical relationships without necessarily denoting a biological one. The term *sister* was sometimes used, as in a case cited by Kristin Mann; see Kristin Mann, *Slavery and the Birth of an African City: Lagos, 1760–1900* (Bloomington: Indiana University Press, 2007), 287. The term *wife* could also conceal a woman's slave status in postabolition societies. See Emily S. Burrill, "'Wives of Circumstance': Gender and Slave Emancipation in Late Nineteenth-Century Senegal," *Slavery and Abolition* 29, no. 1 (March 2008): 49–63. In contemporary Côte d'Ivoire, *petite niece* is commonly used to refer to household servant girls. See Melanie Y. Jacquemin, "'Petites nieces' et petites bonnes: le travail des fillettes en milieu urbain de Coted'Ivoire," *Journal des africanistes* 70, nos. 1/2 (2001): 105–22. Mathias Deshusses, "Du confiage à l'esclavage 'Petites bonnes' ivoiriennes en France (The 'Misfortunes' of Fosterage in France: The Case of 'Little Maids' from the Ivory Coast)," *Cahiers d'Études Africaines* 45, nos. 179/180 (January 1, 2005): 731–50.

26. Jean Bartel, "N. 66 C. Objet: A.S. disparition jeune TELE," June 3, 1937, 8G24 (17), Archives du Sénégal.

27. Roux, "Réquisitoire N. 29 (1937) . . . TELE."

28. Commandant le cercle d'Abomey Bartel, "N. 7/C Objet: Affaire TELE ACAPOVI," February 6, 1938, 8G24 (17), Archives du Sénégal.

29. Aho's position as district chief came with the appointments to the related posts of first assessor to the indigenous tribunal and president of the district's Mutual Aid Society. D. You, "TLO N. 621 D. You Administrateur en Chef à Gouverneur," Telegram, April 29, 1929, 2E1, Archives Nationales du Bénin.

30. Here I am referring to a famous portrait that has been widely reproduced. Frédéric Gadmer's image titled "Dahomey, Abomey, Chef Justin Aho et ses femmes", Oungbégamè, Abomey, Dahomey (actuel Bénin)" is available through the Archives de la Planète at the Musée Albert Kahn at https://collections.albert-kahn.hauts-de-seine.fr/document/abomey-dahomey-actuel-bnin-afrique-portrait-du-chef-justin-aho-entour-de-ses-femmes/617a7a44cf8b8968b3382948?filtrerParDomaine%5B0%5D=Images%20fixes&filtrerParOprateur%5B0%5D=Gadmer,%20Fr%C3%A9d%C3%A9ric&q=dahomey%20aho&pos=503&pgn=33.

31. Toby Green, "Sumptuary Laws in Precolonial West Africa: The Examples of Benin and Dahomey," in *The Right to Dress: Sumptuary Laws in a Global Perspective, c. 1200–1800* (Cambridge: Cambridge University Press, 2019), 461–78.

32. For more information on Dahomean récades, visit the Smithsonian National Museum of African Art see: https://africa.si.edu/collections/objects/10986/recade;jsessionid=25E59D48D968B3746BB54CE9D01327CD. Even in exile in Martinique and Blida, all of these items of his royal stature migrated along with Béhanzin, the former king. The only noticeably absent accoutrement that Béhanzin was frequently pictured with, which is missing in Aho's portrait, was a pipe to smoke Brazilian tobacco.

33. Roberto Zaugg, "The King's Chinese Spittoon: Global Commodities, Court Culture and Vodun in the Kingdoms of Hueda and Dahomey (Seventeenth to Nineteenth Centuries)," *Annales: Histoire, Sciences Sociales* 73, no. 1 (2018): 115–53.

34. Michozounnou, interview. Djimasse, interview. Bachalou, interview. A fundamental element of vodun is the belief that a link exists between the visible world of the living and the invisible world of the spirits. To ensure prosperity in the visible, living world, vodun adherents must communicate with the invisible spirit world through rituals whereby blood sacrifices of animals and, in the case of royal spirits, humans "watered" the graves of the ancestors.

35. Michozzounnou, interview. Melville J. Herskovits, *Dahomey: An Ancient West African Kingdom*, vol. 2 (New York: J. J. Augustin, 1938), 55–57, and Robin Law, "'My Head Belongs to the King': On the Political and Ritual Significance of Decapitation in Precolonial Dahomey," *Journal of African History* 30, no. 3 (January 1, 1989): 399–415.

36. Robin Law, "Human Sacrifice in Precolonial West Africa," *African Affairs* 84, no. 334 (January 1985): 86; Catherine Coquery-Vidrovitch, "La Fête Des Coutumes Au Dahomey: Historique Et Essai D'interprétation," *Annales: Histoire, Sciences Sociales* 19, no. 4 (1964): 696–716.

37. For an outline of the incorporation of chiefs into the colonial power hierarchy and the decline of Abomey within this structure, see Katherine Payne Moseley, "Indigenous and External Factors in Colonial Politics: Southern Dahomey to 1939" (PhD diss., Columbia University, 1975), 210–25. For a discussion of the larger phenomenon of the period whereby France tried to eliminate the "feudal vestiges" of aristocratic rule in West Africa and the hostility of the administration toward the chiefs before World War I, see Alice Conklin, "Colonialism and Human Rights, A Contradiction in Terms? The Case of France and West Africa, 1895–1914," *American Historical Review* 103, no. 2 (April 1998): 425–28.

38. Luc Garcia, "Archives et tradition orale: Á propos d'une enquête sur la politique du royaume de Danhomé à la fin du 19e siècle," *Cahiers d'études africaines*, Histoire Africaine: Constatations, Contestations 16, nos. 61/62 (1976): 198.

39. For more on both Dahomean and French views on human sacrifice and French colonial policies on the ritual, see Lynne Ellsworth Larsen, *Dahomey's Royal Architecture: An Earthen Record of Construction, Subjugation, and Reclamation* (Oxon: Routledge, 2023).

40. "T.L.O. N. 0079 Réponse à 1134 du 26 Novembre," December 3, 1936, 8G24 (17), Archives du Sénégal.

41. It is unclear when this occurred or how extensive it was. Abomeyans mentioned this search when they recalled the Télé Affair, but I found no documentation of who conducted the search or when. Aho was repeatedly interrogated and asked for testimony. Nondichao Bachalou, interview.

42. Eleanor Aho Agoli-Agbo, interview, February 19, 2014.

43. Justin Aho, "Le Chef de Canton d'Oumbégamé, Chevalier de la Légion d'Honneur, à M. l'Inspecteur des Affaires Administratives en mission au Dahomey," July 22, 1936, 8G24 (17), Archives du Sénégal.

44. Martinet, "N. 1035 A.P.A. Objet: COLOMBANI."

45. M. de Coppet, "N. 731 AP/2 Incidents d'Abomey Rapport Colombani, Le Gouverneur Général de l'A.O.F. à Monsieur Le Gouverneur Du Dahomey," September 11, 1937, 4, 5C6, Archives du Sénégal.

46. For Mali, see Marie Rodet, "Continuum of Gendered Violence: The Colonial Invention of Female Desertion as a Customary Criminal Offense, French Soudan, 1900–1949," in *Domestic Violence and the Law in Colonial and Postcolonial Africa*, New African Histories (Athens: Ohio University Press, 2010), 74–93. For a brief discussion of the literature on "runaway" women, see the literature review in the introduction of Brett Lindsay Shadle, *"Girl Cases": Marriage and Colonialism in Gusiiland, Kenya, 1890–1970* (Portsmouth, NH: Heinemann, 2006), xxvi–xxviii.

47. Martinet, "N. 1035 A.P.A. Objet: COLOMBANI."

48. Commandant le cercle d'Abomey Bartel, "N. 7/C Objet: Affaire Tele Acapovi," February 6, 1938, 8G24 (17), Archives du Sénégal.

49. Emilien Darand, "Procès-verbal d'audition de temoins: William Mensah Lawson," November 17, 1936, 8G24 (17), Archives du Sénégal.

50. The legal system in the mandate of Togo was different from that in operation in the colonies of AOF. The criminal tribunal was composed of the district commandant, one European assessor, and one indigenous assessor. For more detail on the legal system in Togo during the 1930s, see the April 21, 1933, decree.

51. Tribunal Criminel d'Anécho, "Jugement n. 4: Affaire AGLAO et Consorts—Meurtres, enlèvement et séquestration de personnes, complot tendant à troubler la peix [sic] intérieure du Territoire complicté," October 18, 1935, Microfiche 3799 Togo, Paris Evangelical Missionary Society. Benjamin Lawrance augments this trial transcript with oral interviews in his analysis of the Affaire Aglao; see "Chapter 4 Vodou and Resistance: Politico-Religious Crises in the Periurban Landscape" Benjamin N. Lawrance, *Locality, Mobility, and "Nation": Periurban Colonialism in Togo's Eweland 1900–1960* (Rochester, NY: Rochester University Press, 2007), 90–120.

52. Tribunal Criminel d'Anécho, "Jugement n. 4: Affaire AGLAO."

53. In total, four defendants were sentenced to death, three to life in prison, and seven to ten years of prison each. One of the four to receive the death penalty was sentenced in absentia. Tribunal Criminel d'Anécho.

54. This investigation into Télé's disappearance was part of a larger inquiry concerning indigenous and French corruption in the circle of Abomey. For more detail on the pressure from Dakar, see Ruth Ginio, "Investigating the Investigators: French Colonial Attempts to Supervise Its Policing System during the 1930s," *Historical Reflections* 46, no. 2 (Summer 2020): 52–58. Ginio's emphasis on the review of murder cases at the federation level presents a slightly different assessment of causal events in the investigation. She is absolutely right in saying that neither the documentation nor oral tradition in Abomey produces a clear and coherent narrative about the Télé Affair. Darand, " Procès-verbal d'audition de temoins."

55. Chef de subdivision, "Fiche des renseignements concernant un chef ou notable indigène: BADOU Jerôme," August 25, 1938, 8G29 (23), Archives du Sénégal. The colonial administration struggled to understand how Abomeyans could be foreigners in areas formerly under the control of the precolonial Kingdom of Dahomey. They did not see this as an important distinction. In the region of Athiémé, this practice of giving chiefly office to Abomeyans was vehemently denounced as "foreign" rule. Badou's status as a lesser member was evident in the fact that he had been unable to secure a chiefly office within the district of Abomey, his ancestral lands. The Adja chiefs and those under his authority in Lonkly believed that Badou had performed human sacrifice in order to silence their opinions that he was a foreign overlord and an illegitimate usurper. However, Badou traced his descent from Ghezo, the ninth king of Abomey.

The prestige of princes declined, as their ancestor receded in the king's line. Badou was greater removed and therefore a less powerful member of the royal lineage than Aho.

56. Sena's disappearance prompted the commandant of Abomey to transfer all of the materials he had gathered on Télé to the district attorney, who finally filed an indictment against an anonymous defendant on April 16, 1937. Roux, "Réquisitoire N. 29 (1937) . . . TELE." Jean Bartel, "N. 192/C. Objet: a/s Disparition TELE ACAPOVI," December 18, 1937, 8G24 (17), Archives du Sénégal.

57. Other missing girls were rumored to have been the victims of sacrifice, but minimal effort was put into investigating these cases, and the rumors were not reported in media coverage. Newspapers did discuss other instances of ritual violence and crime. In 1925, the second-degree tribunal in Djougou convicted nine men for sacrificing a five-year-old boy in a ritual ceremony. The proceedings showed that three men were acquitted of the charges. Djougou was in northwestern Dahomey. Unlike the cases for southern Dahomey in the 1930s, the only evidence on this case was the *état des jugement*'s two-paragraph synopsis and the sentences awarded. Tribunal du 2e degré de Djougou, "État des jugements rendus en matière répressive jugement n. 1: [name illegible] et al.," February 31, 1925, 1M166, Archives Nationales du Bénin.

58. In 1905, France established the French West African Federation, a bureaucratic structure that centrally administered all of France's West African colonial possessions from Dakar, Senegal. The federation included both Côte d'Ivoire and Dahomey, the modern-day Republic of Benin. *Notre Voix*'s coverage of events in Dahomey was uncommon but not unprecedented.

59. Colonial officials and indigenous intermediaries repeatedly described human sacrifice as "barbaric" and an outmoded practice that had ceased with Agoli-Agbo. Ginio, "Investigating the Investigators," 54.

60. For a discussion of the paradoxes of France's identity as a "civilizing" imperial power, see Alice Conklin, *A Mission to Civilize: The Republican Idea of Empire in France and West Africa, 1895–1930* (Stanford, CA: Stanford University Press, 2001). Conklin, "Colonialism and Human Rights."

61. "T.L.O.N. 0079 Réponse à 1134 du 26 Novembre," December 3, 1936, 8G24 (17), Archives du Sénégal.

62. Bartel, "N. 7/C Objet: Affaire Tele Acapovi," February 6, 1938.

63. Nondichao Bachalou, February 21, 2014. Bartel, "N. 7/C Objet: Affaire Tele Acapovi," February 6, 1938.

64. Bartel, "N. 7/C Objet: Affaire TELE ACAPOVI."

65. Bachalou, interview. Michozzounnou, interview.

66. Georges Vigarello, *A History of Rape: Sexual Violence in France from the 16th to the 20th Century*, trans. Jean Birrell (Cambridge: Polity, 2001), 77.

Conclusion

1. For more on Fortier and his photography, see Daniela Moreau and Luis Nicolau Parés, *Images Du Dahomey: Edmond Fortier et Le Colonialisme Français Dans La Terre Des Voduns* (Milan: 5 Continents Editions, 2020).

2. Sarah Maza, "The Kids Aren't All Right: Historians and the Problem of Childhood," *American Historical Review* 125, no. 4 (October 2020): 1262–63.

3. By *imaginable*, I mean the most likely scenario based on oral tradition and an exhaustive excavation of the written records. This approach is inspired by the work of Ada Ferrer. See her reflective essay, Ada Ferrer, "Slavery, Freedom, and the Work of Speculation," *Small Axe* 23, no. 1 (March 2019): 222–23.

4. This approach to archival paucity and the stretching of fragments is based on Marisa Fuentes's research on Black women in colonial Barbados. See Marisa J. Fuentes, *Dispossessed Lives: Enslaved Women, Violence, and the Archive* (Philadelphia: University of Pennsylvania Press, 2016), 146–47.

5. Saheed Aderinto has made this observation in much more general terms in the context of Nigerian childhood; see Saheed Aderinto, ed., *Children and Childhood in Colonial Nigerian Histories* (New York: Palgrave Macmillan, 2015), 2.

6. Grier makes this argument in a gender-neutral sense encompassing all children's labor. Beverly Grier, "Child Labor and Africanist Scholarship: A Critical Overview," *African Studies Review* 47, no. 2 (September 1, 2004): 3.

7. Robin Phylisia Chapdelaine, *The Persistence of Slavery: An Economic History of Child Trafficking in Nigeria* (Amherst: University of Massachusetts Press, 2021), 6.

8. For more information on how rights-in-persons operated in general terms, see Kopytoff and Miers, "Introduction," 7–11. Chapdelaine makes this point in a gender-neutral manner regarding all children in Nigeria; see Chapdelaine, *Persistence*, 6.

9. Office of the High Commissioner of Human Rights (OHCHR), "Benin: Too Many Child Victims of Abuse, Violence and Exploitation, Warns UN Expert," November 8, 2013, http://www.ohchr.org/en/NewsEvents/Pages/DisplayNews.aspx?NewsID=13969&LangID=E. These quotes come from a press release that was published on the website of the United Nations' Office of the High Commissioner of Human Rights and widely circulated via email. Maalla M'jid published a longer report on her visit to Benin in March of 2014. Najat Maalla M'jid, "Report of the Special Rapporteur on the Sale of Children, Child Prostitution and Child Pornography on Her Visit to Benin (28 October–8 November 2013)" (United Nations Human Rights Council, March 5, 2014), www.ohchr.org.

10. Maalla M'jid, "Report of the Special Rapporteur." Law discusses the dominance of precolonial stasis paradigm for the twentieth-century historiography of precolonial Dahomey. Even those scholars who did not fall into this

category of promulgating stasis rarely looked at intimate and personal lives of the nonelite. Robin Law, "'Legitimate' Trade and Gender Relations in Yorubaland and Dahomey," in *From Slave Trade to "Legitimate" Commerce: The Commercial Transition in Nineteenth-Century West Africa*, ed. Robin Law, African Studies Series 86 (Cambridge: Cambridge University Press, 1995), 195. Only recently have scholars begun to challenge this conception of a precolonial stasis in Africa regarding such socially fundamental categories as childhood or motherhood. Rhiannon Stephens challenges the universalism and eternality of motherhood in precolonial Uganda in Rhiannon Stephens, *A History of African Motherhood: The Case of Uganda, 700–1900* (Cambridge: Cambridge University Press, 2013).

11. See Neil Howard, "Is 'Child Placement' Trafficking? Questioning the Validity of an Accepted Discourse," *Anthropology Today* 27, no. 6 (December 2011): 3–7.

12. Office to Monitor and Combat Trafficking in Persons, "2021 Trafficking in Persons Report: Benin" (Washington, DC: US Department of State, 2021), https://www.state.gov/reports/2021-trafficking-in-persons-report/benin/.

13. The Republic of Benin, then known as Dahomey, gained independence from France in 1960 after sixty-six years of colonial rule. Dahomey changed its name to Benin in 1972. Elvire Ahounou-Houenassou interview, January 16, 2014. Marie Noelle Maffon interview, January 16, 2014. Sonia Mahame interview, January 21, 2014. Guirlene March interview, January 20, 2014. This narrative was repeated often in news coverage of these issues in radio, television, and newspaper discussions.

14. Ibid. Beninese people routinely accept and encourage girls as young as ten to leave home as vidomégòn, despite the awareness that some mistresses exploit, abuse, and mistreat these girls.

15. All my informants insisted that residing outside their parents' household or lineage compound was important for a child (*une enfant*) to be well raised (*bien-élevée*). This phenomenon was not limited to West Africa. To understand child circulation from global perspectives, see Suzanne Lallemand, *La circulation des enfants en société traditionnelle: prêt, don, échange* (Paris: Editions L'Harmattan, 1993).

16. For theoretical and comparative studies that support this point, see Jessaca B. Leinaweaver, *The Circulation of Children: Kinship, Adoption, and Morality in Andean Peru* (Durham, NC: Duke University Press, 2008), 2. Lallemand, *La circulation des enfants*, 34. Peter Parkes, "Fostering Fealty: A Comparative Analysis of Tributary Allegiances of Adoptive Kinship," *Comparative Studies in Society and History* 45, no. 4 (October 2003): 741–45.

17. Elodie Razy and Marie Rodet, eds., *Children on the Move in Africa: Past and Present Experiences of Migration* (Suffolk: James Currey, 2016), 5.

18. Niara Sudarkasa, "Interpreting the African Heritage in Afro-American Family Organization," in *Families in the U.S.: Kinship and Domestic Politics*, ed. Karen V. Hansen and Anita Ilta Garey, Women in the Political Economy (Philadelphia: Temple University Press, 1998), 93–97.

19. Oyèrónkẹ́ Oyěwùmí, "Family Bonds/Conceptual Binds: African Notes on Feminist Epistemologies," *Signs* 25, no. 4: Feminisms at a Millennium (2000): 1096.

20. Other ways that African households differed from the nuclear family model included their practice of polygyny, when a husband takes multiple wives. Another example was a preference for matrilineal over patrilineal organizations that were dominant in European and white settler societies.

BIBLIOGRAPHY

Archival Sources

Archives Nationales du Bénin, Porto-Novo, Benin

Le fonds anciens ou du Dahomey colonial: 1840–1960
    Personnel (1C)
    Études générales (1D)
    Politique générale (1E)
    Commandement indigène (2E)
    Justice (1M & 2M)
    Travail et main d'oeuvre (S)
Note on Series M (Justice): Series M had at one point been partially indexed, but before 2012–2014, it had been reorganized. As a result, dossiers and documents no longer corresponded to the handwritten, incomplete index. What had been indexed as 2M or 3M seemed at some point to have been fully or partially incorporated into 1M. I therefore have not listed dossier titles here, as they were list-like and often inaccurate. Between August and December 2013, I analyzed all available judicial documents—1M1–1M190—totaling around 150. This is an estimate because some numbered boxes actually contained two cartons of documents; for example, 1M152-1 and 1M152-2. The following thirty-nine boxes were missing or unavailable, had never existed or had been reorganized but never updated in sequencing in the 1M series: 1M51–1M64, 1M76, 1M80, 1M85, 1M87, 1M90, 1M97, 1M104–1M105, 1M108, 1M111, 1M125, 1M132, 1M137, 1M144, 1M145, 1M149, 1M158, 1M170, 1M175, 1M178–1M181, 1M183, and 1M184.

Archives de la Traite

Archives nationales du Bénin. "Portfolio." *Archives de la traite* 2014–2024. http://www.dan.ilemi.net/Archives-de-la-traite.html.

This digitized collection of Archives nationales du Bénin materials contains selected materials from the following series:
E: Affaires politiques
S: Travail et main d'œuvre
B: Correspondance générale

Archives du Sénégal, Dakar, Senegal

Fonds modernes du A.O.F.
    Affaires Contentieuses (5C)
    Affaires politiques, administratives et musulmanes du Dahomey (8G)
    Affaires politiques, administratives et musulmanes du Togo (14G)
    Service judiciaire de l'A.O.F. (3M)
Savineau, Denise. "Rapport 6: Le Dahomey," March 9, 1938. https://www.francophoneafricaarchive.org/wp-content/uploads/2017/07/rapport6.pdf.

Archives Nationales d'Outre-Mer, Aix-en-Provence, France

Fonds Ministériels (FM)
    Ministère des Colonies séries documentaires Dahomey DAHO I
    Affaires Politiques FM 1AFFPOL
Fonds Moderne A.O.F. Sous Serie G (microfilm)
    Dahomey 8G
    Affaires Politiques A.O.F. 17G
Paris Evangelical Society (microfiche)
    Tribunal Criminel d'Anécho. "Jugement n. 4: Affaire AGLAO et Consorts—Meurtres, enlèvement et séquestration de personnes, complot tendant à troubler la peix [sic] intérieure du Territoire complicté," October 18, 1935. Microfiche 3799 Togo. Paris Evangelical Missionary Society.

Newspapers and Journals

Journal officiel de la République Française
Journal officiel de l'Afrique occidentale française
Journal officiel de la République du Dahomey
Bibliothèque ANOM, Aix-en-Provence, France
    L'Etoile du Dahomey BIB SOM POM/B/251
    La Presse Porto-Novienne BIB SOM POM/C/906
    Le Cœur du Dahomey BIB SOM POM/C/901
    Le Messager du Benin BIB SOM POM/C/933
    Le Trait d'union dahoméen BIB SOM POM/C/902
    Vers la suprême sagesse BIB SOM POM/C/903
Schomburg Center for Research in Black Culture, New York Public Library, New York City, United States. Melville J. and Frances S. Herskovits papers, 1902–1972.

Interviews

Antoine Metodjo, November 28, 2013. Cotonou, Benin.
Elvire Ahounou-Houenassou, January 16, 2014. Cotonou, Benin.
Marie Noelle Maffon, January 16, 2014. Cotonou, Benin.
Guirlene March, January 20, 2014. Cotonou, Benin.
Sonia Mahame, January 21, 2014. Porto-Novo, Benin.
Dr. Euloge Akodjetin, January 28, 2014. Cotonou, Benin.
Dr. Felix Iroko, February 2, 2014. Cotonou, Benin.
Dr. Romuald Michozounnou, February 12, 2014. Cotonou, Benin. February 21, 2014. Abomey, Benin.
Dah Fiossi Behanzin, February 18, 2014. Abomey, Benin.
Morel Behanzin, February 18, 2014. Abomey, Benin.
Gabin Djimasse, February 18 and 21, 2014. Abomey, Benin.
Eleanor Agoli-Agbo (née Aho), February 19, 2014. Abomey, Benin.
Nah Gangnidjè Agoli-Agbo, February 19, 2014. Abomey, Benin.
Dah Ahande Aboli-Agbo, February 19, 2014. Abomey, Benin.
Nondichao Bachalou, February 21, 2014. Abomey, Benin.
Vivi L'Internationale, March 6, 2014. Porto-Novo, Benin.

Published Contemporary Sources

Adams, John. *Remarks on the Country Extending from Cape Palmas to the River Congo*. London: Frank Cass, [1823] 1966.
Albéca, Alexandre L. d'. *La France au Dahomey*. Paris: Hachette, 1895.
Barbot. *Barbot on Guinea*. Vol. 2. Second Series no. 176. Hakluyt Society, n.d.
Béraud, M. "Note Sur Le Dahomé." *Bulletin de La Société de Géographie*, 5th Series, 12 (1866): 374–86.
Beurdeley, E. *La Justice Indigène En Afrique Occidentale Française: Mission d'études 1913–1914*, 1916. http://gallica.bnf.fr/ark:/12148/bpt6k147625h.
Blanchely. "Au Dahomey: Premier voyage de M. Blanchely ainé gérant de la factorerie de M. Régis, de Marseille, à Whydah (1843)." *Les Missions Catholiques* 23 (January–December 1891): 545–48.
———. "Au Dahomey: Relation Du Deuxième Voyage Fait En 1850, Dans Le Royaume Du Dahomey, Par M. Blanchely Ainé, En Compagnie de M. Esprit Cases, Nouvel Agent de La Factorerie Française Régis Ainé, de Whydah." *Les Missions Catholiques* 23 (January–December 1891): 575–76.
Borghero, Francesco. *Journal du premier missionnaire du Dahomey, 1860–1864*. Edited by Renzo Mandirola. Monee, IL: SMA, 2018.
Bosman, William. *A New and Accurate Description of the Coast of Guinea: Divided into the Gold, the Slave, and the Ivory Coasts*. 4th English ed. London: Frank Cass, 1967.
Bouche, Pierre. *Sept Ans En Afrique Occidentale: La Côte Des Esclaves et Le Dahomey*. Paris: Librarie Plon, 1885.

Bouët, Auguste. "Le Royaume de Dahomey: Relation Du Voyage de M. Le Lieutenant de Vaisseau Auguste Bouët, Envoyé En Mission Près Du Roi Du Dahomey, En Mai 1851." *L'Illustration, Journel Universel*. July 17, 1852.

Brunet, Louis, and Louis Giethlen. *Dahomey et Dépendances*. Exposition Universelle de 1900—Les Colonies Françaises. Paris: Augustin Challamel, 1900.

Burton, Richard Francis. *A Mission to Gelele, King of Dahome: With Notices of the So Called*. Vols. 1 & 2. 2 vols. London: Tinsley Brothers, 1864.

Chappet, E. *Études Sur Les Côtes Occidentales de l'Afrique: La Côte Des Esclaves*. Lyon: Imprimerie Générale de Lyon, 1881.

Chaudhuri, Nupur, Sherry J. Katz, and Mary Elizabeth Perry. "Introduction." In *Contesting Archives: Finding Women in the Sources*, edited by Nupur Chaudhuri, Sherry J. Katz, and Mary Elizabeth Perry, xii–xxiv. Urbana: University of Illinois Press, 2010.

Chaudoin, E. *Trois mois de captivité au Dahomey*. Paris: Hachette, 1891.

Chautard, P. *Le Dahomey*. Lyon: Librairie Emmanuel Vitte, 1890.

Crowther, Samuel. *Vocabulary of the Yoruba Language*. London: Seeleys, 1852.

Dalzel, Archibald. *The History of Dahomy an Inland Kingdom of Africa; Compiled from Authentic Memoirs; with an Introduction and Notes*. London: T. Spilsbury and Son, 1793.

Daniel, Jean. *Le palmier à huile au Dahomey*. Revue Coloniale. Paris: Librarie Maritime et Coloniale, 1902.

Dapper, D'O. *Description de l'Afrique*. Johnson Reprint Corporation. Landmarks in Anthropology. Amsterdam: Chez Wolfgang, Waesberge, Boom & van Someren, 1686.

de Chenevert, and Bullet. "Réflexions sur Juda par les Sieurs de Chenevert et abbé Bullet," June 1, 1776. MS 111. Archives Nationale d'Outre Mer.

Delbée. "Journal du voyage du Sieur Delbée, commissaire general de la marine, aux isles, dans la coste de Guynée, pour l'établissement du commerce en ces pays, en l'année 1669." In *Relation de ce qui s'est passé dans les Isles et terre-ferme de l'Amérique, pendant la dernière guerre avec l'Angleterre, et depuis en exécution du traitté de Breda*, by Jean de Clodoré, 347–494. Paris: Chez Gervais Clozier, 1671.

Duncan, John. *Travels in Western Africa in 1845 & 1846: A Journey from Whydah, through the Kingdom of Dahomey, to Adofoodia, in the Interior*. Vol. 1. 2 vols. London: Richard Bentley, 1847.

Foà, Edouard. *Le Dahomey: Histoire, Géographie, Moeurs, Coutumes, Commerce, Industrie, Expeditions Françaises (1891–1894)*. Paris: A. Hennuyer, 1895.

Forbes, Frederick Edwyn. *Dahomey and the Dahomans: Being the Journals of Two Missions of the King of Dahomey . . . in the Years 1849 and 1850*. Vols. 1 & 2. 2 vols. London: Longman, 1851.

Freeman, Thomas B. *Journal of Various Visits to the Kingdoms of Ashanti, Aku and Dahomi, in Western Africa*. 2nd ed. London: John Mason, 1844.

Gellé, Lieutenant de vaisseau. "Notice Sur Porto-Novo (Côte Occidentale d'afrique)." *Revue Maritime et Coloniale*, March 1864, 413–30.

Guillevin, Alfred-Baptiste-Félix. *Voyage dans l'intérieur du royaume de Dahomey*. Nouvelles Annales des Voyages, de la géographie et de l'histoire. Paris: Librarie de la société de géographie, 1862.

Hagen, A. "La Colonie de Porto-Novo et Le Roi Toffa." *Revue d'ethnographie* 6 (March–April 1877): 81–116.

Heywood, Linda M., and John K. Thornton. "Kongo and Dahomey, 1660–1815: African Political Leadership in the Era of the Slave Trade and Its Impact on the Formation of African Identity in Brazil." In *Soundings in Atlantic History: Latent Structures and Intellectual Currents, 1500–1830*, edited by Patricia L. Denault and Bernard Bailyn, 86–111. Cambridge: Harvard University Press, 2009.

Labarthe, Pierre. *Voyage à La Côte de Guinée, Ou Descriptions Des Côtes d'Afrique Depuis Le Cap Tagrin Jusqu'au ca de Lopez-Gonzalves*. Paris: Chez DeBray, 1803.

Labat, Jean Baptiste. *Voyage Du Chevalier Des Marchais En Guinée, Isles Voisines, et à Cayenne, Fait En 1725, 1726 & 1727*. Amsterdam: Aux dépens de la Compagnie, 1731.

Laffitte, J. (Abbé). *Le Dahomé: souvenirs de voyage et de mission*. Tours: Alfred Mame et fils, 1873.

———. *Le Pays Des Nègres*. Tours: Alfred Mame et fils, 1876.

Le Hérissé, Auguste. *L'ancien Royaume Du Dahomey, Moeurs, Religion, Histoire*. 1911. http://gallica.bnf.fr/ark:/12148/bpt6k209284r.

M'Leod, John. *A Voyage to Africa with Some Account of the Manners and Customs of the Dahomian People*. London: John Murray, 1820.

Norris, Robert. *Memoirs of the Reign of Bossa Ahádee, King of Dahomy, an Inland Country of Guiney, to Which Are Added the Author's Journey to Abomey, the Capital, and a Short Account of the African Slave Trade*. 1st ed., new impression. London: Frank Cass, 1966.

Oettinger, Johann Peter. *A German Barber-Surgeon in the Atlantic Slave Trade: The Seventeenth-Century Journal of Johann Peter Oettinger*. Translated by Craig Koslofsky and Roberto Zaugg. Charlottesville: University of Virginia Press, 2020.

Pruneau de Pommegorge, Antoine Edme. *Description de la nigritie*. Amsterdam: Chez Maradan, 1789.

Repin, Pierre-Clément. "Voyage au Dahomey." *Le Tour du monde: nouveau journal des voyages* 7, first semester (1863): 65–112.

Reynier. "Ouidah: Organisation Du Commandement [1917]." *Mémoire Du Bénin* 2 (1993): 28–73.

Ridgway, Archibald R. "Journal of a Visit to Dahomey; or, the Snake Country." *New Monthly Magazine* 81, no. 3 (1847): 187–98, 299–309, 406–14.

Skertchly, J. A. *Dahomey as It Is: Being a Narrative of Eight Months' Residence in That Country* . . . London: Chapman and Hall, 1874.

Smith, William. *A New Voyage to Guinea*. London: Frank Cass, 1967.

Snelgrave, William. *A New Account of Some Parts of Guinea and the Slave-Trade*. 3 vols. London: James, John, and Paul Knapton, 1734.

Vallon, A. "Le Royaume de Dahomey: Côtes occidentales d'Afrique." *Revue Maritime et Coloniale* 59 (August 1861): 332–63.

———. "Le Royaume de Dahomey: Voyage à Abomey." *Revue Maritime et Coloniale* 3 (October 1861): 329–58.

Secondary Sources

Achebe, Nwando. *The Female King of Colonial Nigeria Ahebi Ugbabe*. Bloomington: Indiana University Press, 2011.

———. *Female Monarchs and Merchant Queens in Africa*. Athens: Ohio University Press, 2020.

Aderinto, Saheed, ed. *Children and Childhood in Colonial Nigerian Histories*. New York: Palgrave Macmillan, 2015.

———. *When Sex Threatened the State: Illicit Sexuality, Nationalism, and Politics in Colonial Nigeria, 1900–1958*. Urbana: University of Illinois Press, 2015.

Ajayi, J. F. Ade, and B. O. Olọruntimẹhin. "West Africa in the Anti-Slave Trade Era." In *The Cambridge History of Africa, Volume 5 from c. 1790 to c. 1870*, edited by John E. Flint, 5:200–221. Cambridge: Cambridge University Press, 1976.

Ajayi, J. F. Ade, and Robert Smith. *Yoruba Warfare in the Nineteenth Century*. Cambridge: Cambridge University Press, 1964.

Akinjogbin, I. A. "Archibald Dalzel: Slave Trader and Historian of Dahomey." *Journal of African History* 7, no. 1 (January 1, 1966): 67–78.

———. *Dahomey and Its Neighbours, 1708–1818*. Cambridge: Cambridge University Press, 1967.

———. "The Expansion of Ọyọ and the Rise of Dahomey, 1600–1800." In *History of West Africa*, edited by J. F. A. Ajayi and Michael Crowder, 1:304–43. New York: Columbia University Press, 1972.

———, ed. *War and Peace in Yorùbáland, 1793–1893*. Ibadan: Heinemann Educational Books, 1998.

Akyeampong, Emmanuel. "History, Memory, Slave-Trade and Slavery in Anlo (Ghana)." *Slavery and Abolition* 22, no. 3 (December 2001): 1–24.

Alber, Erdmute. "Denying Biological Parenthood: Fosterage in Northern Benin." *Ethnos* 68, no. 4 (December 2003): 487–506.

———. "No School without Foster Families in Northern Benin: A Social Historical Approach." In *Parenting after the Century of the Child*, 57–78. Burlington, VT: Ashgate, 2010.

———. "The Transfer of Belonging: Theories on Child Fostering in West Africa Reviewed." In *Child Fostering in West Africa: New Perspectives on Theory and Practice*, 79–107. Leiden: Brill, 2013.

———. *Transfers of Belonging: Child Fostering in West Africa in the 20th Century*. Boston: Brill, 2018.

Alber, Erdmute, and Astrid Bochow. "Changes in African Families: A Review of Anthropological and Sociological Approaches towards Family and Kinship in Africa." In *Frontiers of Globalization: Kinship and Family Structures in Africa*, edited by Ana Marta González, Laurie F. DeRose, and Florence Oloo, 1–30. Trenton, NJ: Africa World Press, 2011.

Alber, Erdmute, Jeannett Martin, and Catrien Notermans, eds. *Child Fostering in West Africa: New Perspectives on Theory and Practices*. Vol. 9. Africa-Europe Group for Interdisciplinary Studies. Leiden: Brill, 2013.

Allman, Jean. "Fashioning Africa: Power and the Politics of Dress." In *Fashioning Africa: Power and the Politics of Dress*, edited by Jean Allman, 1–10. Bloomington: Indiana University Press, 2004.

Allman, Jean, and Victoria Tashjian. *"I Will Not Eat Stone": A Women's History of Colonial Asante*. Portsmouth, NH: Heinemann, 2000.

Alpern, Stanley B. *Abson and Company: Slave Traders in Eighteenth-Century West Africa*. London: Hurst, 2019.

Anderson, Richard, and Henry Lovejoy, eds. *Liberated Africans and the Abolition of the Slave Trade, 1807–1896*. Rochester Studies in African History and the Diaspora Book. Rochester: University of Rochester Press, 2020.

Anderson, Richard Peter. *Abolition in Sierra Leone: Re-Building Lives and Identities in Nineteenth-Century West Africa*. African Identities: Past and Present. Cambridge: Cambridge University Press, 2020.

Apter, Andrew. *Odudwa's Chain: Locations of Culture in the Yorùbá-Atlantic*. Chicago: University of Chicago Press, 2017.

Araujo, Ana Lucia. "Dahomey, Portugal and Bahia: King Adandozan and the Atlantic Slave Trade." *Slavery & Abolition* 33, no. 1 (March 2012): 1–19.

Argenti, Nicolas. "Things That Don't Come by the Road: Folktales, Fosterage, and Memories of Slavery in the Cameroon Grassfields." *Comparative Studies in Society and History* 52, no. 2 (2010): 224–54.

Asiwaju, A. I. "Dahomey, Yorubaland, Borgu and Benin in the Nineteenth Century." In *General History of Africa*, vol. 6: Africa in the Nineteenth Century until the 1880s: 699–723. Berkeley: University of California Press, 1989.

Bailey, Moya. "Misogynoir in Medical Media: On Caster Semenya and R. Kelly." *Catalyst: Feminism, Theory, Technoscience* 2, no. 2 (2016): 1–31.

Barnes, Sandra T. "Gender and the Politics of Support and Protection in Precolonial West Africa." *Annals of the New York Academy of Sciences* 810, no. 1 (1997): 1–18.

Bastian, Misty L. "'Vultures of the Marketplace': Southeastern Nigerian Women and the Discourses of the Ogu Umunwaanyi (Women's War) of 1929." In *Women in African Colonial Histories*, edited by Jean Allman, Susan Geiger, and Nakanyike Musisi, 260–81. Bloomington: Indiana University Press, 2002.

Bay, Edna G. "Belief, Legitimacy and the Kpojito: An Institutional History of the 'Queen Mother' in Precolonial Dahomey." *Journal of African History* 36, no. 1 (January 1995): 1–27.

———. "On the Trail of the Bush King: A Dahomean Lesson in the Use of Evidence." *History in Africa* 6 (1979): 1–15.

———. "Protection, Political Exile, and the Atlantic Slave Trade: History and Collective Memory in Dahomey." *Slavery & Abolition* 22, no. 1 (2001): 42–60.

———. *Wives of the Leopard: Gender, Politics, and Culture in the Kingdom of Dahomey*. Charlottesville: University of Virginia Press, 1998.

Bledsoe, Caroline H. *Women and Marriage in Kpelle Society*. Stanford, CA: Stanford University Press, 1980.

Blier, Suzanne Preston. *African Vodun: Art, Psychology, and Power*. Chicago: University of Chicago Press, 1995.

———. "Field Days: Melville J. Herskovits in Dahomey." *History in Africa* 16 (January 1, 1989): 1–22.

———. "The Path of the Leopard: Motherhood and Majesty in Early Danhomè." *Journal of African History* 36, no. 3 (1995): 391–417.

———. *The Royal Arts of Africa: The Majesty of Form*. New York: Harry N. Abrams, 1998.

Boddy, Janice Patricia. *Civilizing Women: British Crusades in Colonial Sudan*. Princeton: Princeton University Press, 2007.

Brady, Ivan A. *Transactions in Kinship: Adoption and Fosterage in Oceania*. Association of Social Anthropology in Oceania. ASAO Monograph; No. 4. Honolulu: University Press of Hawaii, 1976.

Brauner, Christina. "Connecting Things: Trading Companies and Diplomatic Gift-Giving on the Gold and Slave Coasts in the Seventeenth and Eighteenth Centuries." *Journal of Early Modern History* 20 (2016): 408–28.

Bressey, Caroline. "Of Africa's Brightest Ornaments: A Short Biography of Sarah Forbes Bonetta." *Social & Cultural Geography* 6, no. 2 (April 2005): 253–66.

Broc, Numa. *Dictionnaire Illustré Des Explorateurs et Grands Voyageurs Français Du XIXe Siècle*. Vol. I: Afrique. Paris: Editions du C.T.H.S., 1988.

Brooks, George. *Eurafricans in Western Africa : Commerce, Social Status, Gender, and Religious Observance from the Sixteenth to the Eighteenth Century*. Athens: Ohio University Press, 2003.

Brown, Vincent. "Social Death and Political Life in the Study of Slavery." *American Historical Review* 114, no. 5 (2009): 1231–49.

Brunet-La Ruche, Bénédicte. "'Crime et châtiment' aux colonies: poursuivre, juger, sanctionner au Dahomey de 1894 à 1945." Université Toulouse le Mirail—Toulouse 2, 2013. https://tel.archives-ouvertes.fr/tel-00979289.

Burrill, Emily S. *States of Marriage: Gender, Justice, and Rights in Colonial Mali*. Athens: Ohio University Press, 2015.

———. "'Wives of Circumstance': Gender and Slave Emancipation in Late Nineteenth-Century Senegal." *Slavery and Abolition* 29, no. 1 (March 2008): 49–63.

Byfield, Judith. "Pawns and Politics: The Pawnship Debate in Western Nigeria." In *Pawnship, Slavery, and Colonialism in Africa*, edited by Paul E. Lovejoy and Toyin Falola, 357–85. Trenton: Africa World Press, 2003.

Callahan, Michael D. *Mandates and Empire: The League of Nations and Africa, 1914–1931*. Brighton: Sussex Academic Press, 1999.

———. *A Sacred Trust: The League of Nations and Africa, 1929–1946*. Brighton: Sussex Academic Press, 2004.

Cammaert, Jessica. *Undesirable Practices: Women, Children, and the Politics of the Body in Northern Ghana, 1930–1972*. Lincoln: University of Nebraska Press, 2016.

Campbell, Gwyn, Suzanne Miers, and Joseph C. Miller, eds. *Child Slaves in the Modern World*. Athens: Ohio University Press, 2011.

———. *Children in Slavery through the Ages*. Athens: Ohio University Press, 2009.

Campt, Tina M. *Listening to Images*. Durham, NC: Duke University Press, 2017.

Carney, T. F. "Prosopography: Payoffs and Pitfalls." *Phoenix* 27, no. 2 (Summer 1973): 156–79.

Carsten, Janet. "Introduction: Cultures of Relatedness." In *Cultures of Relatedness: New Approaches to the Study of Kinship*, edited by Janet Carsten, 1–36. Cambridge: Cambridge University Press, 2000.

Chapdelaine, Robin Phylisia. *The Persistence of Slavery: An Economic History of Child Trafficking in Nigeria*. Childhoods: Interdisciplinary Perspectives on Children and Youth. Amherst: University of Massachusetts Press, 2021.

Chennells, Rebecca. "Sentencing: The 'Real Rape' Myth." *Agenda: Empowering Women for Gender Equity* 82, Gender and the Legal System (2009): 23–38.

Clark, Gracia. *Onions Are My Husband: Survival and Accumulation by West Africa Market Women*. Chicago: University of Chicago Press, 1994.

Codo, Bellarmin Coffi. "La presse dahoméenne face aux aspirations des 'évolués': 'La Voix du Dahomey' 1927–1957." Thèse de doctorat de 3e cycle: Histoire, Université Paris Diderot—Paris 7, 1978.

Coe, Cati. "Disputes over Transfers of Belonging in the Gold Coast in the 1870s: Fosterage or Debt Pawning?" In *Child Fostering in West Africa: New Perspectives on Theory and Practice*, 201–20. Leiden: Brill, 2013.

———. "Domestic Violence and Child Circulation in the Southeastern Gold Coast, 1905–28." In *Domestic Violence and the Law in Colonial and Postcolonial Africa*, 54–73. New African Histories. Athens: Ohio University Press, 2010.

———. "How Debt Became Care: Child Pawning and Its Transformations in Akuapem, the Gold Coast, 1874–1929." *Africa* 82, no. 2 (May 2012): 287–311.

———. *The Scattered Family: Parenting, African Migrants, and Global Inequality*. Chicago: University of Chicago Press, 2013.

Coles, D. Crystal, F. Ellen Netting, and Mary Katherine O'Connor. "Using Prosopography to Raise the Voices of Those Erased in Social Work History." *Affilia: Journal of Women and Social Work* 33, no. 1 (2018): 85–97.

Collins, Patricia Hill. *Black Feminist Thought: Knowledge, Consciousness, and the Politics of Empowerment*. Perspectives on Gender 2. New York: Routledge, 1991.

Coly, Ayo A. "Un/Clothing African Womanhood: Colonial Statements and Postcolonial Discourses of the African Female Body." *Journal of Contemporary African Studies* 33, no. 1 (2015): 12–26.

Conklin, Alice. "Colonialism and Human Rights, A Contradiction in Terms? The Case of France and West Africa, 1895–1914." *American Historical Review* 103, no. 2 (April 1998): 419–42.

———. *A Mission to Civilize: The Republican Idea of Empire in France and West Africa, 1895–1930*. Stanford, CA: Stanford University Press, 2001.

Cooper, Barbara. *Marriage in Maradi: Gender and Culture in a Hausa Society in Niger, 1900–1989*. Portsmouth, NH: Heinemann, 1997.

Coquery-Vidrovitch, Catherine. "De La Traite Des Esclave à l'exportation de l'huile de Palme et Des Palmistes Au Dahomey: XIXe Siècle." In *The Development of Indigenous Trade and Markets in West Africa*, edited by Claude Meillassoux, 107–23. Oxford: Oxford University Press, 1971.

———. "La Fête Des Coutumes Au Dahomey: Historique Et Essai D'interprétation." *Annales: Histoire, Sciences Sociales* 19, no. 4 (1964): 696–716.

———. "Le Blocus de Whydah (1876–1877) et La Rivalité Franco-Anglaise Au Dahomey: Fin de La Troque, Naissance de l'impérialisme?" *Cahiers d'Études Africaines* 2, no. 7 (1962): 373–419.

Craig, Elaine. "The Inhospitable Court." *University of Toronto Law Journal* 66 (Spring 2016): 197–243.

Cunningham, Hugh. *Children and Childhood in Western Society since 1500*. 2nd ed. New York: Pearson Longman, 2005.

d'Almeida-Topor, Hélène. *Les amazones: Une armée de femmes dans l'Afrique précoloniale*. Paris: Rochevignes, 1984.

———. *Histoire Économique du Dahomey (Bénin) (1890–1920)*. Vol. 1. 2 vols. Collection racines du présent. Paris: L'Harmattan, 1995.

Davis-Marks, Isis. "The Little-Known Story of Queen Victoria's Black Goddaughter." *Smithsonian Magazine*, October 8, 2020. https://www

.smithsonianmag.com/smart-news/english-heritage-presents-portrait-queen-victorias-black-goddaughter-180976008/.

Decker, Corrie. "A Feminist Methodology of Age-Grading and History in Africa." *American Historical Review* 125, no. 2 (April 2020): 418–26.

Deshusses, Mathias. "Du confiage à l'esclavage 'Petites bonnes' ivoiriennes en France (The 'Misfortunes' of Fosterage in France: The Case of 'Little Maids' from the Ivory Coast)." *Cahiers d'Études Africaines* 45, nos. 179/180 (January 1, 2005): 731–50.

Djimassé, Gabin. "Vodun et culture Fon/Vodun and Fon Culture." In *Vodun: African Voodoo*, 200–209. Paris: Fondation Cartier pour l'art contemporain, 2011.

Djivo, Joseph Adrien. *Le refus de la colonisation dans l'ancien royaume de DanxomƐ, 1875–1894*. Vol. 1: GbƐhanzin et Ago-li-Agbo. 2 vols. Langues et cultures du Bénin. Paris: L'Harmattan, 2013.

Duke Bryant, Kelly M. "Runaways, Dutiful Daughters, and Brides: Family Strategies of Formerly Enslaved Girls in Senegal, 1895–1911." *Women, Gender, and Families of Color* 7, no. 1 (Spring 2019): 37–55.

Dunglas, Édouard. "Contribution à l'histoire du Moyen-Dahomey: Royaumes d'Abomey, de Kétou et de Ouidah." *Études Dahoméennes* 19, no. 1 (1957): 17–185.

———. "Contribution à l'histoire du Moyen-Dahomey: Royaumes d'Abomey, de Kétou et de Ouidah." *Études Dahoméennes* 20, no. 2 (1957): 3–152.

Dwyer, Daisy Hilse. "Outside the Courts: Extra-Legal Strategies for Subordinating Women." In *African Women & the Law: Historical Perspectives*, edited by Margaret Jean Hay and Marcia Wright, 90–109. Papers on Africa, 7. Boston: Boston University Press, 1982.

Ekué, Silivi d'Almeida-. *La révolte des loméennes, 24–25 janvier 1933*. Lomé: Nouvelles éditions africaines du Togo, 1992.

Eltis, David, and David Richardson. "West Africa and the Transatlantic Slave Trade: New Evidence of Long-Run Trends." *Slavery & Abolition* 18, no. 1 (April 1997): 16–35.

Etienne, Mona. "Maternité sociale, rapports d'adoption et pouvoir des femmes chez les Baoulé (Côte d'Ivoire)." *L'Homme* 19, nos. 3/4 (1979): 63–107.

Falola, Toyin, ed. *Pawnship in Africa : Debt Bondage in Historical Perspective*. Boulder, CO: Westview Press, 1994.

———. *The Women's War of 1929: A History of Anti-Colonial Resistance in Eastern Nigeria*. Carolina Academic Press African World Series. Durham, NC: Carolina Academic Press, 2011.

Falola, Toyin, and Matt D. Childs, eds. *The Yorùbá Diaspora in the Atlantic World*. Bloomington: Indiana University Press, 2005.

Falola, Toyin, and Paul E. Lovejoy. "Pawnship in Historical Perspective." In *Pawnship in Africa: Debt Bondage in Historical Perspective*, edited by Toyin

Falola and Paul E. Lovejoy, 1–26. African Modernization and Development Series. Boulder, CO: Westview Press, 1994.

Felstiner, William L. F., Richard L. Abel, and Austin Sarat. "The Emergence and Transformation of Disputes: Naming, Blaming, Claiming..." *Law & Society Review* 15, no. 3/4 (1980–1981): 631–54.

Ferrer, Ada. "Slavery, Freedom, and the Work of Speculation." *Small Axe* 23, no. 1 (March 2019): 220–28.

Fretwell. "'Domesticating the Unfamiliar': Afropolitan Dress in the West African Kingdom of Dahomey." *Radical History Review* 2022, no. 144 (October 2022): 19–44.

Fromont, Cécile. *The Art of Conversion: Christian Visual Culture in the Kingdom of Kongo*. Omohundro Institute of Early American History and Culture. Chapel Hill: University of North Carolina Press, 2014.

———. *Images on a Mission in Early Modern Kongo and Angola*. University Park: Pennsylvania State University Press, 2022.

Fuentes, Marisa J. *Dispossessed Lives: Enslaved Women, Violence, and the Archive*. Philadelphia: University of Pennsylvania Press, 2016.

Gage, Kelly Mohs. "Forced Crossing: The Dress of African Slave Women in Rio de Janeiro, Brazil, 1861." *Dress: The Journal of the Costume Society of America* 39, no. 2 (October 1, 2013): 111–33.

Garcia, Luc. "Archives et tradition orale: Á propos d'une enquête sur la politique du royaume de Danhomé à la fin du 19e siècle." *Cahiers d'études africaines*, Histoire Africaine: Constatations, Contestations 16, nos. 61/62 (1976): 189–206.

———. *Le royaume du Dahomé face à la pénétration coloniale: affrontements et incompréhension (1875–1894)*. Paris: Editions Karthala, 1988.

Geary, Christraud M. *In and Out of Focus: Images from Central Africa, 1885–1960*. London: Philip Wilson Publishers, 2002.

George, Abosede A. *Making Modern Girls: A History of Girlhood, Labor, and Social Development in Colonial Lagos*. Athens: Ohio University Press, 2014.

———. "Within Salvation: Girl Hawkers and the Colonial State in Development Era Lagos." *Journal of Social History* 44, no. 3 (2011): 837–59.

Getz, Trevor. *Slavery and Reform in West Africa: Toward Emancipation in Nineteenth-Century Senegal and the Gold Coast*. Athens: Ohio University Press, 2004.

Getz, Trevor R., and Liz Clarke. *Abina and the Important Men: A Graphic History*. 2nd ed. New York: Oxford University Press, 2016.

Getz, Trevor R., and Lindsay Ehrisman. "The Marriages of Abina Mansah: Escaping the Boundaries of 'Slavery' as a Category in Historical Analysis." *Journal of West African History* 1, no. 1 (Spring 2015): 93–118.

Gilman, Sander L. *Difference and Pathology: Stereotypes of Sexuality, Race, and Madness*. Ithaca: Cornell University Press, 1985.

Ginio, Ruth. "Colonial Minds and African Witchcraft: Interpretations of Murder as Seen in Cases from French West Africa in the Interwar Era." In *The French Colonial Mind: Mental Maps of Empire and Colonial Encounters*, edited by Martin Thomas, 1:49–71. France Overseas. Lincoln: University of Nebraska Press, 2011.

———. "Investigating the Investigators: French Colonial Attempts to Supervise Its Policing System during the 1930s." *Historical Reflections* 46, no. 2 (Summer 2020): 43–61.

———. "Negotiating Legal Authority in French West Africa: The Colonial Administration and African Assessors, 1903–1918." In *Intermediaries, Interpreters, and Clerks: African Employees in the Making of Colonial Africa*, edited by Benjamin N. Lawrance, Emily Lynn Osborn, and Richard L. Roberts, 115–38. Madison: University of Wisconsin Press, 2006.

Glélé, Maurice A. *Le Danxomę: du pouvoir Aja à la nation Fon*. Paris: Nubia, 1974.

Goody, Esther. *Parenthood and Social Reproduction: Fostering and Occupational Roles in West Africa*. Cambridge: Cambridge University Press, 1982.

Grant, Kevin. *A Civilised Savagery: Britain and the New Slaveries in Africa, 1884–1926*. New York: Routledge, 2005.

Green, Toby. *The Rise of the Trans-Atlantic Slave Trade in Western Africa, 1300–1589*. Cambridge: Cambridge University Press, 2014.

———. "Sumptuary Laws in Precolonial West Africa: The Examples of Benin and Dahomey." In *The Right to Dress: Sumptuary Laws in a Global Perspective, c. 1200–1800*, 461–78. Cambridge: Cambridge University Press, 2019.

Greene, Sandra E. "Modern 'Trokosi' and the 1807 Abolition in Ghana: Connecting Past and Present." *William and Mary Quarterly* 66, no. 4 (2009): 959–74.

Grier, Beverly. "Child Labor and Africanist Scholarship: A Critical Overview." *African Studies Review* 47, no. 2 (September 1, 2004): 1–25.

———. *Invisible Hands: Child Labor and the State in Colonial Zimbabwe*. Social History of Africa. Portsmouth, NH: Heinemann, 2006.

———. "Pawns, Porters, and Petty Traders: Women in the Transition to Cash Crop Agriculture in Colonial Ghana." *Signs* 17, no. 2 (Winter 1992): 304–28.

Guyer, Jane I. "Wealth in People and Self-Realization in Equatorial Africa." *Man*, New Series, 28, no. 2 (June 1993): 243–65.

———. "Wealth in People, Wealth in Things—Introduction." *Journal of African History* 36, no. 1 (January 1, 1995): 83–90.

Guyer, Jane I., and Samuel M. Eno Belinga. "Wealth in People as Wealth in Knowledge: Accumulation and Composition in Equatorial Africa." *Journal of African History* 36, no. 1 (January 1995): 91–120.

Hayes, Patricia. "Empty Photographs: Ethnography and the Lacunae of African History." In *Ambivalent: Photography and Visibility in African History*, 56–76. Athens: Ohio University Press, 2019.

Hayes, Patricia, and Gary Minkley. *Ambivalent: Photography and Visibility in African History*. Athens: Ohio University Press, 2019.

Hazoumé, Paul. *Le pacte de sang au Dahomey*. Travaux et mémoires de l'Institut d'ethnologie; 25. Paris: Institut d'ethnologie, 1937.

Herskovits, Melville J. *Dahomey: An Ancient West African Kingdom*. Vol. 1. 2 vols. New York: J. J. Augustin, 1938.

Higman, B. W. "The Sugar Revolution." *Economic History Review* LIII, no. 2 (2000): 213–36.

Hopkins, A. G. *An Economic History of West Africa*. New York: Columbia University Press, 1976.

Hounyoton, Hospice. "Child Slaves: The Case of Vidomegon Children in Benin." In *Child Exploitation in the Global South*, edited by J. Ballet and A. Bhukuth, 173–201. London: Palgrave Macmillan, 2019.

Howard, Neil. "Is 'Child Placement' Trafficking? Questioning the Validity of an Accepted Discourse." *Anthropology Today* 27, no. 6 (December 2011): 3–7.

Hurston, Zora Neale. *Barracoon: The Story of the Last "Black Cargo."* Edited by Deborah G. Plant. London: Amistad, 2018.

Ipsen, Pernille. *Daughters of the Trade: Atlantic Slavers and Interracial Marriage on the Gold Coast*. Philadelphia: University of Pennsylvania Press, 2014.

Jacquemin, Melanie Y. "'Petites nieces' et petites bonnes: le travail des fillettes en milieu urbain de Cote-d'Ivoire." *Journal des africanistes* 70, nos. 1/2 (2001): 105–22.

Jaksch, Marla L., Catherine Cymone Fourshey, and Relebohile Moletsane. "A Turn to the African Girl." *Girlhood Studies* 16, no. 1 (Spring 2023): vii–xv.

Jean-Baptiste, Rachel. *Conjugal Rights: Marriage, Sexuality, and Urban Life in Colonial Libreville, Gabon*. New African Histories. Athens: Ohio University Press, 2014.

Jeater, Diana. *Marriage, Perversion, and Power: The Construction of Moral Discourse in Southern Rhodesia, 1894–1930*. Oxford: Clarendon, 1993.

Johnson, Jessica Marie. *Wicked Flesh: Black Women, Intimacy, and Freedom in the Atlantic World*. Philadelphia: University of Pennsylvania Press, 2020.

Johnson, Samuel. *The History of the Yorubas from the Earliest Times to the Beginning of the British Protectorate*. Reprint. London: Forgotten Books, 2012.

Jones, Adam. "Decompiling Dapper: A Preliminary Search for Evidence." *History in Africa* 17 (1990): 171–209.

———. "Prostitution, Polyandry or Rape? On the Ambiguity of European Sources for the West African Coast 1660–1860." In *African Women in the Atlantic World: Property, Vulnerability, & Mobility, 1660–1880*, edited by Mariana P. Candido and Adam Jones, 89–108. Suffolk: James Currey, 2019.

Jones, Hilary. "From Mariage à La Mode to Weddings at Town Hall: Marriage, Colonialism, and Mixed-Race Society in Nineteenth-Century Senegal." *International Journal of African Historical Studies* 38, no. 1 (2005): 27–48.

———. *The Métis of Senegal: Urban Life and Politics in French West Africa*. Bloomington: Indiana University Press, 2013.
Kane, Aminata. "Violences sur les femmes, violences des femmes en Afrique Occidentale Francaise (1895–1960): Histoire des femmes d'apres les registres judiciaires." Doctoral thesis, University of Provence-Aix-Marseille 1, 2008.
Kastner, Kristin. "Fashioning Dakar's Urban Society: Sartorial Code-Mixing in Senegal." *Sociologus* 69, no. 2 (2019): 167–88.
Katz, Jonathan G. *Murder in Marrakesh: Émile Mauchamp and the French Colonial Adventure*. Bloomington: Indiana University Press, 2006.
Kea, Ray A. "From Catholicism to Moravian Pietism: The World of Marotta/Magdalena, a Woman of Popo and St. Thomas." In *The Creation of the British Atlantic World*, 115–37. Baltimore: Johns Hopkins University Press, 2005.
Keller, Candace M. *Imaging Culture: Photography in Mali, West Africa*. Bloomington: Indiana University Press, 2021.
Kirk, Jackie, Claudia Mitchell, and Jacqueline Reid-Walsh. "Toward Political Agency for Girls: Mapping the Discourses of Girlhood Globally." In *Girlhood: A Global History*, edited by Jennifer Helgren and Colleen A. Vasconcellos. Rutgers Series in Childhood Studies. New Brunswick, NJ: Rutgers University Press, 2010.
Klein, Martin. "Children and Slavery in the Western Sudan." In *Child Slaves in the Modern World*, edited by Gwyn Campbell, Suzanne Miers, and Joseph C. Miller, 124–39. Athens: Ohio University Press, 2011.
———. "Sex, Power, and Family Life in the Harem: A Comparative Study." In *Women and Slavery: Africa, The Indian Ocean World, and the Medieval North Atlantic*, edited by Gwyn Campbell, Suzanne Miers, and Joseph C. Miller, 1:62–81. Athens: Ohio University Press, 2007.
———. *Slavery and Colonial Rule in French West Africa*. Cambridge: Cambridge University Press, 1998.
Klein, Martin, and Richard Roberts. "Gender and Emancipation in French West Africa." In *Gender and Slave Emancipation in the Atlantic World*, edited by Pamela Scully and Diana Paton, 162–80. Durham, NC: Duke University Press, 2005.
———. "The Resurgence of Pawning in French West Africa during the Depression of the 1930s." In *Pawnship, Slavery, and Colonialism in Africa*, edited by Paul Lovejoy and Toyin Falola, 409–26. Trenton, NJ: Africa World, 2003.
Knott, Sarah. "Theorizing and Historicizing Mothering's Many Labours." *Past and Present* Supplement 15 (2020): 1–23.
Kopytoff, Igor, and Suzanne Miers. "Introduction: African 'Slavery' as an Institution of Marginality." In *Slavery in Africa: Historical and Anthropological Perspectives*, edited by Suzanne Miers and Igor Kopytoff. Madison: University of Wisconsin Press, 1977.

Kriger, Colleen E. *Cloth in West African History*. The African Archaeology Series. Lanham, MD: AltaMira, 2006.

Lallemand, Suzanne. *Adoption et Mariage: Les Kotokoli du centre du Togo*. Anthropologie—Connaissance des hommes. Paris: Éditions L'Harmattan, 1994.

———. *La circulation des enfants en société traditionnelle: prêt, don, échange*. Paris: Editions L'Harmattan, 1993.

Larsen, Lynne Ellsworth. *Dahomey's Royal Architecture: An Earthen Record of Construction, Subjugation, and Reclamation*. Oxon: Routledge, 2023.

Law, Robin. "An Alternative Text of King Agaja of Dahomey's Letter to King George I of England, 1726." *History in Africa* 29 (2002): 257–71.

———. *Consul John Beecroft's Journal of His Mission to Dahomey, 1850*. Fontes Historiae Africanae 17. Oxford: Oxford University Press, 2019.

———, ed. *Dahomey and the Ending of the Trans-Atlantic Slave Trade: The Journals and Correspondence of Vice-Consul Louis Fraser, 1851–1852*. Fontes Historiae Africanae 10. Oxford: Oxford University Press, 2012.

———. "The English Interpreters in Dahomey, 1843–1852." *Journal of Imperial and Commonwealth History* 44, no. 5 (2016): 730–51.

———, ed. *The English in West Africa, 1685–1688: The Local Correspondence of the Royal African Company of England 1681–1699 Part 2*. Vol. 2. 3 vols. Oxford: Oxford University Press, 2001.

———. "Ethnicity and the Slave Trade: 'Lucumi' and 'Nago' as Ethnonyms in West Africa." *History in Africa* 24 (1997): 205–19.

———. "Finance and Credit in Precolonial Dahomey." In *Credit, Currencies, and Culture: African Financial Institutions in Historical Perspective*, edited by Endre Stiansen and Jane I. Guyer, 21–43. Uppsala: Nordiska Afrikainstitutet, 1999.

———. *From Slave Trade to Legitimate Commerce: The Commercial Transition in Nineteenth-Century West Africa*. Cambridge: Cambridge University Press, 2002.

———. "Further Light on Bulfinch Lambe and the 'Emperor of Pawpaw:' King Agaja of Dahomey's Letter to King George I of England, 1726." *History in Africa* 17 (1990): 211–26.

———. "History and Legitimacy: Aspects of the Use of the Past in Precolonial Dahomey." *History in Africa* 15 (1988): 431–56.

———. "Human Sacrifice in Precolonial West Africa." *African Affairs* 84, no. 334 (January 1985): 53–87.

———. "Ideologies of Royal Power: The Dissolution and Reconstruction of Political Authority on the 'Slave Coast,' 1680–1750." *Africa: Journal of the International African Institute* 57, no. 3 (1987): 321–44.

———. "'Legitimate' Trade and Gender Relations in Yorubaland and Dahomey." In *From Slave Trade to "Legitimate" Commerce: The Commercial Transition in Nineteenth-Century West Africa*, edited by Robin Law, 195–214. African Studies Series 86. Cambridge: Cambridge University Press, 1995.

———. "Madiki Lemon, the 'English Captain' at Ouidah, 1843–1852: An Exploration in Biography." *History in Africa* 37 (2010): 107–23.

———. "'My Head Belongs to the King': On the Political and Ritual Significance of Decapitation in Precolonial Dahomey." *Journal of African History* 30, no. 3 (January 1, 1989): 399–415.

———. "On Pawning and Enslavement for Debt in the Precolonial Slave Coast." In *Pawnship, Slavery, and Colonialism in Africa*, 55–69. Trenton, NJ: African World Press, 2003.

———. "Ouidah as a Multiethnic Community." In *The Black Urban Atlantic in the Age of the Slave Trade*, edited by Jorge Cañizares-Esguerra, Matt D. Childs, and James Sidbury, 42–62. Philadelphia: University of Pennsylvania Press, 2013.

———. *Ouidah: The Social History of a West African Slaving "Port," 1727–1892*. Athens: Ohio University Press, 2004.

———. *The Qyọ Empire, c. 1600–c. 1836: A West African Imperialism in the Era of the Atlantic Slave Trade*. Oxford: Clarendon, 1977.

———. *The Slave Coast of West Africa, 1550–1750: The Impact of the Atlantic Slave Trade on an African Society*. Oxford: Oxford University Press, 1991.

———. "The Slave-Trader as Historian: Robert Norris and the History of Dahomey." *History in Africa* 16 (1989): 21–35.

Lawrance, Benjamin N. "La Révolte des Femmes: Economic Upheaval and the Gender of Political Authority in Lomé, Togo, 1931–33." *African Studies Review* 46, no. 1 (April 2003): 43–67.

———. *Locality, Mobility, and "Nation": Periurban Colonialism in Togo's Eweland 1900–1960*. Rochester, NY: Rochester University Press, 2007.

Lawrance, Benjamin N., and Richard L. Roberts, eds. *Trafficking in Slavery's Wake: Law and the Experience of Women and Children in Africa*. New African Histories. Athens: Ohio University Press, 2012.

Leinaweaver, Jessaca B. *The Circulation of Children: Kinship, Adoption, and Morality in Andean Peru*. Durham, NC: Duke University Press, 2008.

Lempereur, Samuel. "A Path from Slavery to Freedom: The Case of the Ologuoudou Family in Southern Benin." *African Economic History* 48, no. 1 (2020): 20–45.

Lindsay, Lisa A. *Atlantic Bonds: A Nineteenth-Century Odyssey from America to Africa*. Chapel Hill: University of North Carolina Press, 2017.

———. "Remembering His Country Marks: A Nigerian American Family and Its 'African' Ancestor." In *Biography and the Black Atlantic*, 192–208. Philadelphia: University of Pennsylvania Press, 2014.

Lindsay, Lisa A., and John Wood Sweet, eds. *Biography and the Black Atlantic*. Philadelphia: University of Pennsylvania Press, 2013.

Lokossou, Clément Koudessa. "La Presse au Dahomey 1894–1960: Évolution et réaction face à l'administration coloniale." PhD diss., École des hautes études en sciences sociales, 1976.

Lovejoy, Paul E. "Pawnship, Debt, and 'Freedom' in Atlantic Africa during the Era of the Slave Trade: A Reassessment." *Journal of African History* 55, no. 1 (March 2014): 55–78.

———. *Transformations in Slavery: A History of Slavery in Africa.* 2nd ed. Cambridge: Cambridge University Press, 2000.

Lovejoy, Paul E., and David Richardson. "The Business of Slaving: Pawnship in Western Africa, c. 1600–1810." *Journal of African History* 42, no. 1 (2001): 67–89.

Lovejoy, Paul, and Suzanne Schwarz, eds. *Slavery, Abolition and the Transition to Colonisation in Sierra Leone.* Trenton, NJ: African World Press, 2014.

Lugones, María. "The Coloniality of Gender." In *The Palgrave Handbook of Gender and Development*, 1–17. London: Palgrave Macmillan, 2016.

———. "Heterosexualism and the Colonial/Modern Gender System." *Hypatia* 22, no. 1: Writing against Heterosexism (Winter 2007): 186–209.

Lydon, Ghislaine. "The Unraveling of a Neglected Source: A Report on Women in Francophone West Africa in the 1930s (La re-decouverte d'une source negligee: un rapport sur la condition des femmes en AOF dans les annees 1930)." *Cahiers d'études africaines* 37, no. 147 (1997): 555–84.

———. "Women, Children and the Popular Front's Mission of Inquiry in French West Africa." In *French Colonial Empire and the Popular Front: Hope and Disillusion*, edited by Tony Chafer and Amanda Sackur, 170–87. London: Macmillan, 1999.

Lynn, Martin. *Commerce and Economic Change in West Africa: The Palm Oil Trade in the Nineteenth Century.* African Studies Series 93. Cambridge: Cambridge University Press, 1997.

Maalla M'jid, Najat. "Report of the Special Rapporteur on the Sale of Children, Child Prostitution and Child Pornography on Her Visit to Benin (28 October–8 November 2013)." United Nations Human Rights Council, March 5, 2014. https://digitallibrary.un.org/record/766861?ln=ar&v=pdf.

Maier, Donna J. E. "Precolonial Palm Oil Production and Gender Division of Labor in Nineteenth-Century Gold Coast and Togoland." *African Economic History* 37 (2009): 1–32.

Manière, Laurent. "Popular Unrest and the Press Campaign against the Capitation Tax in Dahomey, 1929–1935." *Journal of Policy History* 25, no. 3 (July 2013): 385–403.

Mann, Kristin. *Marrying Well: Marriage, Status, and Social Change among the Educated Elite in Colonial Lagos.* Cambridge: Cambridge University Press, 1985.

———. "Shifting Paradigms in the Study of the African Diaspora and of Atlantic History and Culture." In *Rethinking the African Diaspora: The Making of a Black Atlantic World in the Bight of Benin and Brazil*, 3–21. London: Frank Cass, 2001.

———. *Slavery and the Birth of an African City: Lagos, 1760–1900*. Bloomington: Indiana University Press, 2007.

Mann, Kristin, and Richard Roberts, eds. *Law in Colonial Africa*. Social History of Africa. Portsmouth, NH: Heinemann, 1991.

Manning, Patrick. *Slavery, Colonialism, and Economic Growth in Dahomey, 1640–1960*. Cambridge: Cambridge University Press, 1982.

Martin, Susan M. *Palm Oil and Protest: An Economic History of the Ngwa Region, South-Eastern Nigeria, 1800–1980*. Cambridge: Cambridge University Press, 1988.

Martino, Enrique. "Dash-Peonage: The Contradictions of Debt Bondage in the Colonial Plantations of Fernando Pó." *Africa* 87, no. 1 (February 2017): 53–78.

Matera, Marc, Misty L. Bastian, and Susan Kingsley Kent. *The Women's War of 1929: Gender and Violence in Colonial Nigeria*. Basingstoke: Palgrave Macmillan, 2012.

Mauss, Marcel. *The Gift: Expanded Edition*. Translated by Jane I. Guyer. Chicago: Hau Books, 2016.

Maza, Sarah. "The Kids Aren't All Right: Historians and the Problem of Childhood." *American Historical Review* 125, no. 4 (October 2020): 1261–85.

Mbah, Ndubueze L. *Emergent Masculinities: Gendered Power and Social Change in the Biafran Atlantic Age*. Athens: Ohio University Press, 2019.

Medenouvo, Firmin, ed. *Coutumier Du Dahomey*. Paris: Presence Beninoise, 2004.

McDougall, E. Ann. "'To Marry One's Slave Is as Easy as Eating a Meal': The Dynamics of Carnal Relations within Saharan Slavery." In *Sex, Power, and Slavery*, edited by Gwyn Campbell and Elizabeth Elbourne, 140–66. Athens: Ohio University Press, 2014.

McMahon, Elisabeth. "Trafficking and Reenslavement: The Social Vulnerability of Women and Children in Nineteenth-Century East Africa." In *Trafficking in Slavery's Wake: Law and the Experience of Women and Children in Africa*, 29–44. New African Histories. Athens: Ohio University Press, 2012.

Meillassoux, Claude. *The Anthropology of Slavery: The Womb of Iron and Gold*. Translated by Alide Dasnois. Chicago: University of Chicago Press, 1991. Originally published as *Anthropologie de l'esclavage: Le ventre de fer et d'argent* (Paris: Presses Universitaires de France, 1986).

Miers, Suzanne. "Slavery and the Slave Trade as International Issues 1890–1939." In *Slavery and Colonial Rule in Africa*, 16–37. Routledge: Frank Cass, 1999.

Miller, Joseph C. "A Historical Appreciation of the Biographical Turn." In *Biography and the Black Atlantic*, edited by Lisa A. Lindsay and John Wood Sweet, 19–47. Philadelphia: University of Pennsylvania Press, 2014.

Mitchell, Robin. *Vénus Noire: Black Women and Colonial Fantasies in Nineteenth-Century France*. Race in the Atlantic World, 1700–1900. Athens: University of Georgia Press, 2020.

Moitt, Bernard. *Child Slavery and Guardianship in Colonial Senegal*. Cambridge: Cambridge University Press, 2023.

———. "Slavery and Guardianship in Postemancipation Senegal: Colonial Legislation and Minors in Tutelle, 1848–1905." In *Child Slaves in the Modern World*, edited by Gwyn Campbell, Suzanne Miers, and Joseph C. Miller, 140–56. Athens: Ohio University Press, 2011.

Monroe, J. Cameron. *The Precolonial State in West Africa: Building Power in Dahomey*. New York: Cambridge University Press, 2014.

Monroe, J. Cameron, and Anneke Janzen. "The Dahomean Feast: Royal Women, Private Politics, and Culinary Practices in Atlantic West Africa." *African Archaeological Review* 31, no. 2 (June 2014): 299–337.

Moreau, Daniela, and Luis Nicolau Parés. *Images du Dahomey: Edmond Fortier et le colonialisme Français dans la terre des voduns*. Milan: 5 Continents Editions. 2020.

Morgan, Jennifer L. *Laboring Women: Reproduction and Gender in New World Slavery*. Philadelphia: University of Pennsylvania Press, 2004.

Morton-Williams, Peter. "A Yoruba Woman Remembers Servitude in a Palace of Dahomey, in the Reigns of Kings Glele and Behanzin." *Africa: Journal of the International African Institute* 63, no. 1 (1993): 102–17.

Moseley, Katherine Payne. "Indigenous and External Factors in Colonial Politics: Southern Dahomey to 1939." PhD diss., Columbia University, 1975.

Myers, Walter Dean. *At Her Majesty's Request: An African Princess in Victorian England*. New York: Scholastic, 1999.

Nast, Heidi. *Concubines and Power Five Hundred Years in a Northern Nigerian Palace*. Minneapolis: University of Minnesota Press, 2005.

Nelson, Margaret K. "Whither Fictive Kin? Or, What's in a Name." *Journal of Family Issues* 32, no. 2 (2014): 201–22.

Newbury, Colin W. *The Western Slave Coast and Its Rulers: European Trade and Administration among the Yoruba and Adja-Speaking Peoples of South-Western Nigeria, Southern Dahomey, and Togo*. Oxford: Clarendon, 1961.

Noret, Joël. "Between Authenticity and Nostalgia: The Making of a Yoruba Tradition in Southern Benin." *African Arts* 41, no. 4 (Winter 2008): 26–31.

Nzegwu, Nkiru Uwechia. *Family Matters: Feminist Concepts in African Philosophy of Culture*. SUNY Series, Feminist Philosophy. Albany: State University of New York Press, 2006.

Obichere, Boniface I. "Women and Slavery in the Kingdom of Dahomey." *Revue Française d'histoire d'outre mer* 65, no. 1 (1978): 5–20.

Ochonu, Moses E. *Colonial Meltdown: Northern Nigeria in the Great Depression*. Athens: Ohio University Press, 2009.

Ogundiran, Akinwumi. *The Yorùbá: A New History*. Bloomington: Indiana University Press, 2020.

Ojo, Olatunji. "Beyond Diversity: Women, Scarification and Yoruba Identity." *History in Africa* 35 (2008): 347–74.

———. "Child Slaves in Precolonial Nigeria, c. 1725–1860." *Slavery and Abolition* 33, no. 3 (September 2012): 417–34.

———. "'Èmú' (Àmúyá): The Yorùbá Institution of Panyarring or Seizure for Debt." *African Economic History* 35 (2007): 31–58.

Oliveira, Vanessa S. "Spouses & Commercial Partners: Immigrant Men & Locally Born Women in Luanda, 1831–1859." In *African Women in the Atlantic World: Property, Vulnerability, & Mobility, 1660–1880*, edited by Mariana P. Candido and Adam Jones, 217–32. Suffolk: James Currey, 2019.

Osborn, Emily. *Our New Husbands Are Here: Households, Gender, and Politics in a West African State from the Slave Trade to Colonial Rule*. Athens: Ohio University Press, 2011.

Oyěwùmí, Oyèrónkẹ́. "Family Bonds/Conceptual Binds: African Notes on Feminist Epistemologies." *Signs* 25, no. 4: Feminisms at a Millennium (2000): 1093–98.

Pande, Ishita. "Is the History of Childhood Ready for the World? A Response to 'The Kids Aren't All Right.'" *American Historical Review* 125, no. 4 (October 21, 2020): 1300–1305.

Parkes, Peter. "Fostering Fealty: A Comparative Analysis of Tributary Allegiances of Adoptive Kinship." *Comparative Studies in Society and History* 45, no. 4 (October 2003): 741–82.

Patterson, Orlando. *Slavery and Social Death: A Comparative Study*. Cambridge, MA: Harvard University Press, 1982.

Peirce, Leslie P. *The Imperial Harem: Women and Sovereignty in the Ottoman Empire*. Oxford: Oxford University Press, 1993.

Peiretti-Courtis, Delphine. *Corps noirs et médecins blancs: La fabrique du préjugé racial XIXe–XXe Siècles*. Paris: La Decouverte, 2021.

Perry, Mary Elizabeth. "Finding Fatima, a Slave Woman of Early Modern Spain." In *Contesting Archives: Finding Women in the Sources*, 3–19. Urbana: University of Illinois Press, 2010.

Pétré-Grenouilleau, Olivier. *Dictionnaire des esclavages*. Paris: Larousse, 2010.

Pinto, Pedro, and Robin Law. "New Evidence on Relations between Portugal and the Kingdom of Allada in the Sixteenth Century." *History in Africa* 47 (2020): 37–50.

Razy, Elodie, and Marie Rodet, eds. *Children on the Move in Africa: Past and Present Experiences of Migration*. Suffolk: James Currey, 2016.

Reid, Anthony. "'Closed' and 'Open' Slave Systems in Pre-Colonial Southeast Asia." In *Critical Readings on Global Slavery*, 1462–85. Leiden: Brill, 2018.

Renne, Elisha P. "Childhood Memories and Contemporary Parenting in Ekiti, Nigeria." *Africa (Edinburgh University Press)* 75, no. 1 (March 2005): 63–82.

Reuther, Jessica. "Irresponsible Boys, Promiscuous Girls: Maturity, Gender, and Rape Myths in the Criminal Tribunals of Colonial Dahomey, 1924–1940." *La Revue d'histoire de l'enfance "irrégulière"* 20 (November 2018): 67–84.

———. "Street Hawking or Street Walking in Dahomey? Debates about Girls' Sexual Assaults in Colonial Tribunals, 1924–1941." *Journal of African History* 63, no. 3 (November 2022): 368–83.

———. "Women in Benin." In *Oxford Research Encyclopedia of African Women's History*. Oxford: Oxford University Press, 2019.

Roberts, Richard. *Litigants and Households: African Disputes and Colonial Courts in the French Soudan, 1895–1912*. Social History of Africa. Portsmouth, NH: Heinemann, 2005.

Robertson, Claire C. *Sharing the Same Bowl? A Socioeconomic History of Women and Class in Accra, Ghana*. Bloomington: Indiana University Press, 1984.

Robertson, Claire C., and Iris Berger, eds. *Women and Class in Africa*. New York: Africana, 1986.

Robertson, Claire C., and Martin A. Klein, eds. *Women and Slavery in Africa*. Portsmouth, NH: Heinemann, 1997.

Robertson, Claire C., and Marsha Robinson. "Re-Modeling Slavery as if Women Mattered." In *Women and Slavery: The Modern Atlantic*, 2:253–83. Athens: Ohio University Press, 2007.

Robins, Jonathon E. *Oil Palm: A Global History*. Chapel Hill: University of North Carolina Press, 2021.

Rodet, Marie. "Continuum of Gendered Violence: The Colonial Invention of Female Desertion as a Customary Criminal Offense, French Soudan, 1900–1949." In *Domestic Violence and the Law in Colonial and Postcolonial Africa*, 74–93. New African Histories. Athens: Ohio University Press, 2010.

———. "'I Ask for Divorce Because My Husband Does Not Let Me Go Back to My Country of Origin with My Brother:' Gender, Family, and the End of Slavery in the Region of Kayes, French Sudan, 1890–1920." In *Sex, Power, and Slavery*, edited by Gwyn Campbell and Elizabeth Elbourne, 182–202. Athens: Ohio University Press, 2014.

———. "'Under the Guise of Guardianship and Marriage': Mobilizing Juvenile and Female Labor in the Aftermath of Slavery in Kayes, French Soudan, 1900–1939." In *Trafficking in Slavery's Wake: Law and the Experience of Women and Children in Africa*, edited by Benjamin N. Lawrance and Richard L. Roberts, 86–100. Athens: Ohio University Press, 2012.

Ross, David. "Mid-Nineteenth Century Dahomey: Recent Views vs. Contemporary Evidence." *History in Africa* 12 (1985): 307–23.

Rubin, Gayle S. "The Traffic in Women: Notes on the 'Political Economy' of Sex." In *Deviations: A Gayle Rubin Reader*, 33–65. Durham, NC: Duke University Press, 2011.

Rucker, Walter C. *Gold Coast Diasporas: Identity, Culture, and Power*. Bloomington: Indiana University Press, 2015.
Sagbo, Bernard Fidèle. "Pouvoir politique et cultes vodun dans le Dahomey pré- et post-colonial." *Hemispheres* 11 (1997): 33–41.
Sahlins, Marshall. "What Kinship Is (Part One)." *Journal of the Royal Anthropological Institute* 17, no. 1 (March 2011): 2–19.
Sandall, Roger. "Herskovits' Last Day in Dahomey." *Anthropology Today* 15, no. 6 (1999): 18–20.
Scanlan, Padraic X. *Freedom's Debtors: British Antislavery in Sierra Leone in the Age of Revolution*. New Haven, CT: Yale University Press, 2017.
Schildkrout, Enid. "Age and Gender in Hausa Society Socio-Economic Roles of Children in Urban Kano." *Childhood* 9, no. 3 (August 1, 2002): 342–68.
Schnapper, Bernard. *La Politique et Le Commerce Français Dans Le Golfe de Guinée de 1838 à 1871*. Paris: Mouton, 1961.
Semley, Lorelle D. *Mother Is Gold, Father Is Glass: Gender and Colonialism in a Yoruba Town*. Bloomington: Indiana University Press, 2011.
———. "Public Motherhood in West Africa as Theory and Practice." *Gender & History* 24, no. 3 (November 2012): 600–616.
Shadle, Brett Lindsay. *"Girl Cases": Marriage and Colonialism in Gusiiland, Kenya, 1890–1970*. Portsmouth, NH: Heinemann, 2006.
———. "Rape in the Courts of Gusiiland, Kenya, 1940s–1960s." *African Studies Review* 51, no. 2 (September 1, 2008): 27–50.
Sharpley-Whiting, T. Denean. *Black Venus: Sexualized Savages, Primal Fears, and Primitive Narratives in French*. Durham, NC: Duke University Press, 1999.
Shaw, Rosalind. *Memories of the Slave Trade: Ritual and the Historical Imagination in Sierra Leone*. Chicago: University of Chicago Press, 2002.
Shipton, Parker MacDonald. *The Nature of Entrustment: Intimacy, Exchange, and the Sacred in Africa*. Yale Agrarian Studies. New Haven, CT: Yale University Press, 2007.
Shumway, Rebecca. "Castle Slaves of the Eighteenth-Century Gold Coast (Ghana)." *Slavery & Abolition* 35, no. 1 (2014): 84–98.
Smith, Shawn Michelle. "Introduction: First Photographs." In *At the Edge of Sight: Photography and the Unseen*, 1–19. Raleigh: Duke University Press, 2013.
Soumonni, Elisée A. "The Compatibility of the Slave and Palm Oil Trades in Dahomey, 1818–1858." In *From Slave Trade to "Legitimate" Commerce: The Commercial Transition in Nineteenth-Century West Africa*, edited by Robin Law, 78–92. Cambridge: Cambridge University Press, 1995.
———. "Dahomean Economic Policy under Ghezo 1818–1858: A Reconsideration." *Journal of the Historical Society of Nigeria* 10, no. 2 (June 1980): 1–11.
———. "Disease, Religion and Medicine: Smallpox in Nineteenth-Century Benin." *História, Ciências, Saúde—Manguinhos* 19 (December 2012): 35–45.

———. "Porto-Novo, Between the French and the British, 1861–1884." *Journal of the Historical Society of Nigeria* 12, nos. 3/4 (December 1984): 53–60.

Sparks, Randy J. "Gold Coast Merchant Families, Pawning, and the Eighteenth-Century British Slave Trade." *William and Mary Quarterly* 70, no. 2 (April 2013): 317–40.

Stearns, Peter N. *Childhood in World History*. 2nd ed. New York: Routledge, 2010.

Stephens, Rhiannon. *A History of African Motherhood: The Case of Uganda, 700–1900*. Cambridge: Cambridge University Press, 2013.

Strickrodt, Silke. *Afro-European Trade in the Atlantic World: The Western Slave Coast, c. 1550–c. 1885*. Western Africa Series. Suffolk: James Currey, 2015.

Sudarkasa, Niara. "Interpreting the African Heritage in Afro-American Family Organization." In *Families in the U.S.: Kinship and Domestic Politics*, edited by Karen V. Hansen and Anita Ilta Garey, 91–104. Women in the Political Economy. Philadelphia: Temple University Press, 1998.

Svorenčik, Andrej. "The Missing Link: Prosopography in the History of Economics." *History of Political Economy* 50, no. 3 (September 2018): 605–13.

Sweet, James H. *Domingos Álvares, African Healing, and the Intellectual History of the Atlantic World*. Chapel Hill: University of North Carolina Press, 2011.

———. *Recreating Africa: Culture, Kinship, and Religion in the African-Portuguese World, 1441–1770*. Chapel Hill: University of North Carolina Press, 2003.

———. "Reimagining the African-Atlantic Archive: Method, Concept, Epistemology, Ontology." *Journal of African History* 55, no. 2 (July 2014): 147–59.

Thelen, Tatjana, and Erdmute Alber. "Reconnecting State and Kinship: Temporalities, Scales, Classifications." In *Reconnecting State and Kinship*, edited by Tatjana Thelen and Erdmute Alber, 1–35. Philadelphia: University of Pennsylvania Press, 2018.

Thomas, Lynn M. "The Modern Girl and Racial Respectability in 1930s South Africa." In *The Modern Girl Around the World: Consumption, Modernity, and Globalization*, edited by Alys Eve Weinbaum, Lynn M. Thomas, Priti Ramamurthy, Uta G. Poiger, and Madeleine Yue Dong, 96–119. Durham, NC: Duke University Press, 2008.

———. *Politics of the Womb: Women, Reproduction, and the State in Kenya*. Berkeley: University of California Press, 2003.

Thornberry, Elizabeth. *Colonizing Consent: Rape and Governance in South Africa's Eastern Cape*. Cambridge: Cambridge University Press, 2019.

———. "Defining Crime through Punishment: Sexual Assault in the Eastern Cape, c. 1835–1900." *Journal of Southern African Studies* 37, no. 3 (September 2011): 415–30.

———. "Virginity Testing, History, and the Nostalgia for Custom in Contemporary South Africa." *African Studies Review* 58, no. 3 (December 2015): 129–48. https://doi.org/10.1017/asr.2015.79.

Thornton, John K. *A Cultural History of the Atlantic World, 1250–1820*. Cambridge: Cambridge University Press, 2012.

———. *The Kongolese Saint Anthony: Dona Beatriz Kimpa Vita and the Antonian Movement, 1684–1706*. Cambridge: Cambridge University Press, 1998.

Trouillot, Michel-Rolph. *Silencing the Past: Power and Production of History*. Boston: Beacon, 1995.

Tucker, Jennifer, Matthew Fox-Amato, Zeynep Devrim Gürsel, Marius Kothor, Sumathi Ramaswamy, and Olga Shevchenko. "AHR Review Roundtable: Ambivalent: Photography and Visibility in African History." *American Historical Review* 126, no. 4 (December 2021): 1552–73.

Usman, Aribidesi, and Toyin Falola. *The Yoruba: From Prehistory to the Present*. Cambridge: Cambridge University Press, 2019.

Vaughan, Megan. "Which Family? Problems in the Reconstruction of the History of the Family as an Economic and Cultural Unit." *Journal of African History* 24, no. 2 (1983): 275–83.

Venkatachalam, Meera. *Slavery, Memory, and Religion in Southeastern Ghana, c. 1850–Present*. New York: Cambridge University Press, 2015.

Verger, Pierre. *Dieux d'Afrique: culte des Orishas et Vodouns à l'ancienne Côte des esclaves en Afrique et à Bahia, la baie de tous les saints au Brésil*. Paris: P. Hartmann, 1954.

Verhoef, Heidi. "'A Child Has Many Mothers': Views of Child Fostering in Northwestern Cameroon." *Childhood* 12, no. 3 (2005): 369–90.

Videgla, Michel D. K. *Un état ouest-africain: le royaume Goun de Hogbonou (Porto-Novo) des origines à 1908*. 2 vols. PhD diss., University of Paris 1-Panthéon-Sorbonne 1999, 2002.

Vigarello, Georges. *A History of Rape: Sexual Violence in France from the 16th to the 20th Century*. Translated by Jean Birrell. Cambridge: Polity, 2001.

Weismantel, Mary. "Making Kin: Kinship Theory and Zumbagua Adoptions." *American Ethnologist* 22, no. 4 (November 1995): 685–704.

White, Deborah Gray. *Ar'n't I a Woman? Female Slaves in the Plantation South*. Rev. ed. New York: W. W. Norton, 1999.

White, Luise. *Speaking with Vampires: Rumor and History in Colonial Africa*. Berkeley: University of California Press, 2008.

Whyte, Christine. "Mothering Solidarity: Infant-Feeding, Vulnerability and Poverty in West Africa since the Seventeenth Century." *Past and Present*, 246, no. suppl. 15 (2020): 54–91.

Yemitan, Oladipo. *Madame Tinubu: Merchant and King-Maker*. Ibadan: University Press Limited, 1987.

Zaugg, Roberto. "The King's Chinese Spittoon: Global Commodities, Court Culture and Vodun in the Kingdoms of Hueda and Dahomey (Seventeenth to Nineteenth Centuries)." *Annales: Histoire, Sciences Sociales* 73, no. 1 (2018): 115–53.

INDEX

abolition, 5–6, 45, 50, 56, 58, 62–63, 70, 107, 161, 176n34, 193n47

Abomey, 50, 59, 69, 112–13, 149–50, 205n10, 208n35; and Agbessipé, 82–83; and Aholoupé, 88, 90, 93–95, 101; and Cana, 53; decline of, 119, 224n37; and France, 92, 98, 100, 152–54, 225n54; and girls, 19, 42; and John Beecroft, 60; and King Béhanzin, 93; plateau, 6, 32, 74, 203n78; and Porto-Novo, 93, 95; and royal family, 20, 89, 98, 100, 141–42; and slavery, 48; and Télé, 141–49, 151–52, 155–56; and Thomas Freeman, 60; and water, 41–42; and women, 42, 74

Acapovi, Télé, 17, 19, 142, 144–52, 155–56, 159, 222n19

Agbessipé, 18, 63, 65–75, 77–85, 105, 162, 196nn1–2, 203n78

agojie, 39–44, 106, 180n14, 186n103, 188n130, 188n132

Aho, Justin, 20, 142, 150–56, 222n18, 223n30, 224n41, 226n55

Aholoupé, 19, 88–101, 156, 159, 204n4, 205n8

Akouéle, 125–27, 129–30, 135, 159, 218n9

Aledjessi, 104, 115–19, 216n56

Bight of Benin, 13, 70, 79, 85, 165; and Agaja, 25, 32; and Allada, 28; and alliances, 29; and coastal waters, 71; and culture, 173n16; and economic transformations, 161; and France, 89; and girlhood, 8, 34; and girls, 39; and Hueda, 28; and labor, 163; and National Archives, 128; and princes, 30; and royal households, 31; and status markers, 15; and transfer, 162–63; and violence, 162

Boco, Kadja, 112, 214n39

bondage, 4, 6, 45, 52, 78, 84; debt, 10, 105; and dependence, 9, 15, 88, 120, 159; and gender, 12, 18–19; and kinship, 12, 146; status, 7

Bonetta, Sarah Forbes, 49, 62

Borghero, Francesco, 61, 187n108

Burton, Francis, 41

Burton, Richard, 55–56, 188n132, 191n29, 205n7

INDEX

colonial economy, 19, 85, 118–20, 122
colonial tribunals, 99, 103, 107–11, 115–16, 127, 128, 133–38, 139, 153
commerce, 70, 76, 82–83, 98, 133–34
Convention to Suppress Slavery and the Slave Trade, 111

dash, 47, 55–56, 62, 188n1
dashed people, 4, 6, 47, 49, 51–52, 54–63, 88, 194n59
dashing, 47–49, 55, 57–58, 61

economic hardship, 139, 147, 151, 156, 160
economic policy, 47, 83
economic power, 85
economic productivity, 7, 43, 138; and colonialism, 98, 119, 165; and households, 24, 41, 120; and Kingdom of Dahomey, 32, 38, 69–70; and Ouidah, 81, 84; and palm products, 94; and women, 69, 74, 89
economic "roles", 18; and Dahomean girls, 26, 32–33, 35, 39
economic systems, 58, 85; and trade, 48
economic transformations, 10, 19, 34–35, 44, 68, 72, 89, 156, 161
economic value, 9, 27
economy, 29, 96, 161; and agriculture, 63; household, 101, 118, 122; industrialization, 79; informal, 76; and Kingdom of Dahomey, 38, 63, 68, 83; monoculture, 97; plantation, 54; and Porto-Novo, 94; slave export, 53, 68; and trade, 68–70
enslaved people, 15, 71–72, 97, 110, 120, 191n29, 192n35, 202n78, 208nn35–36, 213n25; and Abomey, 100; and Adjohoun, 103; and ancestry, 66; and children, 56–57; commerce of, 76; and Dahomey, 52, 66, 70, 73, 95, 99, 115, 122; and *dashing*, 47, 56–57, 61; and dependent status, 84, 113; domestic, 88, 104; girls, 4–6, 9, 18, 34, 44, 48, 59, 69, 82–84, 90, 94, 104, 106–8, 112, 115, 161–62; and households, 44; and kinship, 176n34, 176n36; and marriage, 106–8; and masters, 9; and mistresses, 9, 82; and Ouidah, 81–82; and palm products, 95, 80; and pawning, 82, 88; purchase of, 75, 81, 99–100, 105, 109; and sexuality, 82; and social mobility, 196n5; and status, 12, 58, 176n34; vulnerability of, 80–81; and West Africa, 95; and women, 34, 65–66, 75, 80–82, 91, 94–96, 101, 103, 106–8, 177n46, 178n59, 205n5, 205n8; and Yorùbá, 18, 50–51, 53–54, 62, 70, 78
Europeans, 18, 32, 82, 110, 151, 164, 197n15, 207n26; and abolition, 63; and African children, 29, 45, 59, 146; and African communities, 71–72; and African girls, 13; and African practices, 10, 29; and agojie, 40, 188n132; and Àìná, 49; and archives, 13; and Bight of Benin, 13; and Christianity, 30; and colonists, 15, 101, 121; and diplomats, 60–61; and doctors, 139; and education, 29; and Gezo, 49; and *gohento*, 41; and Kingdom of Allada, 27, 29; and Kingdom of Dahomey, 14, 27, 34, 38–40, 47–52, 55–61, 63, 65, 79, 91, 97, 177n46, 209n44; and Kingdom of Hogbonou, 208n36; and Kingdom of Hueda, 27; and languages, 29, 60, 88; and masculine gaze, 14; and missionaries, 61, 173n13, 181n33; and morality, 51, 219n24; and officials, 24; and Ouidah, 50, 53, 66, 72, 77, 81,

146; and palm oil, 79–80; and Pierre Johnson, 116; and Robert Norris, 35; and slavery, 3–4, 24, 50, 56, 70, 71–74, 88, 101, 199n33, 208n36; and social mothers, 121; and trade, 69–75, 77–80, 173n13; and trading forts, 69, 72, 198n25; and West Africa, 55–56, 62; and Yorùbá, 50, 53–56, 62, 78

female children (girls), 38, 40–42, 45, 91–92, 97, 100, 108, 125; and Abomey, 42; and abuse, 143; and adolescence, 26; and agojie, 41; and agriculture, 33; and ahosi, 25; dashed, 51, 57–58, 60–62; and Dahomean kings, 18, 37, 47, 142; and dependence, 31, 43–44, 103, 118–20, 159; enslaved, 6–7, 18, 45, 58, 69, 80, 82–84, 99, 101, 103–4, 107, 122; and entrustment, 6, 85, 112, 115–22, 132–33, 147, 152, 157, 164, 178n59; experiences of, 13; and food preparation, 8, 34, 92; and guardians, 111–12; and households, 32; and identity, 19–20; and Kingdom of Allada, 33; and Kingdom of Hueda, 31–32; and King Gezo, 39–40, 45; and King Glèlè, 41, 45; and kinship, 12; and labor, 7–8, 19, 35, 57, 79, 89, 91, 95–96, 119, 121, 126, 145, 156, 161–62, 165; and marriage, 173n11; and maturation, 8, 10, 114, 145; and men, 13–14; and missing cases, 153–54; and Ouidah, 74; and Oyo Empire, 38; and palaces, 25–26, 34, 48; and pawning, 18, 77–82, 88; representations of, 14; and royal households, 44; runaway, 88, 90, 93, 178n62; and servitude, 18–19, 25–26; and sexual exploitation, 9, 32, 130–32, 135–38; and socialization, 7, 12–13; and social mothers, 6, 121, 127–30; 133, 139; as soldiers, 42; trafficking of, 19, 104–7, 119, 157; transfers of, 4, 8, 28, 31, 62, 68, 113, 145, 149, 162; value of, 27; and womanhood, 7; and women, 5, 18–19, 25–26, 47–48, 87–88, 106; Yorùbá, 50–54, 63, 83

Fohoumbo, 112–15, 117–21, 162

France: and abolition, 107; and Abomey, 90, 93; and Aholoupé, 98–99; and Allada, 99; and army, 155; and Bight of Benin, 89; and civilizing mission, 109; Caribbean colonies, 70; Compagnie des Indes, 27; and colonial administration, 3, 85, 87, 89, 101, 104, 106–10, 113, 118–19, 122, 132, 141–44, 151–56, 161, 173n11; and colonial legal system, 104, 107; and colonial rule, 14; and colonial tribunals, 103, 111, 115, 120; and Cotonou, 98; and entrustment, 112; and French West Africa (AOF), 67, 103, 107–9, 118, 133, 155; and Hogbonou, 94; and identity, 155; and indigenous assessors, 110; and Indigenous chiefs, 143; and Kingdom of Dahomey, 5, 49, 85, 90, 92, 94–95, 98, 100, 106, 111–12, 149; and King Gezo, 60–61; and Kodokoué, 98; and League of Nations, 111; and missionaries, 56; and naval officers, 60; and Navy, 95; and Ouidah, 69; and pawning, 112; and Port-Novo, 17, 95–96; and Resident Guestard, 36; Saint Louis fort, 27, 73; and slave trading, 38, 137; and Sophia Olivier (d'Oliviera), 73–74; and Télé, 142–43; and Togoland, 145, 156; and transfers, 105; and troops, 90, 92

Freeman, Thomas, 57, 59–60, 193n52

gender, 10, 12–13, 33, 97, 209n44; and class, 28; ideology, 172n10; and labor, 12; neutral, 31, 48, 78, 163, 227n6, 227n8; norms, 80

girlhood, 5, 13–14, 17, 26, 66, 92, 143, 152, 165, 172n5, 175n24; and Bight of Benin, 34; colonial, 10; Dahomean, 4, 6–7, 162, 172n10; experiences of, 89–90, 160–61; and social norms, 4, 6, 156, 163; stages of, 8–10, 173n13

hawkers, 94, 127–28, 130–31, 134, 142, 147, 150, 160

Houmé, 103–4, 106–9, 115, 120, 159, 212n18

households, 67, 77–78, 94–96, 112, 114–16, 126, 131–33, 157, 202n70, 229n20; and Abomey, 93; and children, 48, 180n23, 205n8, 228n15; colonial, 118; credit-giving, 5, 69; and Dahomeans, 9–10, 18, 25–26, 31–33, 58, 90–94, 100, 105, 122, 146; and dependent status, 4, 10, 54, 62, 107, 111, 161, 165; and economics, 41, 122; and Fohoumbo, 104; formation of, 12; and Gezo, 59–60, 195n67; and girls, 4, 7, 9, 28, 34, 104, 117, 129, 156, 161, 164, 173n13; and hierarchy, 44, 63; and Kodokoué, 101; and labor, 4, 8, 44, 83–84; and marriage, 12, 72; and mistresses, 147–48; and pawning, 5–6, 9, 68, 78–79, 81–82, 88, 198n20; and relationships, 128; and servile relationships, 16, 87–88, 101, 156, 222n25; and slavery, 25–26, 101, 106, 120, 147–48, 205n5; and women, 6–7, 74, 84, 127, 142, 144–49, 178n62; and workers, 88

human trafficking, 19, 48, 105, 108–10, 116, 121–22, 163, 214n36, 216n56, 220n6; and Aholoupé, 93; and children, 119–20; and Dahomeans, 111; and Fohoumbo, 112, 115; and Houmé, 107; and marriage, 101, 103–4; and sexual violence, 157; victims of, 98–99

indigenous people, 54–55, 99, 116, 133, 137, 139, 143, 155–57, 226n59; and activist, 219n24; and assessors, 109–11, 213n30, 214n35, 225n50; and civil servants, 126; and factories, 53; and girlhood, 10; and Gold Coast, 71; and fort personnel, 73; and hierarchy, 55; and justice, 109; and language, 25, 198n20; and leadership, 67; and networks, 29; and practices, 104; and religion, 154; and territories, 146; and tribunals, 223n29; and *vodun*, 60, 142

International Convention on the Suppression of Traffic in Women and Children, 111

Kingdom of Allada, 5, 25–26, 27–33, 43, 75, 99, 216n51, 220n30

Kingdom of Hogbonou, 5, 51, 87, 89–90, 93–101

Kingdom of Hueda, 5, 26–33, 37, 43, 69, 75, 182n39, 183n52, 198n25

King Agaja, 23, 25–26, 31–35, 47, 75, 150, 182n45

King Gezo, 18, 39–40, 49, 59–61, 82–83, 99, 142, 154, 191n17, 195n67, 203n89; and child transfer, 51; and dashing, 47–48, 57; and death, 84; and economy, 45; and Leflefun, 53; and Ouidah, 81; palace of, 141, 150; and pawning, 76; and slave trade, 55–56; and traders, 76

King Glèlè, 18, 45, 57–58, 61, 83–85, 90–91, 99; and agojie troops, 187n108; and agriculture, 53; and Dahomey, 41; and human captives, 47; and King

Gezo, 39, 49; and military, 40–42; and prerogative, 203n90; and royal family, 192n35; and Tegbesu, 27; and transfer, 45; and vidaho, 205n9

kinship, 174n18, 176n32, 176nn37–39, 218n7, 222n25; bonds, 146; creation of, 4; and Dahomey, 12; definition of, 11–12; and enslavement, 12; and networks, 35, 61, 81, 118, 162, 164; social, 4, 66, 77; studies, 11

Kodokoué, 89, 91–94, 98–101, 205n8, 205n10

Lawson, Mathilde, 142, 144–45, 155–56

Lawson, William, 142, 145, 152, 221n7

monarchy, 6–7, 18, 26, 35–39, 43, 51, 53, 69, 73, 84–85, 97, 105, 151, 161

Nigeria, 39, 103, 106

Norris, Robert, 27, 35–38, 180n19, 184n68

Ouidah, 5, 28, 50, 71, 95, 99–100, 113–14, 190n14, 195n75; and Agbessipé, 18, 66–67, 72, 75, 78, 83–84; and Charles Marcadé, 112; and Christian missionaries, 51, 60–61, 195n73; and colonial authorities, 131; as commercial center, 18; and community, 69; and English Fort, 53; and enslaved people, 66, 81–82; and entrepreneurs, 67–68; and Europeans, 73, 77; and factories, 54; and girl runaways, 17; and girls, 131; and Gold Coast, 73; and iwofa, 83; and John Beecham, 57; and merchants, 67, 82–85, 203n89; and oral traditions, 197n16; and palm products, 96–97; and Saint Louis fort, 27; and Sierra Leone, 209n43; and slave trade, 38, 61, 70, 190n9; 205n10, 208n35; and trade, 73, 76; and urban community, 146; and white community, 81; and William's Fort, 23, 193n50; and women, 67, 74, 119; and Yorùbá, 68, 75, 79

palm products, 52–54, 95, 105, 161–62; and kernels, 65, 87–88, 96–97, 125, 208n40; and palm oil, 54, 68, 72–77, 79–85, 89, 96–97, 187n121, 202n68, 204n3, 206n14, 208n40, 209n43; and plantations, 77, 85, 205n10; and trade, 69, 74, 82, 94, 161; and women laborers, 79

pawning, 6, 68–69, 75–79, 104, 111–12, 117, 121–22, 162; and France, 198n20, 215n42; and girls, 9, 105; and Kingdom of Dahomey, 76; and law, 201n53; process of, 75; as slavery, 214n38, 216n51; and West Africa, 5, 197n20

pawnship, 5, 68, 75, 105, 116–17, 122, 172n7, 198n21, 215n51

political economy, 18–19, 26, 156, 161, 165; and child transfers, 31; and dashes, 55; and Gezo, 45; and Kingdom of Dahomey, 26, 34, 39, 61

Porto-Novo, 5, 51, 87, 125, 133, 207n26, 208n36; and Abomey, 88, 93–94; and Adjohoun, 103; and Aholoupé, 93–98, 100; and children, 99, 146; and colonial capital, 119; and colonial tribunal, 107–8; and commercial community, 209n43; and economy, 94; and girl runaways, 17, 101; and Hogbonou, 96, 182n40; and indigenous, quarter, 133; and King Dahomey, 98; and Kodokoué, 93; and labor supply, 96; and markets, 103; and Ouidah, 96–97, 99, 119, 190n9; and Oumé River, 106; and regional markets, 97; and Sierra Leone, 97, 209n43; and slave trade, 72 power, 4, 15, 28, 83, 161, 189n3, 207n26, 215n49, 226n55; abuses of, 152; and Abomey, 141–43, 151; and Agbangla, 30; and Agaja, 33; and Allada, 29, 32; colonial, 104, 141, 224n37; and Dahomey, 35, 38, 43, 49, 110, 151; economic, 69, 85; and European trade, 72; and France, 85, 213n35; and governance, 25; and Hogbonou, 94; and Hueda, 32; imperial, 155, 226n60; and indigenous chiefs, 143; and Justin Aho, 142, 150, 152, 156; and King Gezo, 61; and King Glèlè, 61, 85; and kings, 36; and Kodokoué, 91; and labor, 77, 79; monarchical, 84; and Ouidah, 84; and Oyo Empire, 52, 94; and palaces, 18; regional, 5, 35; and slaveholders, 177n46; and Tegbesu, 27, 35, 38; and West Africa, 73; and women, 85

rape, 9, 19, 122, 126–28, 131–39, 218n6, 218n11, 219n25
ritual, 18, 34, 42, 69, 142–43, 153–55, 157, 226n57; exotic, 14; Hwetanu, 34; palace, 34; vodun, 151
royal households, 25–26, 28, 31–34, 43–44, 49, 51–52, 58, 60, 63, 69, 89, 144; and ancestry, 34; and authority, 36, 141–42, 151–52; and celebrations, 41; and children, 61; and courts, 48, 91; and girls, 40, 99; and ideology, 76; and ministers, 91, 98; and monopolies, 42; and palaces, 34, 41–42, 48, 188n132; and plantations, 53–54, 83; and power, 83; and prerogative, 47, 83; and royal lineages, 29–30, 36, 154, 156, 165, 226n55; and slavery, 93, 100, 152, 192n35; and status, 94, 101, 142, 151,

156; and wives, 33; and women, 77, 82–83, 185n89

sexual abuse, 9, 161, 163
sexual assault, 9, 19, 127–33, 137–39, 161, 218n6
sexual desires, 70, 82, 108
sexual exploitation, 9, 12, 32, 119, 156, 162; and slavery, 175n21
sexual maturity, 9, 136
Skertchly, J.A., 42, 57–58, 188n128, 188n132
slave raids, 50, 52, 106
slavery, 45, 52, 56, 77, 104, 110, 113, 117, 184n68, 204n4, 212n16, 214n42; abolition of, 107, 217n64; and African forts, 71–72; and British views of, 81; chattel, 192n35; child, 50, 83, 103; and child entrustment, 121; colonial, 107; and Dahomeans, 115; "dashed", 61; domestic, 13, 104; and Europeans, 50, 105; evolution of, 161; female, 65, 69, 222n25; and freedom, 12–13; and French colonial authorities, 106, 215n42; and gender, 210n6; and iwofa, 78; and kinship, 176n34, 176n37; legitimacy of, 82; and Ouidah, 66, 71; and pawning, 111–12, 198n21, 216n51; and sexuality, 9; and slave trade, 58, 93, 109; and Yorùbá people, 70, 72, 83. *See also* enslaved people
slave societies, 12, 50, 53, 66, 68, 107, 192n35
slave status, 56, 222n25
social age marker, 10, 173n11
social capital, 33, 77, 162
social kinship, 4, 66, 77
social maturity, 9
social mobility, 12, 79, 81, 84, 160, 192n35, 196n5

social mothers, 5–6, 19, 67, 112, 114, 120–22, 127–30, 132–33, 138–39, 144, 163, 215n49, 218n7

Tegbesu, 23, 25, 27, 35–40, 43, 53, 73, 184n68, 185n79
Télé Affair, 143–44, 153, 157, 224n41, 225n54
trade, 78, 163; and Africa, 71–72, 75; and Dahomey, 14; and Europe, 72; "export", 6, 70, 74, 101, 209n43; international, 48; kernel, 89, 96, 101; "legitimate", 68–69, 74, 82, 161; palm oil, 73–74, 80, 82–84, 94, 96, 161–62; and Yorùbá, 51–52
transatlantic slave trade, 5–6, 52, 71, 75, 80, 184n68, 186n93, 189n2; abolition of, 50, 56, 58, 62, 70; and Bight of Benin, 79; and *dash*, 47; and girls, 96; and Great Britain, 56, 190n9; and elites, 76; and Europe, 77; and France, 95; and human pawning, 105; and Kingdom of Dahomey, 32, 44, 49–50, 66, 68, 72, 76, 98–99, 105, 161; and King Tezifon, 29; and Ouidah, 28, 190n9; and Robert Norris, 27, 180n19; and traders, 14; and women, 43–44
transfer: and alliances, 29; child, 43–44, 49, 52, 58, 61–62, 75–77, 105, 112, 117–19, 121–22, 139, 147–48, 150, 157, 161–64, 180n23, 185n82, 198n20; coerced, 18; and colonial households, 149; control of, 35; and Dahomean kings, 26, 35; girl, 4–6, 8–9, 20, 28, 31, 33, 39, 43–45, 63, 68, 76, 104–5, 113, 116, 144–46, 152, 163–64; and households, 8, 30; institutionalized, 6, 37; and King Gezo, 51; legitimization of, 61, 150;

and Mathilde Lawson, 220n6; and natal homes, 76; voluntary, 9

violence, 4, 9, 137, 143, 162, 219n15, 226n57
vodun, 60, 142, 151–54, 180n18, 223n34

West Africa, 34, 36, 51, 71, 74, 78, 164, 181n27, 205n12, 220n2; and aristocratic rule, 224n37; and Atlantic Coast, 29, 47, 55, 190n14; and Chesham, Francis, 23; and child fostering, 11, 29; and children, 28, 57, 118, 219n24, 228n15; and colonial taxation, 145, 161; and economies, 50; and export commodities, 95; and girlhood, 4; girls, 3, 8, 13, 62, 148, 159; and families, 20; and France, 67, 103–4, 107, 109, 118, 133, 155, 173n11, 197n20, 213n31, 213n35, 217n66, 226n58; and households, 33; and identity, 56; and indigenous practices, 104; and *iwofa*, 68; kingdoms, 151; and men, 14; and palm oil, 79; and pawning, 69; and Republic of Benin, 5, 162; and Robert Norris, 27; and slave trade, 50, 104–5; and social mothers, 215n49; and society, 6, 58; and women, 24, 69, 73, 84
wives: and *ahosi*, 23; of Adjokpalo, 36; and Aholoupé, 91; and Aledjessi, 116; of circumstance, 106, 108; and "country wife", 67–68, 72–74, 77–78, 197n16; and glési, 54; and Houmé, 106; and households, 100; and Justin Aho, 150–51; of kings, 24–26, 31, 33–34, 42, 74; and palaces, 35; and pawning, 105; as record-keepers, 25; roles of, 24; and royal ministers, 98; and slavery, 107; of Tegbesu, 36; and Yossago, 131

women, 38, 41–42, 44–45, 67, 94, 100, 132, 149, 153, 162–63; and agriculture, 33, 113; and ahosi, 25, 33; and colonization, 101; and dependence, 5, 120; and economic independence, 161, 165; enslaved, 35, 65, 80, 82, 90, 99–101, 103, 176n37, 178n59, 222n25; as entrepreneurs, 18, 67–68, 81, 85, 112; and entrustment, 115, 121–22, 129; and Europeans, 14, 73–74; and food preparation, 8, 34; as fort slaves, 70; and France, 111, 118, 120; and gendered identities, 7; as guardians, 4, 19, 91–92, 115, 120, 127, 132, 138, 149, 159; and hierarchies, 16, 35, 44; as householders, 9, 17, 32, 67–68, 73, 82, 178n62; and kings, 47; as laborers, 44, 57, 106; market, 3, 117, 119, 121; and marriage, 106–7; as moneylenders, 77; and motherhood, 8, 65; and palaces, 44, 48; and palm oil, 74, 76, 79–80, 84–85, 89, 96; as parents, 114; and pawning, 5–6, 78, 105; representations of, 14, 24; and royal families, 25–26; runaway, 90, 152; and sexual assault, 127–28, 133, 135, 138–39; as social mothers, 127–28; and soldiers, 39–43, 95, 101; and status, 15; as traders, 74, 76, 80, 84, 128, 202n76; trafficking of, 104, 107; value of, 24; and wealth, 76–79; Yorùbá, 52–55, 63, 68–69, 75, 79, 83

Yorùbáland, 5, 18, 56, 61, 95, 99, 193n44, 200n49; and agricultural laborers, 52; and Àìná, 48, 50, 189n4; and children, 52–55; and culture, 66, 196n1; and diaspora, 54, 62, 68, 84–85; and enslaved people, 72, 78; and glési, 54; and *ifolé*, 88; and *iwofa*, 68, 76, 198n20; and Kingdom of Dahomey, 51, 66, 69–70, 192n34; and Mahi, 55; and men, 75; and Middle Pasage, 50; and migrants, 51, 83, 191n23; and Ouidah, 79; and pawning, 78; and religion, 66; and villages, 52; and women, 63, 65–66, 68, 79, 197n18; and Yorùbá Revolutionary Wars, 94

Jessica Catherine Reuther is Associate Professor of History at Ball State University. Her articles have appeared in the *Journal of African History* and the *Revue d'histoire de l'enfance "irrégulière"* (*RHEI*). She has contributed to the *Oxford Encyclopedia of African Women's History* and the *Oxford Encyclopedia of African Slavery, Slave Trade, and the Diaspora*.

For Indiana University Press
Tony Brewer, Artist and Book Designer
Anna Francis, Assistant Acquisitions Editor
Anna Garnai, Editorial Assistant
Samantha Heffner, Marketing and Publicity Manager
Brenna Hosman, Production Coordinator
Katie Huggins, Production Manager
Darja Malcolm-Clarke, Project Manager/Editor
Bethany Mowry, Acquisitions Editor
Dan Pyle, Online Publishing Manager
Pamela Rude, Senior Artist and Book Designer
Stephen Williams, Assistant Director of Marketing

www.ingramcontent.com/pod-product-compliance
Lightning Source LLC
Chambersburg PA
CBHW022003220426
43663CB00007B/937